Were They Pushed or Did ...?

Were They Pushed or Did They Jump?

Individual Decision Mechanisms in Education

Diego Gambetta

WestviewPress

A Division of HarperCollins*Publishers*

Copyright © 1996 by Westview Press, Inc., A Division of HarperCollins Publishers, Inc.

Published in 1996 in the United States of America by Westview Press, Inc., 5500 Central Avenue,
Boulder, Colorado 80301-2877, and in the United Kingdom by Westview Press, 12 Hid's Copse
Road, Cumnor Hill, Oxford OX2 9JJ

Library of Congress Cataloging-in-Publication Data
Gambetta, Diego, 1952–
Were they pushed or did they jump?
Individual decision mechanisms in education.
Bibliography.
Includes index.
ISBN   0-8133-3154-4
1. Educational Psychology.   2. Educational equalization.
I. Title.
LC191.G26   1996
370.19—dc20   86-21589
                                                                      CIP

The paper used in this publication meets the requirements of the American National Standard for
Permanence of Paper for Printed Library Materials Z39.48-1984.

a Nini e Carletto

Contents

Preface

I am deeply grateful to Cathie Marsh, who throughout the research reported in this book was a constant source of stimulating criticism, to Jon Elster for his invaluable help towards greater conceptual clarity, and to John Craig, who by offering me an impressive array of micro critical comments had an important part in improving the macro results.

I am also most grateful to Gordon A. Hughes, who spent a substantial share of his time and patience acquainting me with the use of the logit model. In addition, Pat Altham and Ugo Colombino gave me important statistical advice. I received comments on various versions of this work from several persons, and I would like to express my appreciation to Alberto Baldissera, Bob Blackburn, Flavio Bonifacio, Daniela Del Boca, Elisabetta Galeotti, Tony Giddens, A. H. Halsey, Geoffrey Hawthorn, Anthony Heath, Angelo Pichierri, Ken Prandy, Luca Ricolfi, Loredana Sciolla, David Voas, and Jonathan Zeitlin.

My friend Andy Martin gained my special gratitude for attempting to improve my style. Lynda Ball was patient and accurate in typing this work on the computer. To her go my thanks.

The research presented in this study has been possible thanks to a British Council scholarship, which supported me during a period of over two years in Cambridge.

Figures

Introduction

Individual decisions in education are what this book is about. I shall be focusing on the mechanisms that govern individuals' choices at and beyond school-leaving age and trying to explain why some pupils leave while others stay on, and what it is that make the latter choose one type of school rather than another. The empirical material is drawn from two surveys carried out in North-West Italy, but as far as the substantive implications of this study are concerned – and with the obvious exception of the institutional arrangements of the educational system specific to that country (chapter 2) – it could have come from anywhere else in the Western world. The relevant educational decisions – to stay on in education or leave – are common to most educational systems, and the conditions under which these decisions are made, such as inequality of cultural and economic resources and problems of employment are broadly similar in many Western countries.

There is little need to remind the reader of the crucial effects of educational behaviour from both an individual and a social viewpoint. Sociologists (Hyman, Wright & Reed 1975) and economists (Juster 1975) have explored the wide range of consequences that follow from education, from private and social monetary returns to child-rearing practices, from saving behaviour to occupational destinations. The interest of educational choices, however, lies not merely in their long-term effects, but also in some of their inherent features, which make them both individually non-trivial and socially complex events. Like few other decisions in life, they are encountered by virtually everyone living in Western societies. At the same time, they are treacherous in that they have to be made by persons in their teens, an age when preferences are unstable and little past experience can be drawn upon; and although they require long-term planning there is often no going back, the arrangements of the educational system or the pressure 'to enter into adult life' making a change of mind too costly or difficult to be translated into action (Boudon 1979).

Moreover, from a statistical point of view, the aggregation of educational choices often shows neat and significantly differentiated patterns across sections of the population, a fact which raises the question of what micro mechanisms are producing such patterns. The most important of these patterns is the positive correlation between the proportion of children staying longer in school and the level of social origin, no matter how the latter is measured; this suggests the presence of some reproductive force. Even though such correlations are far from perfect, the inertia produced by one's allotted position in society, especially if it is at one of the extremes, has an impact, first of all, on educational destinations. But how is this inertia created? This is the crucial question. Since there are no overt forces of coercion, educational destinations have somehow to be reached through individual preferences and decisions, which leaves one wondering how it comes about that what at a macro level takes the form of a partially reproductive pattern can, at the same time, be the result of decisions individually taken. The question that Paul Willis (1977) poses concerning occupational choices also seems appropriate when applied to educational choices: 'The difficult thing to explain about how working class kids get working class jobs is why they let themselves' (p. 1). Similarly, though, one can raise the converse question – which is equally crucial – and ask how it comes about that many manage to escape the forces of social reproduction and the destinations that their ascribed status would predict.

The dominant tendency in studies of educational behaviour has been to concentrate on either of these two questions, tacitly disregarding or openly rejecting the other as irrelevant. Most authors, in other words, have either embraced the idea that reproductive forces are overwhelming and that therefore there is little doubt that people are exclusively *pushed* into given destinations or, on the contrary, the idea that people are rational and *jump* towards the destinations that attract them most. The basic theoretical problem (chapter 1) – whether and to what extent it is more realistic to think of educational decisions 'as, so to speak, non-decisions, as pure individual manifestations of social forces that constrain or act *behind the backs* of agents, or whether it is rather the case that people act rationally and try to act according to what they genuinely want – has been lifted from the realm of rational discussion open to empirical test and dropped unfruitfully into that of insuperable ideological oppositions.

This book seeks to reverse that tendency and to bring the question back to its proper domain. It aims to be of some use also to those who have an interest in socially relevant decisions other than educational decisions. The means which sustain this enterprise are a comprehensive set of empirical tests, which in turn are founded upon two surveys and a particular statistical method. Let us briefly review them.

The empirical testing endeavours to bring numerical life into specific questions which articulate the broader theoretical problem in manageable statements. Thus, for example, on the *push* side the questions are: is the cultural capital one is endowed with through the family an essential ingredient for reaching higher education? What is the relative importance of economic constraints on educational decisions? Whereas on the *jump* side we have: when deciding about their education, do people respond rationally to their past achievement and to labour market opportunities? And, finally, do their personal preferences and aspirations make a difference in themselves to educational choices irrespective of social origin?

The surveys were both conducted in a predominantly non-academic environment. The first survey (Appendix 1) was organized jointly by the University of Turin and by two associations, one of parents and one of former Second World War resistance partisans. During spring 1977, 1,031 high school pupils were interviewed in the city of Turin, mainly in order to ascertain their political and cultural orientations. The questionnaire contained some items – such as post-high school intentions – which were not considered by the original researchers and which have been analysed for this study.

The second survey (Appendix 2) – which constitutes the major source – was directly sponsored by the Regional Government of Piemonte. In December 1978, 1,739 respondents were interviewed; they were young people of both sexes, between the ages of 14 and 29, who a year before had registered in the lists specially set up by the so called '285 Act'. The Act, passed by Parliament at the beginning of 1977, aimed at helping young people to find a job.[1] The subjects therefore were a cohort of young people who had started to look for a job not later than a year before the time of the interviews, and indeed the general aim of the survey was to gather information about what had happened during that year of searching. This sample will be referred to as 'the youth unemployment sample', but the reader should be aware that this is a definition based on the past condition of the subjects rather than on that found at the time of the interviews, at which point 56% had in fact already found a job, 7% had stopped searching for one, and 'only' 37% were still unemployed.

The fact that this study is based generally on survey data and in particular on these two surveys inevitably implies certain limitations. First, the survey method does not allow one to pick up the subtleties which are within the reach of in-depth interviews and participant observation. While obviously lacking in statistical significance these would give more insight into character traits and psychological interactions, which are beyond the scope of this book. Secondly, variations across time in educational behaviour cannot be observed through the samples used, for they refer to just one point in time. However, to bridge the gap between the rich and synchronic survey data on the one hand and the diachronic but poor or highly aggregated data of official educational statistics on the other would require another study.[2]

A further limitation of surveys conducted at one point in time is that causal-temporal sequences cannot be directly tested, but only inferred; thus it is difficult to judge in which direction the arrow of causation between events is actually pointing, and it is easy to end up with problems such as: is a given level of family income the independent variable acting on educational choices or is it rather the need to keep children at school that induces an effort to earn more by parents?

Finally, among the variables that are not under consideration in this book is a direct measure of ability. This is not, however, because original

[1] It provided benefits for firms employing young people, specially financed public projects, and made possible particular agreements between employers and employees, such as on-the-job training and temporary jobs. Any young unemployed person of 14 to 29 years of age was entitled to register in the lists set up by the bill in addition to the ordinary unemployment lists. Subjects were ranked in order of priority, according to age, marital status, number of children, family income and so on. The lists did not provide any pecuniary benefits to those who registered.

[2] For an attempt in this direction, see Boudon 1974. Starting from micro behavioural assumptions, he applies a simulation model to try to produce results consistent with the actual trends as shown by educational statistics.

researchers were not interested in it, but is just a consequence of the fact that IQ or similar tests have never succeeded in gaining any ground in Italy and they certainly have no connection with the world of education and with the subjects' perception of their ability. Several measures of past achievement are, however, closely considered.

The method of analysis is the *logit model* (section 3.1), which represents a considerable advancement over methods previously adopted. It is a multivariate technique which makes it possible to measure the effects of several independent variables, simultaneously considered, over the probability of making a given choice. It also allows – and this is one of its most innovative features – the treatment of decisions as *discrete* events, as choices, that is, where the basic question is 'which' rather than 'how much'. Although this may appear rather obvious to the lay person, the way most frequently adopted by both sociologists and economists when analysing educational choices has been to consider as the indicator the *number* of years of education experienced by individuals, as if the basic question subjects ask were 'how many years of education am I going to take?'. Thus they have used models that tell us the effects of a set of independent variables upon the probability of staying on at school for an additional year rather than the overall probability of an individual's choosing a given course of education (see for instance Sewell & Hauser 1975 among sociologists, and Psacharopoulos & Tinbergen 1978 among economists).

While this approach can, to some extent, be adequate for those few educational systems – notably the American system – which operate on a yearly basis, it is certainly inappropriate for most European systems.[3] Here people are likely to encounter choices that come in bundles, i.e. they often have to choose between no education at all and a course of education, which, among other attributes, has an institutionally given length of more than one year. Moreover, people not only choose between binary alternatives, but are often faced with more than two options – and obviously there is no way of transforming more than two qualitatively different alternatives into a continuous variable. Even if all options had the same length and could in principle be reduced to a binary choice

---

[3] Scholars in Europe have attempted to use methods other than log-linear or logit which seem to be able to maintain the discreteness of choices. Path analysis has been, so to speak, the most trodden alternative. However, it is a technique whose applicability to non-continuous variables is dubious when the choice contains two alternatives, and impossible when the alternatives are more than two.

opposing zero years to some amount of education, length would still be only one attribute among many that are considered by individuals when making decisions, and the reduction could therefore be misleading.[4] In this light the adoption of the logit model brings the analysis of decisions closer to the way subjects experience them in reality.

There is a further reason why analysing educational decisions as discrete choices is of considerable importance. In those models that use 'years' as the indicator, any particular year in which school is abandoned or continued becomes like any other, whereas a year soon after compulsory education may be qualitatively different from a year after high school, or similarly, the decision to leave before the beginning of a course may differ considerably from the decision to leave during it. In technical terms, it is very plausible to expect major *interactions* to occur between the level of education at which the choice takes place and the factors considered in the decision.

The book is organized in the following way. Chapter 1 is devoted to the theoretical question and discusses three approaches to the individual agent. In chapter 2 I describe the major institutional features of the Italian educational system which define the set of choices formally available, i.e. the 'dependent variable' of the study. The exposition of the empirical analysis is divided into two parts, developed in chapters 3 and 4. Chapter 3 deals with predominantly *pushing* forces and discusses the effects of a set of independent variables – cultural and economic resources of the family variously measured – which expressed such forces. Chapter 4, on the other hand, concentrates on *pulling* forces and considers whether subjects – when deciding about their education – adjust rationally to their expected probability of success, both in school and in the labour market, as well as whether they take account of their personal preferences and aspirations.

---

[4] There is also the possibility of *scaling* the multiple set of alternatives by the 'value' of what is to be chosen, e.g. educational quality or access to further education or particular occupations. Yet associated with this technique there are two problems: first one needs to know how people evaluate alternatives, and secondly alternatives often present countervailing attributes, so that an option that scores low on one attribute may score high on another.

1 The theoretical question

The basic theoretical question – which will provide a regulative idea around which the analysis presented in this book will be organized – can be stated as follows: to what extent can educational behaviour be represented as a product of intentional choice or, conversely, to what extent is it the result of processes which, in one way or another, minimize the scope for a socially meaningful choice at the individual level?

In this chapter I shall outline three major views of the individual agent, which will help in elaborating this question. According to two views, the individual agents are essentially inactive, since they are seen either as constrained by a lack of relevant alternatives or as pushed from behind by causal factors that escape their awareness; whereas in the third view they are regarded as capable of purposive action and of weighing the available alternatives with respect to some future reward. The two former views pertain to the realm of causality, the latter to intentionality. These three approaches have all been applied, often in mutual disregard or opposition, to educational choices as well as to many other choices of social relevance. They raise a great number of problems and are discussed in an equally wide field of literature. In the exposition that follows, therefore, I shall have to be selective and rely partially on the work of others who have already simplified the terms of a complex debate.[1]

In the first section of this chapter I shall introduce the three approaches: the argument will be kept mainly at a theoretical level, using some examples outside the sociology of education. In the second section the controversy surrounding the three approaches will be considered as it applies to the latter field.

---

[1] Particularly the work of Elster (1979: chs. 1 and 3; 1978: 157–63).

1.1 Three views of the individual agent

1.1.1 The structuralist view

The first view, which has been called *structuralist* (Elster 1979: 113), considers man's action as channelled by external constraints which do not leave any substantial room for choice: people would not pick, but would grab what they could. This view has been presented in a variety of ways, only a few of which are theoretically acceptable. The main dividing-line separates the 'strong' version of the structuralist approach, which holds this to be a generalized, even ontological state of affairs, from the 'weak' one, which underlines its intrinsically contingent nature, the latter being a far more acceptable viewpoint. In other words, the structuralist approach cannot really claim to represent a generalized explanation of human action. At most it may work under particular circumstances.

One of the most extreme and assertive versions is provided by Louis Althusser, for whom subjects are to be seen merely as 'supports' of social practices, as their 'occupants' and 'functionaries' (Althusser & Balibar 1970: 180). In Althusser's vision there is no scope or relevance for beliefs, preferences and intentions, for these are not only pre-empted by constraints as in weaker versions of the structuralist approach, but are also shaped by the structure of society and by its fundamental system of relations of production. Although this view may have leaked out of scholarly circles to achieve some degree of popularity among a number of Marxist militants, it is not on the whole of any great importance in the social sciences. Few people have shaped their analysis of society on the basis of this conception, and even fewer have explicitly acknowledged its theoretical merits. Above all, the various criticisms – the most recent as well as the most lucid of which is provided by Susan James (1985) – have shown the flaws of Althusser's approach and demolished its inescapable determinism.

A somewhat more common and less assertive – if still unacceptable – version of the structuralist approach, rather than boldly prescribing the theoretical value of ignoring people's motives for action, takes the pragmatic line of ignoring them *de facto*. It can be seen as the tendency to focus on the fence rather than on what the cows do within it (Elster 1979: 114). Outstanding examples can be found in certain studies of the labour market, whether these are Marxist in methodology or treat the functioning of the economy as mainly shaped by macro-economic and institutional forces (Gordon 1972; Barbagli 1974; Edwards *et al.* 1975; Rubery 1978; Rubery and Wilkinson 1981).

For instance, in some of the literature about the Italian labour market and particularly the 'black economy', workers tend to be seen as 'victims' of particularly nasty features of capitalism, or at least as passive components in the demand side of the economy, while their active behaviour and motivations are completely neglected.[2] People's behaviour in general seems to be mechanically deducible from the structure of the economy and from the decisions of government and employers.[3] I am obviously not suggesting that this is never the case, but rather that the social sciences should not neglect the more intriguing question of why people put up with such conditions, in this case why workers accept and very often actively look for jobs in the 'black economy'. The structuralist view usually avoids the problem of making hypotheses about models of man, although of course it must be based on assumptions about how people behave and what they want. These assumptions, which are often left implicit, seem sometimes obvious, for example the view that no one spends more money than his budget permits or that unemployment is always an unpleasant state; however, as we shall see later, there are cases when these assumptions, once spelled out, can be highly problematic and at least worthy of specific attention.

If we focus instead on a weaker version of the structuralist approach we can conceivably state that – *under given circumstances* in the outside world as it presents itself to the individual – it is possible that either (1) the feasible set of alternatives is reduced to one outstanding option only or that (2) the available alternatives are not alternatives at all, that is to say that with respect to the important attributes each alternative is like the other(s), so that they tend to collapse into one outstanding course of action only, as in (1).

The first statement is exemplified by Marx's words that proletarians 'are forced to sell themselves' (Marx & Engels 1930: 34). It seems difficult

---

[2] For a more extensive treatment of this point see Gambetta & Ricolfi (1978: 102–3 and 157–8). For texts in English which give some idea of the Italian black economy and of the 'subjective' side of it see Contini (1982) and Brusco (1982).

[3] Elster has observed that such an approach often grants the capacity of rational pursuit of interests to those in power while it denies it to the rest; this shows that unless it is self-contradictory the view is not in principle opposed to a rational action.

to understand this kind of statement as literally meaning that there is no choice. Unless one is directly treated as an object, notional alternatives always exist. It seems more plausible to interpret them as referring to the lack of minimally *acceptable* alternatives. If the alternatives are of an extreme kind, such as death, starvation, prison and the like, we can plausibly expect most people to choose to avoid them and we can sensibly describe their choices as largely forced, even though many counter-examples in which people choose the 'worst' alternative suggest that this statement cannot be taken literally.

The second statement stresses the lack of *relevant* rather than of acceptable alternatives. It can be exemplified by offering someone the old choice of which way they would like to die; this underlines paradoxically that, in given circumstances, one's preferences can only be expressed about details while the final outcome of each alternative remains unchanged and out of one's control. A good sociological example is provided by Blackburn & Mann (1979). These authors, with respect to the choice of occupation of manual workers in England, show that the scope for choice and meaningful trade-offs among jobs that are available for unskilled workers is very restricted and that according to a range of attributes all jobs look very much the same.

In both cases – i.e. whether there are no acceptable alternatives or whether those that there are do not differ substantially from one another – the number of relevant alternatives and the extent to which they can be sensibly distinguished very much depend on how (and by whom) the problem is defined, namely on which alternatives are thought to be unacceptable and on which attributes are thought to be insufficiently discriminating to make alternatives really distinct. Thus, for instance, if we consider the selling of our labour power as the crucial social event, then the amount for which it is sold and whether we sell it as school-leavers or as university graduates, in so far as we are selling it, will become relatively irrelevant. On the other hand, even choosing how to die can be very important if what we value is not merely the final result.

The judgements of the actors involved and those of the outside observers are often in conflict with one another, as in the case of Blackburn and Mann, whose workers do not subjectively perceive the lack of relevant differences among the alternatives at their disposal and 'no matter how restricted the choice, they treat it as real' (p. 288). Whenever such conflict occurs the observers are tempted to postulate the presence of some degree of 'false consciousness', whereby some causal mechanism prevents people from seeing that the choice is not quite 'real'.[4] The result, in other words, is that of combining the structuralist view with some of the difficult notions related to the second general view – the *pushed-from-behind view* – which we shall consider below.

In conclusion, to say that there is no choice seems to be too easy a way out, and I believe one should not treat actors as structural puppets: the structuralist view – by focusing on the constraints of behaviour rather than on behaviour itself – tends, so to speak, to *shortcircuit* the agent and attribute, often implicitly, a zero weight *a priori* to his preferences, expectations, and decision mechanisms. True, there are cases where the circumstances themselves – rather than the view – shortcircuit the agent, but such cases can be detected, and the conclusion that there is no choice reached, only *after* empirical work has been able to show the presence neither of acceptable nor of relevant alternatives. To adopt such a conclusion is not logically incompatible with considering individuals as potentially rational actors. It does not constitute an alternative to the rational theory of action: the point being that, in some but not all circumstances, the agents may have very little chance to show their rationality in action, since constraints channel their behaviour to a large extent.

1.1.2 The pushed-from-behind view

The second general view arrives at the same conclusion, namely that individual decisions are of minimal importance. It does so, however, by a different route, and makes much stronger assumptions about human nature. Broadly speaking, it assumes that a given piece of behaviour follows from causes, either social or psychological, that are opaque to the individual consciousness and, by acting *behind their backs*, push the agents towards a given course of action. Many views can be fitted in with this general conception: from unconscious behaviour to conditioned reaction to stimuli, from 'traditional' behaviour to internalization of social norms and constraints. In one way or another an individual's actions are seen as *propelled* (Elster 1979: 137; Elster 1978: 161) by forces that are not within the immediate reach of his or her conscious state. The

---

[4] Blackburn & Mann, however, do not explain how this mechanism comes about. See especially pp. 287ff.

point here is not to examine how many alternatives there really are for the individual; he or she does not weigh them and choose, but tends to select the course of action according to some inner mechanism, either behaving as if the feasible set were more restricted than it is objectively or, more frequently, acting independently of it.[5]

In other words, here the agents do not clearly perceive the alternatives they face – however many there may be – but are moved by causes that act independently of their awareness. According to the structuralist view it is largely irrelevant whether people are or are not aware of the constraints governing them, whereas the present approach assumes some limitation to consciousness: it is the inverse of Sartre's words that 'Il n'y a pas de l'inertie dans la conscience.'

The standard social example of this approach is perhaps that of people becoming criminals as a consequence of 'subculture-specific norms that more or less inexorably force some individuals into crime' (Elster 1979: 137).[6] Within sociology, which is the area where the *pushed-from-behind* view has been developed most explicitly, the father of this approach is probably Emile Durkheim. Although there is no general agreement as to how much emphasis he places on the individual as an intentional actor, it seems fair to trace to some of his writings the origins of the passive view of *homo sociologicus*,[7] which has been mainly though not exclusively developed by functionalism, notably through the work of Parsons.[8] As

---

[5] Also the case of behaving as if the feasible set contained real alternatives while these are actually very similar to each other falls partly under this approach, at least as far as opaqueness of consciousness is concerned.

[6] For an example in political theory cf. the work of Barry (1970), where the two approaches – the 'sociological' (that of values) and the 'economic' (that of rational actors) – are confronted. They more or less correspond to the distinction I am outlining in the text between the push-from-behind and the pull-from-the-front views. For a collection of examples in fertility decisions where again something like the rational approach is opposed to norms and the like see Hawthorn (1970), Easterlin (1978), and Andorka (1978). Also closely related is the recent debate on peasants' behaviour; see the review by Cumings (1981).

[7] The following quotation seems to suggest a radically different interpretation of Durkheim's views: in 'all forms of human behaviour into which reflection is introduced we see, to the degree that reflection is so developed, that tradition becomes more malleable and more amenable to innovations. Reflection in fact is the natural antagonist, the born enemy of routine. It alone can prevent habits from being caught in an immutable, rigid form, which prevents them from changing; it alone can keep them adaptable, maintain them in the state of necessary adaptability and flexibility in order that they may vary, evolve, adapt to the diversity and the changes of circumstances and milieux. Conversely, the less is the part of reflection, the greater is that of resistance to change.' (*Durkheim 1956: 137*) For a discussion of the work of Durkheim and its relationship to a passive view of man see Boudon (1979, particularly ch. 1).

[8] For a critique of Parsons' work precisely on these grounds see Barry (1970: ch. 4).

A. Giddens has recently pointed out,[9] 'a common tendency of many otherwise divergent schools of sociological thought is to adopt the methodological tactic of beginning their analysis by discounting agents' reasons for their action . . . in order to discover the "real stimuli" to their activity, of which they are ignorant'.

My point here is that it is not necessarily wrong to think of some forms of behaviour as caused by forces that are not perceived by the subject, but that it would be mistaken to think of all relevant social behaviour as explicable in this way and, even more so, to discount people's reasons for action *a priori*. We might conclude that under given circumstances people tend to behave like 'automata', but it is not something that can be assumed.[10]

Here there is also a logical and perhaps ethical fallacy which deserves to be mentioned: every time outside observers show that somebody else's behaviour follows from causes that are somehow unknown to the person, they assume at the same time that their view is superior to that of the observed person,[11] and this is a very strong assumption indeed. The sole logical ground on which in normal circumstances such an assumption can be justified is of an informative and contingent character, and it does not have a substantive and ontological status. More simply this is only justified if the observers can say that if the observed person had the

---

[9] Giddens (1979: 71; also the introduction). For a critique of this sociological view, particularly in its extreme version, see also Bourricaud (1975), Boudon (1977: ch. 7) and Heath (1976, especially the introduction).
  This tactic of starting off by looking for causes that act behind the back of the agent is also typical of psychoanalysis, where one explains and interprets somebody else's action by imputing some unconscious motives which might be totally alien to the other person's intentions and can be equally well thought of as a projection. It is instead interesting to note that psychoanalysis in order to be effective as a therapy *must* first of all be based on some kind of contingent agreement between the two parties involved, whereby the therapist's redefinition of the patient's situation in terms of unconscious reasons that were transformed in neurotic behaviour are accepted by the patient himself *as if* they were the 'true' motives. For a discussion of this problem in Freud see for instance Alexander (1974) and the well-known remarks by Popper (1963: 33ff).
[10] G. Tullock has argued that many who started off thinking that criminal behaviour can be explained by the 'sickness hypothesis' ended up by finding instead that a rational choice approach fitted the data better. Quoted by Elster (1979: 138). A very striking instance of this is in Downes (1966).
[11] This presumption of superiority takes on a particularly disturbing character in some work of Marxist origin where the argument runs more or less in the following way: 'When you fellows finally come to realize what we have long known are the real sources of your troubled and unhappy lives then . . . some kind of political upheaval will follow.' Cf. the otherwise interesting work of Bowles and Gintis (1976: 222–3). But this presumption is often held outside extreme Marxist views, and many authors – whenever they believe themselves to have a theory of the *real* interests – tend to slip into it.

same amount of information they have, the person would significantly alter his self-knowledge and perhaps modify his behaviour accordingly. In this connection one of the sound reasons that has been suggested as a ground for claiming the contingent superiority of the social scientists' viewpoint with respect to ordinary people is that they can actually observe a much wider range of behaviour and therefore of *variance* than ordinary people conceivably can (Marsh 1983).

Binmore[12] has raised a similar criticism in a rather witty manner with respect to behaviourism:

Man does often behave like a laboratory rat and the examination of this type of behaviour is clearly a worthwhile and absorbing activity and to this extent it is possible to have some sympathy with the views of its followers. But to claim that the whole truth can be incorporated within this viewpoint is a travesty. Not only can a man reason, he can also read. In particular he can read the work of Psychologists and modify his behaviour as a result of what he reads there.

Binmore's argument suggests that the causality affecting people's awareness does not necessarily identify immutable laws of human nature. Humans are certainly trapped in many causal circuits which cannot be interrupted without 'interrupting' humans themselves: whatever their preferences in terms of food, they must eat something. However, most causal circuits governing individuals' actions go through preferences and beliefs and can in principle be interrupted by the agents

---

[12] Binmore (1977) also says that 'any formal theory of human behaviour must take into account the effect that theories of human behaviour have upon human behaviour. In particular any such theory must take into account the effect which it itself would have on human behaviour if generally accepted. Otherwise the theory would of necessity contain the seeds of its own destruction.' To this, two things could be added. The first is that the effects of a theory when widely accepted can also be self-fulfilling – though it is improper to speak of a theory as self-fulfilling, because for this very reason the theory must have been wrong beforehand, or tested in non-generalizable conditions. Secondly, for a theory to contain the seeds of its own destruction can be part of its central significance. Suppose a theory predicted that certain effects would follow from advertisements capable of acting at the subliminal level and creating undesirable consequences. In principle this could make it less difficult for people to detect consciously such effects and intervene through higher-order processes that undermine the very causal circuit identified by the theory. Within the psychological literature cf. Nisbett & Wilson (1977: 247): 'at least some psychological phenomena probably would not occur if in the first place people were aware of the influence of certain critical stimuli'. At a philosophical level cf. Husserl (1970: 6): 'Mere fact minded science created mere fact minded men.'

themselves – they can, as it were, switch off one circuit and switch on an alternative one.

This notional possibility, which lays the foundations of thoughtful and intentional action itself, does not of course rule out the existence and the pervasiveness of mechanisms which constrain subjects' awareness and shape their intentions behind their backs. It simply indicates that such mechanisms cannot constitute a generalized explanation of human action. Here I shall mention some of such mechanisms which will be relevant to the analysis of decisions developed in this book.

We can mainly distinguish between mechanisms that are related to *cultural causation* and mechanisms which are related to *economic causation*. The former involve those inertial forces embodied in norms, beliefs and sub-cultural values[13] – which can shape preferences as well as the perception of the set of feasible alternatives, leading to a somewhat socially 'biased' or rigid evaluation of costs and benefits. In other words, class-related inertial forces can affect the preference structure by altering the values attached to any given option: the working-class belief, for instance, that academically oriented schools are not 'for people like us', or, vice versa, the upper-class belief that only academically oriented schools are 'for people like us'.

Similarly, inertial forces can act on the perception of the available alternatives by restricting the possibilities of evaluating and processing relevant information about available options. Cognitive constraints and a short time-perspective can lead to ruling out certain options 'automatically' through ignorance of the advantages associated with them.

These possible mechanisms, however, do not imply – as particularly crude sociological accounts seem to imply – that inertial forces directly govern agents' behaviour by singling out the final outcome. Subjects can still compare alternatives and choose rationally between them even if

---

[13] 'Values' are not always examples of pushing forces: they, in fact, may be present in one's own mind and act as pulling elements of action, as in the notion of 'value-oriented action' of Weberian origin. In the latter sense 'values' are probably better treated as lexicographic preferences (cf. Elster 1979: 137), for they imply some degree of awareness on the part of the agent. They are in a sense freely chosen values according to which the subject orientates his or her action. With respect to values, however, lexicographic preferences have something in common: they are both related to the action selected by an attribute which is non-trade-offable, i.e. no additional quantity of any other attribute can compensate for it. As a consequence action that follows from lexicographic preferences and from values is particularly inflexible to all changes in circumstances which do not concern the valued attribute. This footnote originates from comments I received from G. Hawthorn.

through a socially 'biased' preference structure. A working-class child can perceive as alien to his or her interests the *liceo* – the Italian secondary school of classical education – but still choose whether to leave after compulsory education or stay on in other types of secondary education on the basis of the expected returns. Similarly, the occurrence of certain events can shake up a 'numbed' perception of feasible alternatives. Thus, an exceptionally good school performance can convince a working-class child that he or she could be well suited to attend *liceo*; or, alternatively, an exceptionally bad school performance can still force unwilling upper-class parents to send their children to less demanding secondary schools, in spite of the strong drive to keep up with family status.

The second type of mechanisms, which revolves around structural or economic causation, can be well exemplified by the process of *sour grapes* (Elster 1983), whereby preferences, independently of actors' awareness, are shaped by external constraints. It can be that people come to prefer only what constraints allow them to achieve either by adjusting *ex post*, after having actually experienced the impossibility of pursuing the desired goal, or by adjusting *ex ante*, i.e. by not even cultivating preferences or goals that are outside their feasible set of alternatives.

A conspicuous share of the empirical analysis conducted in chapters 3 and 4 will be devoted to discussing this set of behind-the-back mechanisms as a possible explanation of part of the inter-class differences in educational decisions.

1.1.3 The pulled-from-the-front view

The third approach in general assumes that individuals act purposively in accordance with their intentions: when they are faced with multiple courses of action, it predicts that they will weigh them up and choose according to some expected future reward attached to each course of action. Individuals are here viewed not so much as pushed from behind as *attracted from the front*.[14] The basic assumptions of this approach have recently been unravelled by Jon Elster (1979):

[14] Though this approach usually assumes that people will *maximize* expected rewards this is not necessary, as the work of H. Simon showed in his justifiably famous *Models of man*; he argued that it is the *satisficing* course of action which is chosen rather than the maximizing one more often than not. See Simon (1957, especially ch. 14; 1976, especially pp. xxviii–xxxi and pp. 80–1).

The specifically human rationality is characterized by the capacity to relate to the future in contradistinction with the myopic gradient-climbing in natural selection. (p. vii)

We may say that *in creating men natural selection has transcended itself.* This leap implies a transition from non intentional adaptation, be it local or accidentally global, to intentional and deliberate adaptation. (p. 16)

Man, again in contrast [with animals], can choose between unactualized possibles. (p. 17)[15]

The capacity to relate to one's future can be regarded as the fundamental feature of the *rational-intentional* approach; but one can probably distinguish further between two versions of this approach to human behaviour. The first posits an intentional actor capable of behaving according to his preferences. Such preferences do not necessarily coincide with those of economic maximization. The second version, by contrast, tends to stress the adaptive features of rational choice. Constraints and preferences are taken as given; furthermore, preferences are often considered to be irrelevant for explaining differences in behaviour. The latter version is also that which has been more developed – often to the detriment of the former – and the problems related to it need some attention.

[15] Similar considerations were put forward by H. Simon some 35 years ago: 'The animal learning is primarily of trial and error character, that is learning does not show itself until he has had an opportunity, by actually experiencing them, to observe the consequences of his behaviours. . .[Man] may trace in his mind the consequences of each behaviour alternative and select one of them without actually trying any of them out' (Simon 1976: 86). Simon seems, however, more doubtful as to whether the differences between animal and man are a matter of kind, whereby a leap in natural selection is implied, or rather just a matter of degree.
  Also K. Popper moves generally along very similar lines when he says that: 'consciousness will assume evolutionary significance – and increasing significance – when it begins *to anticipate* possible ways of reacting: possible trial and error movements, and their possible outcomes . . . Our conscious states anticipate our behaviour, working out, by trial and error, its likely consequences: thus they not only control but they try out, *deliberate*' (Popper 1965: 29).
  On the difference between animal and man cf. Marx's words: 'what from the very first distinguishes the most incompetent architect from the best of bees, is that the architect has built a cell in his head *before* it constructs it in wax' (1974: 170; my italics).

Homans, for instance – to take a view which has been developed within sociology – does not view rational choice as stemming necessarily from conscious deliberation; he holds rather that expectations about the future merely incorporate past experience and bases the main propositions of his theory on a behaviouristic model of man, that is on a model that assumes behaviour as the result *par excellence* of causes operating behind the backs of agents (Homans 1961, 1967. G. Becker holds a similar viewpoint, 1976: 7).[16]

Although not as extreme as Homans', within economics too – a field in which the pulled-from-the-front view of action has been further developed – the version of rationality which has been stressed tends to view agents as passive creatures, with no more outstanding intentions than to adjust to market prices; this version 'can be used to eliminate the agent altogether, by guaranteeing a smooth fit between changes in prices and effective preferences at the margin. This is, so to speak, plastic interpretation, making the agent the creature of market conditions' (Hollis 1976: 17; cf. Heath 1976: 82–3). In this particular version rational choice theory tends to resemble the previous approaches, where causal rather than intentional forces shape human behaviour.

Here people's reasons for action are not discounted in the same way as in the pushed-from-behind approach, but rather subjects' relations with their future are assumed to obey a stable rule (for instance 'everything has its price') and can be derived from a set of preferences which are considered stable over time and similar among individuals, and therefore irrelevant for explaining differences in behaviour: everyone is seen as acting according to the objective 'the more the better', where 'the more' is overwhelmingly taken to refer to material goods and well-being. Particularly striking in this context are the words of one of the outstanding exponents of the 'economic approach to human behaviour': 'Since natural selection determines simple and identical preferences for other [non-human] species, the economic approach may well be *more* powerful in understanding the long-run behaviour of other species even though it was developed for human behaviour' (Becker 1981b: 217).

Of course, to varying extents, market forces can indeed make individuals their own creatures in a very rat-like fashion. Whether and to what extent this may be so is a matter for empirical analysis to

[16] For a critic of Homans' position on this point see Heath (1976: 14 and 78).

establish.[17] We can be sure, however, that many forms of behaviour cannot be explained within an 'economic approach',[18] for they do not simply imply an adjustment to the rationality assumptions of a market economy. Consider one of the basic theorems of economics, that is that the demand for a given commodity will diminish when the price of that commodity rises; inelasticities in the responses to change in prices – i.e. some people behaving differently from what is expected – are usually taken as deviations from rational behaviour and explained through some residual assumptions such as imperfect market conditions, limited information, and impulsiveness. But the famous paradox by Groucho Marx – 'I would not dream of belonging to a club that is willing to have me as a member'– can give some idea of how low- or even negative-demand elasticities can hide equally rational though not economic behaviour. (Cf. also Elster 1979: 166, 'I would not dream of loving someone who would stoop so low as to love me.') Applying the economic approach to 'club market behaviour' (or to 'marriage market behaviour') – where according to Groucho (cf. Hirsch 1977 about positional goods) the rule holds that the more *costly* the better – can be done only at the expense of denying importance to some of the most appealing subtleties of mankind. On less amusing, though still quite exciting grounds, A. O. Hirschman, in his remarkable book *Exit Voice and Loyalty*, has shown that the option *Exit* (i.e. stop buying a commodity, quit an organization, change college when dissatisfied with it) can be far less valuable, both individually and socially, than the alternative option

[17] This argument certainly has an historical weight. As has been pointed out recently by A. O. Hirschman, one of the arguments 'in favour of capitalism before its triumph' was that from the point of view of the Prince, the activity of money-making, of pursuing one's private interest, could make the behaviour of his subjects considerably more predictable, whereas other passions not as 'calm' as economic 'rationality and calculations' were much more dangerous for political stability. Behaviour governed by economic interest was seen since the beginning of capitalism as displaying a strongly bounded rationality, a rationality, that is, that did not question the rules within which it was expected to be applied. Now, to the extent that the force of economic interest is still successful at the micro level as a *governing rule* for decision-making, the scope for an 'economic approach to human behaviour' is still wide and its 'reductionist' view well grounded in reality. Marxist critics of neoclassical economics often forget this point, rejecting everything coming from that side, more or less as if Marx had rejected Adam Smith because the latter supported capitalism. On the pervasiveness of money interest as introduced by the bourgeoisie, Marx himself made some memorable comments in *The communist manifesto* (1930: 28).

[18] Elster (1979: 126–7) argues that there can be rational non-economic behaviour mainly because there are behaviours that follow 'non-Archimedean' preferences, i.e. they do not allow the rule 'everything has its price' to work.

of raising one's *Voice* (i.e. when not satisfied with goods etc. complaining, bringing pressure, rebelling and so on).

On the whole much of the rational choice theory has confined itself to the rather narrow interstices between preferences and constraints, both of which are taken as given. Nonetheless, even though it is very rewarding to concentrate on how people make their choices, treating both preferences and constraints as exogenous variables,[19] it should not be overlooked that intentional action can also be directed towards one's preferences or towards the (social) constraints one is facing.

It is easy to understand why the rational choice theorist avoids questioning preferences, for indeed one of the most difficult problems in the social sciences is related to preference-formation: can people be active subjects only *after* their preferences are formed? Are preferences created as a result of a causal mechanism that more often than not escapes subjects' awareness? Though some convincing arguments in favour of viewing man as active also with respect to his preferences have been put forward (Taylor 1964; Elster 1978, especially p. 162; Boudon 1979, especially ch. 3), questions of this sort are not easy to answer.[20] In general, however, by taking preferences as given the rational choice theory lends itself to the harsh criticism that J. S. Mill addressed to Bentham, the father of the calculus approach:[21] 'Knowing so little – he said – of human feelings, he knew still less of the influences by which those feelings are formed: all the more subtle workings of the mind upon itself, and the external things upon the mind escaped him.'[22]

By taking constraints as given the rational choice approach seems to

---

[19] Within these limits economists have usually contented themselves with the further assumption that the choice takes place in a compensatory mode, that is that an alternative can always be supplied in sufficient quantity to offset any deficiencies in any of the other alternatives. However, current research is showing how much can still be done about actual mode of choice; in contrast to the compensatory model others are discussed, such as the conjunctive and the lexicographic. See Tversky (1972); Tversky & Sattath (1979); Foerster (1979).

[20] On the economists' side an interesting attempt not to take preferences as given is provided by C. C. von Weizsäcker (1971). He ends his paper with a remark that concerns education and preferences: 'one of the functions of education seems to be to reduce people's mental and emotional dependence on the continuation of the *status quo* or in economic terms to increase the elasticity of substitution of their preferences. An adult person may have sufficient insight to educate himself, to work on his own preferences' (p. 371). Among those who have questioned some of the relevant subtleties that come to be neglected by a simplistic connection between preferences and behaviour is Sen (1973).

[21] Such paternity has been more recently acknowledged by G. Becker (1976: 18).

[22] Mill (1979: 97). For a critic of Utilitarianism, especially as far as the 'subtle working of the mind' is concerned, see Taylor (1969).

ignore much of the historical flavour of conflict and change, that is when people do not choose among 'the alternatives open to them', but try either to open more for themselves or – and sometimes it amounts to the same thing – to close some to other people (cf. Parkin 1974). The rational choice theorist is more likely to ask which course of action an individual is likely to choose among those open to him, rather than how and when individuals will take action for changing the available alternatives.[23] In Hirschman's terminology the rational choice theorist is more at ease with the *Exit* type of situation (going from one alternative to another) than with *Voice* type situations (complaining about the quality of the chosen alternative) (Hirschman 1970). Thus 'if any degree of creativity were required or shown by the actors, the sociologist [faithful to the rational choice theory] is likely to be in trouble' (Heath 1976: 182). Although it would be a mistake to neglect the fact that people make calculations as to the best (or the most satisfying) alternatives within those open to them,[24] it would also be a mistake to believe that the rationality they are capable of displaying is exclusively of an adjusting character, which takes social constraints as naturally given. How useful an approach this is depends on the subject under consideration.

The problems with the rational choice approach that I have outlined above point towards some of the reasons why perhaps many social scientists have regarded it as unappealing and preferred to have recourse to arguments about either structural constraints or pushing-from-behind causes. However, despite such problems Elster is surely right to argue that at the very least as *regulative ideas* the notion of rationality or in a weaker sense that of intentionality are of central importance for understanding and explaining human agency.[25] There is now a growing degree of agreement on this importance, even though it is not quite clear on which basis it should be founded. Some, like Hollis, emphasize that an active view of man's actions has to be taken at the level of metaphysics, and advocate the idea that 'rational action is its own explanation' (Hollis 1976: 21). Others, like Elster, argue on somewhat more empirical

[23] Even though one could in principle include among the alternatives the option of rejecting the existing ones and struggling for new ones, and although one could evaluate this course of action with the same cost-benefit analysis, this is not usually the way in which rational choice theory has been applied (the most notable exceptions are Olson 1965 and Coleman 1973).

[24] For a case where this neglect has led to disastrous consequences for the trade union movement in Italy see Gambetta (1981).

[25] For a distinction between the two concepts see Elster (1979: 150–6).

grounds that though not all human behaviour is rational or intentional 'there is a well grounded presumption that this will typically be the case' (Elster 1979: ix).

Whichever the basis, and I find the latter more appealing, it is a good tactic to begin one's analysis by presuming that in principle people act intentionally in the sense that they know something of what they want, of what may stand in their way of getting it, and of the likelihood of getting it. Such logical priority, though, does not imply that the purposive view systematically explains better given events: logical superiority does not confer an attribute of explanatory superiority to the approach, but simply reflects the possible superiority of its object.

But finally, having assumed a higher-order view of men, perhaps the most challenging task for social science is to look at how far we are in 'real life' from that ideal, or in other words to look at the *limits* of our rationality and the forces that prevent and pervert our intentions.[26]

1.2 The three views and the sociology of education

We can now take a further step and provide a brief outline of how the three approaches described in the previous section have been applied to the sociology of education. In this section I shall first consider a particular example which lends itself to clarifying the differences as well as the relationships between the three general views; next I shall introduce the major hypotheses which have been put forward in order to explain educational decisions and which will be discussed in greater detail in chapters 3 and 4.

1.2.1 The case of the student-workers

Suppose we observe that among students the proportion of student-workers has increased over a period of time, and that we would like to

[26] Among those who, starting with a regulative notion of perfect and improbable rationality, have given major contributions to the analysis of its limits are Simon (1957, 1976, 1979); Lindblom (1965); Hirschman (1967); and March (1974). These authors, however, tend to come more from an economic than a sociological background. On the sociological side, although Pareto defined sociology as the science of limited, problematic and contradictory rationality, his line of thought has not until recently been developed extensively. Boudon (1979) seems the sociologist most inclined to do so explicitly and to try to insert it in a wide and coherent sociological framework.

explain this growth. Depending on which of the three views we take, different sets of hypotheses are likely to be put forward.[27]

The structuralist-inclined observer is likely to put forward two types of hypotheses: (1) the number of student-workers has increased as a consequence of an increase in the demand for marginal, part-time and temporary labour that can be easily filled by students; (2) their number has increased because over the same period of time the number of working-class low-income students has increased, therefore the number of those who need to work in order to support themselves or help their families has also gone up. Here the assumption is: they work because they are poor.[28]

The first type of structuralist hypothesis is a good example of what it means to focus on the fence rather than on what the cows do within it: when the fence is widened (increase in demand), all the cows (the students) will automatically spread out and eat the extra grass (jobs) which has become available. It can provide only a partial explanation, for it picks out just a necessary condition and not a sufficient one: if there is no suitable demand obviously there will be no student-workers, but if there is demand it is far from obvious that there will also be student-workers. In other words some additional mechanism *at the level of the agent* must be introduced. Arguing that an increase in the level of demand will be followed by an increase in the supply of student-workers, one needs implicitly to assume that students *always* wanted to work but in the past they were constrained and had no chance of doing so. The key question of why they wanted to work remains in the shadows, along with questions of why students and not some other member of their family – such as the mother or the father taking up a second job – went to fill the new demand. To relate mechanically 'boxes' like demand, social classes and so on with particular forms of behaviour does not constitute a sufficient explanation, and the underlying processes are still in need of being spelled out.

Although explanations of this type are often presented as structuralist explanations, when looked at more closely they seem to be rather

---

[27] Here I shall not pursue this question in substantive terms. For an empirical test of the various hypotheses concerning student-workers at the level of secondary school see Gambetta & Moretti (1981).

[28] These hypotheses are not fabrications but are popular among Italian trade union and left-wing 'sub-cultures'. See Consiglio di Zona CGIL–CISL–UIL (1977) and Foa *et al.* (1969).

impoverished versions of rational choice models (cf. section 4.2 for an example). One could in fact conceivably argue that an increase in demand gave students more scope for *choosing* what they wanted, lifting some of the previously existing constraints.

The second type of structuralist explanation is not so obviously insufficient. The 'poverty hypothesis' is already at the level of the agent and can in principle provide an understandable and compelling reason for students to take up jobs. Here the problem is rather empirical: since clearly there is no *a priori* reason to believe that absolute need for money is the only plausible explanation, it remains to be seen how much of the overtime variance in the student-workers phenomenon is explained by this hypothesis. Avoiding the methodological intricacies of how this can be done, the logical conclusion is that only if residuals are small – granting that we are somehow measuring net effects and not spurious ones – will our hypothesis gain strength; otherwise some of the other hypotheses reviewed below must be simultaneously at work.

But even if the results were highly positive for the hypothesis it would still be virtually impossible to show that we are really dealing with necessitating constraints and that work for the students was the unique available option. We may ask: why have they not borrowed the money? Why have their families obtained the needed additional income from the students' efforts rather than from those of the mother or the father's second job? Often what appears to be a compelling course of action for a single individual can be the result of previous decisions taken within the family and whose source may well be some kind of opportunity calculations rather than straightforward compulsion. In conclusion, we can observe that the crucial difficulty with this view is that it tends to be generally inadequate at the level of the agent and of the mechanisms governing his responses. A structuralist hypothesis makes much more sense if it is stated in probabilistic rather than necessitating terms: the presence of income constraints makes it more likely for students to *choose*, rather than to be forced, to work while in education. It is not very realistic to expect that the structuralist hypotheses alone would typically constitute an exhaustive explanation of behaviour, and this leaves room for the other two approaches.

If we are inclined towards the pulled-from-the-front approach and we believe that agents' decisions are predominantly made on the basis of some rational calculation combining personal preferences and future rewards, then an increase in the proportion of student-workers would be interpreted either as a consequence (1) of a decrease in rates of return or other rewards connected with investing in education a small enough amount for it still to be an attractive option, but enough to make the immediate returns provided by work more attractive than a full-time devotion to studying in view of purely future returns (cf. Levy Garboua 1976); and/or as a consequence (2) of a generalized shift in tastes which, say, makes the young prefer earlier economic independence from their family (Ricolfi & Sciolla 1980: 96–102). Both hypotheses are theoretically plausible, not necessarily incompatible and are liable to be tested through empirical analysis.[29] Furthermore, there is nothing to prevent either or both representing, at least in principle, an exhaustive explanation of the decision process.

However, when looking at the same event the observer inclined towards the pushed-from-behind idea would put forward radically different hypotheses from those advanced by the rational theorist. They would resemble the following: the increase of student-workers follows from an increase over the same period of those groups, such as working-class students, who have different values concerning the place of work in life and its relationship with studying. More people, that is, come from a sub-culture that considers early work experience as more important and as not quite separate from studying, which in turn could be valued more instrumentally.[30]

This hypothesis can be tested empirically, in the first instance by checking whether the increase in student-workers is accounted for exclusively by individuals of working-class background. If this were the case, it would not constitute sufficient evidence to conclude that the increase is due to the effect of sub-cultural values, for, among other things, the same evidence is also compatible with the structuralist hypothesis (see above) whereby working-class students would tend to work because they needed the money to finance their education. But, for

---

[29] Similar explanations have been advanced in the literature by Ricolfi & Sciolla (1980: 93–4) and by Turner (1960: 264), the latter with respect to the difference in numbers of student-workers between the UK and the US. It is worth noticing that – as John Craig pointed out to me – in theory the first hypothesis could be reversed and still yield the same result: an *increase* in returns could attract into education individuals who would not have enrolled otherwise, but they may belong to social groups that need to work in order to pay for their education.

[30] For similar arguments developed with respect to educational choices in general see Lane (1972: 255).

the sake of argument, let us assume that among working-class students income is irrelevant in determining whether or not they are also simultaneously working and that we are in the position to infer from the evidence that the explanatory factor could well be sub-cultural values.

How theoretically plausible this hypothesis is and to what extent it is compatible with the hypotheses derived from the other approaches still depends on further specifications which are not usually found in the literature that takes this line. By saying that sub-cultural values push one to choose a certain option we can have in mind at least two states of affairs: either that (1) independently of any other consideration subjects who share those values tend automatically to select a particular option or that (2) those values tend to interact with other considerations and make it more likely for agents who entertain them to choose a particular option.

The latter specification is distinctly more plausible than the former. The former disregards on the one hand the importance of constraints and on the other that of purposive action. First, as Becker (1976) has shown, one may be governed by a wide range of non-rational inclinations, but if the option towards which one is inclined happens to fall out of the feasible set then there is no way in which that particular option can be chosen. If there are no jobs available for students then, irrespective of sub-cultural values, there will be no increase in student-workers. Secondly, it seems theoretically not very plausible to believe that sub-cultural values can single out directly, independently of preferences and irrespective of the structure of rewards, the course of action actually taken. It would seem more plausible – particularly if data showed an extra increase among students of working-class origins not accounted for by differences in income – to explain the increase in student-workers by a two-step model, which, while taking the impact of constraints into account, also involved rational and less rational mechanisms. Thus, a change in the structure of rewards and/or a change in preferences could generally account for the increase. However, within particular sub-cultural groups such as the working class, the 'over-evaluation' of work as an attractive option could alter the preference structure and, through the latter, enhance the response to changes in the rewards structure, leading relatively more working-class students to take up employment while in education. If we express the same model in counter-factual terms we can say that had the changes in the reward structure not taken place, working-class students too would not have considered the possibility of working. The presence of sub-cultural values is likely to affect the preference structure by giving more weight to certain options, but is far less likely to push subjects mechanically towards a certain option and to make them altogether insensitive to the rewards structure.

1.2.2 The main controversy

How the controversy surrounding the three approaches applies to educational choices in general will be extensively discussed in the following chapters. Here I shall provide the reader with a preliminary outline and a few methodological remarks.

A surprising circumstance which emerges from reading through the studies of educational choices is that, in contrast with what is suggested by the example of the student-workers discussed above, most authors have had the tendency to cluster around one of the three approaches, while ignoring or *a priori* rejecting the others. Empirical testing has been carried out within the hypotheses consistent with one particular approach rather than between different hypotheses derived from more than one approach.[31] Thus we find those who have stressed the importance of constraints, whether cultural (e.g. Bourdieu & Passeron 1977) or economic (e.g. Barbagli 1973); those who have highlighted the role of sub-cultural values and experiences (e.g. Hyman 1966, Lane 1972), those who have pointed out that it would be mainly a matter of rational decisions taken on the basis of costs and benefits (e.g. Boudon 1979), and finally those who have boldly insisted that there would be no hard evidence to prove that educational choices are other than the result of genuine preferences (Murphy 1981). Only a few authors have attempted some integrated tests (e.g. Halsey, Heath & Ridge 1980).

Perhaps the main controversy has been between the cultural capital hypothesis and the rational choice hypothesis. The former, represented mainly by Pierre Bourdieu, can be seen as a particular version of the structuralist approach. The latter, represented mainly by Raimond Boudon, can be seen essentially as an adaptive version of the pulled-from-the-front approach in which a socially uneven distribution of costs and benefits explains inequality in educational decisions. Both have been

---

[31] Perhaps the same three approaches could be applied in order to explain the scholars' choice of approach: scholars may have found cultural or economic constraints, or they may have been propelled by ideological biases, or, finally, given the available 'technology' for analysing data, it may have been relatively costly for them to go to the trouble of testing the general approaches against one another.

forcefully argued and have deeply divergent implications with respect to educational policies. In one case a lower degree of educational inequality could be brought about by acting on the class biases of school culture, which should become better able to accommodate the features of working-class culture rather than selecting their bearers out of education. In the other case the same result would be achieved by acting on the structure of unevenly distributed economic incentives, which at present make it both less possible and attractive for a working-class child to continue in education as long as his middle-class counterpart.

Here it is important to stress that *a priori* there is no reason to expect that any of the above-mentioned hypotheses should constitute a more plausible or more general explanation of educational choices. Above all, there is no reason to believe that the final aggregate outcome of individual decisions should be the result of just one mechanism. This can be understood in at least three possible ways. First, different agents can make their decisions according to different mechanisms. Thus, some can rationally choose whether or not to stay on at university given their preferences and the expected advantages, while others can be so deprived as to have serious computational difficulties in forming an idea about the possible advantages associated with education. Secondly, the same agent can decide simultaneously on the basis of more than one mechanism: a working-class child can exclude academically oriented high school because 'that is not for us', and still choose rationally among the remaining options. Thirdly, the same agent can choose according to different mechanisms at different educational stages. Upper-class children can be 'automatically' sent to *liceo* after compulsory education but later on when they face the choice of university they may decide on the basis of how satisfactory their past academic achievement was and of how attractive the prospects for immediate employment look.

All these possible combinations will be considered below. Here it suffices to say that what constitutes the specificity of this book is its unusual lack of obsession with any one in particular of the three approaches and the attempt at providing a comprehensive test of the decision processes in education.

1.3 Conclusions

The theoretical stance which I shall take in this book can now be more clearly stated: it is certainly insufficient to generalize the statement that

there is no choice, as structuralists are often tempted to do, or to discount people's reasons for action, as does the pushed-from-behind view, but it would be over-optimistic to think either that all relevant social behaviour takes place always within some relevant degree of freedom or that our motives and causes for action are always transparent to our consciousness; having a structure of preferences and acting accordingly does not necessarily mean being aware of how this structure has come about.

To start with I shall assume that people try to achieve intended and expected results and above all reflect on their future and the alternatives they face.[32] At the same time I shall also try to consider pushing factors that may be at work: norms, tradition, and class values – though it is unlikely that they will single out directly the course of education to be taken – can be quite important, independently of any rational calculation, in narrowing down the feasible set from its logical to its perceived extension. Furthermore, sub-intentional processes like *sour grapes* can act causally upon the formation of preferences. Finally, structural constraints either concerning the institutions (for example the educational system) or the individual (for example income) or, again, the labour market (for example the number of available jobs) define what is feasible both for each single individual and for all individuals taken together.

It is now possible to recapitulate the initial question. The path leading from totally heterodetermined behaviour to perfect rationality seems to be rather twisting, steep at some points and gentler at others. Structural constraints, by defining the feasible set, also define how far the individual can climb uphill before being blocked by an obstacle which only a collective effort can eventually remove. However, it is a slope and not a precipice, and in this sense the question is not so much at which extreme individuals tend to cluster – whether they jumped or were pushed – but rather where on the slope they are likely to stop. It is only through empirical analysis that an answer to this question can be provided.

[32] Whether they will actually get their intended results is another matter: lack of knowledge and information (Simon 1957, 1976; Haystead 1974) plus unintended consequences (Merton 1932, Boudon 1977, Elster 1978) can prevent individuals from fulfilling their intentions, in spite of their attempts to incorporate probabilities into their rational calculations.

2 Institutional constraints and educational choices

In chapter 1 three approaches to individuals' decisions were outlined and it was argued that although the intentional view is in principle the most important, external constraints and non-rational forces can also be expected to affect educational choices. Before trying to develop those three approaches empirically through the analysis of the survey data and to focus on individuals' mechanisms of decision, it is necessary to introduce the present institutional context of Italian education and the educational choices which it makes available to individuals. The latter constitute the 'dependent variable' of this study. This task, to which this chapter is devoted, requires a few words of introduction.

In general an educational system constitutes an external constraint on individual behaviour, in the sense that it provides the organization for a given type of education and sets the rules and the procedures which regulate admission, selection, certification and so on. Single individuals, when making a decision, have to adjust to the institutionally feasible set of alternatives that the system offers and, depending on how an educational system is set up and its streaming and selecting mechanisms arranged, individuals may face considerably different routes. For example, during term-time few British university students can seriously consider the idea of a job, whereas in Italy many students do work simultaneously. The educational system in Britain enforces a clear-cut decision: either one goes to university or one goes to work.[1] In Italy both options are open at the same time: there are no residence requirements to be fulfilled, fees are low, and students can obtain their degree over a much longer period than the normal length of the course of study; besides, students can more or less freely decide when to take their exams

[1] In the UK there is some possibility of adopting a 'mixed strategy' of studying and working at the same time, but it involves, for instance, sandwich courses, the Open University or some technical colleges, instead of traditional university courses.

and when to submit their final dissertation. In Britain, by contrast, the demarcation between working and studying periods is far more strict: the length of the course of study as much as the timing of the final exams is externally determined.[2]

There is another sense in which educational institutions represent a constraint: the purposive action of isolated individuals can do very little to change them and they are more often the result of political conflicts[3] and of purposive collective action.[4]

Yet the fact that individual actions are shaped and constrained by existing institutions does not make micro decisions irrelevant. This can be understood in the light of two considerations. Firstly, individuals' decisions are governed by economic and cultural mechanisms which are independent of and sometimes in conflict with institutional obligations and arrangements. This is suggested by the fact – considered in detail in section 2.1 – that until the mid seventies compulsory education up to 14 years remained no more than a formal principle and many pupils left before reaching the legal minimum leaving age. For institutional obligations to be effective either the obedience to the rule must be enforced by some punitive sanction or the non-institutional mechanisms which, say, keep people from sending children to school must be broken (stronger control against child labour, economic aids, compensatory education and so on).[5]

---

[2] Superficially it would seem as if the Italian educational system were leaving more room for choice to students than the British system. However, if we consider that in the UK every student whose parents cannot afford to pay receives a grant and has his fees paid by the State, we may also wonder how many Italian students would still work if the educational system of their country intervened to cover living costs.

[3] General remarks on conflict and educational systems can be found in Banks (1976) and Archer (1979). For an attempt to write a history of the Italian educational system from this perspective see Barbagli (1974).

[4] For instance, the engineering workers – to pick an example from Italy at the beginning of the seventies – obtained from their employers the right to 150 hours a year paid work leave in order to facilitate, for those among them who had not had the chance when young, the completion of compulsory education; they also managed to obtain from the State free courses, which were organized specially for that purpose. In the following years this entitlement spread throughout most of the other industrial sectors and the number of hours was increased to 250. Since 1975, access to the courses has been extended to housewives and the unemployed. From the beginning of the initiative to the end of 1979, over 400,000 workers have benefited from the courses and received their final certificate (CENSIS 1980). Clearly, this is one of those cases where, rather than passively adjusting to their constraints, people took collective action in order to change their feasible set of alternatives and the relative costs of going back to school.

[5] In Italy neither strategy was followed and the institutions, *de facto*, waited until the governing mechanisms themselves became compatible with staying on at school until 14 years of age.

Secondly, educational systems in Western countries often give individuals some freedom of choice *within* the limits established by their rules. There are two ways in which we can see a relative lack of constraint: educational systems almost invariably (1) provide a certain variety of educational routes of different lengths and content (this aspect will be discussed in section 2.2) and within a particular educational system individuals' choices cannot be explained simply by institutional mechanisms; more importantly, (2) they frequently let the supply of school and college places be determined by the demand so that all qualified people who wish to do so can choose to continue their education.

The relative autonomy of educational decisions can also be evaluated by comparison with occupational choices. The latter are to a large extent the product of two simultaneous decisions, that of the applicant and that of the employer. The former, by contrast, are taken in a much more stable and formalized environment which sets the rules and leaves individuals free – within the limits of what might influence their decisions extra-institutionally – to conform to the rules and on that basis decide their educational career. As Boudon puts it, 'an individual cannot create a job just because he wants it, but he can go to college if he wants to, provided he is qualified' (Boudon 1974: 21). Even though there are Western countries where the supply of school and college places is not entirely determined by the demand (Britain, the USA), in most European countries, especially those like France and Italy which have a highly centralized system, the so-called 'Robbins principle', i.e. universal access to higher education, has been long since adopted.

A final remark should be made on the importance of micro decisions in their aggregate and unintended effects. Simple shifts in taste can unintentionally move giant manufacturing industries (Sabel 1982: especially part 5), and individual decisions can have much the same effect on institutions. Educational system decision-makers, but also each single individual facing a decision, have implicitly to rely upon the aggregate decisions of everybody else;[6] if everyone should suddenly shift to only one among the many possible alternative routes offered by, say, a university system, it could be difficult both for the system to adjust and find the appropriate means to alter the flow of new and unexpected

---

[6] By this I do not mean necessarily in any game-theoretical situations like the ones suggested by Boudon (1974) and Elster (1976), but simply in mechanical terms, as in the game of musical chairs.

demand, and for each single individual not to be crowded out. The fact that educational systems seldom break down or individuals are rejected on the basis of sudden over-crowding suggests that the risk is rather potential and limited in terms of its effects; and, at the same time, that relatively stable mechanisms are probably governing educational decisions.

In general this chapter will consider how the Italian educational system constrains, circumscribes and promotes individual types of behaviour. Section 2.1 deals with the postwar development of compulsory education and with the discrepancy between the legal and actual minimum leaving age; it also discusses the reform which in 1962 introduced comprehensive education and questions its theoretical premises. Section 2.2 introduces the set of educational choices which are available in the Italian educational system after compulsory education and the way in which they will be represented in the analysis, i.e. as a set of hierarchically ordered discrete choices.

2.1 Compulsory education and individual choices

In the Italian educational system children up to the age of 14 have no other choice than attendance at school, and their overall educational behaviour appears to be institutionally determined. Since 1962, when a major reform was introduced, the comprehensive course of compulsory education of eight years – from 6 to 14 – has been divided into five years of elementary school and three years of middle school. At the end of the third year of middle school, the pupils who pass the state examination obtain a certificate, which, besides being required for access to many occupations, allows them to enrol in high school. Thus, after the end of middle school, those who have met the standards can exercise their right of choice: a choice between leaving and staying on, and a choice among several possible routes of post-compulsory education.[7]

However, leaving school before the 14th birthday has been a widespread phenomenon until recent years and legislation has been quite insufficient to compel attendance at school up to the prescribed age. Furthermore, at the compulsory level there is a considerable degree of

[7] A full description of the Italian educational system can be found in Fadiga Zanatta (1978). An important feature is that education is mainly provided by the State and financed through public spending. Fewer than 10% of pupils attend private schools.

selection, which has a very important bearing on future choices. Before considering the set of post-compulsory feasible choices, a task which will be undertaken in section 2.2, it is therefore essential to consider in some detail the way in which the compulsory system operates and the extent to which it may influence educational decisions later on.

2.1.1 Trends and selection mechanisms

Compulsory education was formally extended up to the age of 14 in 1923 through the *Riforma Gentile*,[8] but thirty years later, Italy still had an extremely low participation rate in education, especially at the lower levels: in 1952–3 (table 2.1) at 11 years of age 27% of children were already out of school and by 13 those who had left totalled 64.4%. Italy was also far behind other countries: according to OECD estimates (quoted by Boudon 1974: 42) in 1950 the enrolment rate, in Italian primary and secondary education considered together, was 56% of the relevant age groups and was ahead only of the rates of Turkey (24%), Portugal (31%), Yugoslavia (42%), and Spain (43%); all other OECD countries had higher school attendance rates.

It would, I think, be wrong to attribute such a state of affairs merely to a low level of economic development: other countries like Belgium, Finland, Austria and Japan, which economically were not very far ahead of Italy, had far higher rates of school attendance. Certainly one of the historical reasons for such massive 'distaste' for formal education, as can be found after the war among Italians, comes from the institutional arrangements introduced by the Fascist regime in the educational system. The *Riforma Gentile*, which was one of the first initiatives to be taken by the Fascists, while formally raising the minimum leaving age to 14, actually and intentionally blocked and depressed the growing demand for education by introducing ferocious selection mechanisms which had immediate and drastic consequences on the enrolment rate in middle school:[9] the number of pupils at this level of education was

8 The Act was named after the idealist philosopher Giovanni Gentile, who was Minister of Education at that time. The compulsory leaving age at 14 was for some time limited only to those pupils who were living within 2 kilometres of a school. For a recent discussion on the *Riforma Gentile* see Barbagli (1974: ch. 5); for a bibliography and a description see Fadiga Zanatta (1978).
9 In every type of middle school, for instance, it introduced an entry examination and Latin became a compulsory subject, even for those who did not intend to follow a course of study in the humanities. In addition it limited the supply of middle school places.

Table 2.1. *School attendance rates by age in Italy*

age	1952–3	1959–60	1966–7	1972–3	1975–6
6–7	94.1	97.0	98.6	100.5	96.9
7–8	96.7	98.4	98.4	100.5	99.2
8–9	97.8	98.5	98.5	100.4	98.5
9–10	96.0	97.6	98.0	100.0	98.3
10–11	92.5	96.3	97.6	99.4	98.6
11–12	73.0	81.4	90.9	99.5	98.5
12–13	55.0	65.4	84.3	96.3	99.5
13–14	35.6	51.0	74.0	89.8	96.5
14–15	n.a.	33.0	56.4	72.7	76.2
15–16	n.a.	24.1	42.1	56.9	57.6
16–17	n.a.	20.3	33.6	47.1	51.5
17–18	n.a.	16.8	27.4	38.1	43.2
18–19	n.a.	12.3	19.7	31.8	36.2

Source: until 1966–7 ISTAT (1968); for 1972–3 and 1975–6, EUROSTAT 1978: 140–1

around 340,000 in 1922, a year before the reform, while only a year after the reform, in 1924, this had become 240,000, a decrease of more than 30%. The decline was not merely the result of institutional forces that forced people out directly. The reform in fact changed the set of opportunities linked with one type of middle school, provoking a rational, albeit negative, response on the side of the people. Over half of the decrease took place in fact in the *scuola complementare*, which was mainly attended by working-class and lower-middle-class children and previously entitled pupils to continue into some of the branches of high school. The reform had transformed it into an educational *cul de sac*, and since no equivalent alternative was provided by the reform, people simply failed to enrol their children. The negative response was so massive that the regime had to retreat and restored some form of openness at the end of the *scuola complementare* (see Barbagli 1974: 202ff).

Since the war the situation has improved dramatically: in 1978 the number of pupils enrolled in middle school was five and a half times as great as in 1946. This massive increase is to a large extent genuine and very little of it is due to an increase in the corresponding birth cohorts. From table 2.1 we can see, in terms of school attendance rates by age, the upward shift over time of the first main selection point, and more generally the increase of survival rates across age-groups. From the fifth column of the table we can see that, despite the increase, it is only since 1975–6 that the actual minimum leaving age has begun to correspond approximately to the legal leaving age. Even in 1972–3, 1 out of 10 of those 13–14-year-olds had already left school.

The disappearance since the mid seventies of the long-standing discrepancy between the formal and actual leaving age does not imply, however, that everybody in fact successfully reaches the end of compulsory education, thereby acquiring the right to go to high school. Some pupils, although they stay at school until they are 14, never manage to pass the final examination and obtain the certificate. In 1975, 6.8% of pupils leaving school did so before reaching the final certificate. The proportion of early *dropouts* is, however, declining very fast – in 1974 it was 10.8% – and such pupils are almost entirely concentrated in the South of Italy. Here in 1975 18% left compulsory education before obtaining the certificate, whereas in the rest of the country virtually no one did so (CENSIS 1976–7). This is no consolation, yet it means that in two-thirds of the country nowadays all pupils actually reach the point where they qualify to choose whether to stay on at high school and which school to go to.

There remains the problem of children who are kept down, which probably constitutes one of the major sources of interaction between institutional selection mechanisms and individuals' behaviour. The system is such that at every level of education, from elementary school to high school, pupils whose school performance is judged as seriously deficient by teachers can be kept down at the end of a given year and they have to repeat the year. Such pupils are known as *ripetenti*, 'repeaters'.

The possibility of failing is thus not occasioned only by a final examination falling at the end of each full stage of education, but can occur at the end of every intermediate year. There is no formal limit to the number of times a pupil can be kept down, and there is no limit either to the number of times a pupil can attempt once more to pass into the next year. In this way selection never takes place explicitly by turning the pupil out of school; it is always left up to the child and his family whether to withdraw or to stay on, despite one or more failures. The proportion of children kept down at elementary school has been declining constantly over the postwar period: it was 16% in the school year 1952–3 and is now (1977–8) 2.2%. In middle school the proportion of repeaters, though it

Table 2.2. *Annual percentages of 'repeaters' by*
level of education in four school years

	elementary school	middle school	high school
1952–3	16.0	—	—
1962–3	11.8	13.9	9.5
1972–3	5.2	7.4	7.1
1977–8	2.2	6.9	7.1

Source: CENSIS 1980

declined during the fifties and sixties, has stayed constant in the last decade at around 6–7% (table 2.2).

Put this way these figures would seem reasonably low; but, if we realize that these rates are annual and that the bulk of repeaters are pupils who are kept down only once,[10] the cumulative effect is substantial and the proportion of pupils who reach a certain age but are one or more years behind is high. The most recent estimate I could obtain of the number of pupils who are behind at the age of 13 yielded a figure of 38% for the school year 1972–3 (ISTAT 1976a). It is likely that since that year the rate of pupils who are behind has declined, particularly as a consequence of the declining selectivity in elementary school; however, no less than 25–30% of children who reach the middle school certificate and the key decision point concerning high school still suffer from the considerable disadvantage of being older than their 'regular' fellow pupils.

In what way this is a disadvantage should be intuitively clear and it will be dealt with more extensively later, especially in terms of the consequences of a failure for future educational decisions (section 4.1). Here it is important to point out that this method of selection is both institutionally contradictory and economically unjust, especially when applied to compulsory education.[11]

At an institutional level, the application of the keeping-down mechanism raises contentious ambiguities: some have argued that, since

[10] In 1972–3 out of 100 13-year-old pupils who were behind, 60 were behind one year, 29, two years and 11, more than two years (ISTAT 1976a). The reason for the high proportion of pupils kept behind 'only' one year is probably that they are unlikely to face this failure a second time without leaving school as a consequence. For a full quantitative assessment of selection in Italy see Gattullo (1976).

[11] The injustice is similar to that which takes place when the school-leaving age is raised without simultaneously providing financial aid for poorer families to keep their children at school longer (Blaug 1970: 170).

the schooling is compulsory and pupils have not chosen to attend, the system ought to be non-selective.[12] Certainly what is problematic is that the reform of 1962, while talking explicitly of compulsory education up to the end of middle school, left the minimum leaving age at 14 and did not abolish the keeping-down selective device; as a consequence, repeaters may be far behind their supposed compulsory attainments, although they may leave 'compulsory' education on their 14th birthday.

At an economic level, repeaters suffer from a doubling of the costs – both forgone earnings and direct costs – of one year of education which adds to the financial burden of education; a burden which is already unevenly confronted by families according to their level of income. Thus being kept down is only formally a similar measure in different cases: in reality it represents a very differentiated punishment and can be expected to have a considerable discouraging effect for poorer families.

To talk of forgone earnings for boys and girls younger than 14 years of age may seem rather odd, and we need to dwell a little on this issue. It has been argued (Blaug 1970) that the disappearance of child employment and the institutionalization of the leaving age have abolished any real opportunity cost of schooling up to the end of compulsory education and that, at this stage, work and school no longer represent competing alternatives.[13] This, however, does not apply to Italy, even though the law formally forbids child labour.

According to a survey carried out over all middle school pupils in Lombardy by the Regional Administration in 1975–6 as many as 25.4% of middle school pupils are involved in working activities, associated mainly with their families. Lombardy is one of the three most industrialized regions of the country and it would be difficult to argue that this striking phenomenon is a consequence of a rural and backward economic structure for which it is convenient to have recourse to the marginal sections of the labour force. Nor, according to the researchers who analysed the data of the survey (Tagliaferri 1980), does the work involvement of children appear to be the result of sheer poverty; rather, it seems to spring from the peculiarities of the productive system and from its reliance on family-based economic activities, which provide many opportunities for employing children.

[12] This is not so much an academic argument as a widespread idea in the Italian left, which makes itself felt in Italian education through one of the largest teachers' unions (CGIL).

[13] For a different view see Schultz' Nobel lecture (1980).

If a quarter of middle school pupils are to some extent involved in working activities it is plausible to assume that, even during compulsory school, forgone earnings – or forgone working time in the family business – can be of considerable importance for family educational decisions and that school and work are partially competing alternatives from very early in life.[14]

2.1.2 Institutional constraints and children's aspirations

The *Riforma Gentile* introduced six types of middle school, two of which survived until 1962: the *scuola media*, which was essentially a way to upper secondary education, and the *scuola di avviamento professionale*, which aimed at training for manual and ordinary non-manual occupations. The latter was a dead-end school with respect to the main branches of high school and gave access only to vocational education. This *bipartite system*, whose main feature was to enforce an early and key choice at the age of 11, lasted until 1962 when a new Act, passed by the new government of the centre-left, introduced *La scuola media unica*, essentially by abolishing the *scuola di avviamento professionale* and by rearranging the subjects taught in the old *scuola media*. The new middle school, the one we still have today, was essentially devoted to general education and did not aim at providing occupational training.

Before describing the way in which Italian post-compulsory schooling is organized it is worth dwelling on the 1962 Act, which has been the most important institutional move of the postwar period. This will help to raise some of the questions concerning the relevant selection mechanisms that will be dealt with later.

The introduction of the new middle school was generally welcome as a progressive reform: by shifting the age of the relevant bifurcation point from 11 to 14 and by enforcing a higher degree of mixing between children from different social backgrounds, the new middle school was thought to be potentially less discriminatory. To a large extent the Act appeared to be the result of the left-wing forces' initiative (Barbagli 1974: 391–454).

The tendency in favour of abolishing early decision points and the rigid boundaries between 'cultural' and 'technical' branches has cer-

---

[14] For an estimate of the value of children's forgone earnings in Italy, see Padoa Schioppa (1974: 191–6).

tainly not been unique to Italy. At the international level, OECD expressed a view in 1969 which seems to summarize quite clearly the reasons why reformers in various countries followed such lines:

> The radical solution adopted – they said – by Italy, Norway, Sweden and Yugoslavia – and already practised though in a different way in the United States, parts of Canada and Japan – consisting of an amalgamation of all syllabuses at junior secondary level, has the *great advantage of breaking away from the influence exerted by the tradition and prestige* of the several parallel junior syllabuses . . . it is certainly the most interesting and radical attempt to deal with the new needs created by wider participation in secondary education and by the quest for full educational opportunities for all. (OECD 1969: 97)

In Italy the legislators – and their view is still supported by recent academic opinions (Barbagli 1974: 406) – seemed to believe that the bipartite system represented the chief obstacle and constraint preventing working-class children from having an equal opportunity to further their education. However, the mechanism which was thought to make the bipartite system discriminatory was never spelled out very clearly, apart from unending discussions on whether Latin, which was taught as a subject in the old *scuola media*, was or was not 'digestible' by the lower classes or essential for 'opening the minds' of the pupils.[15] The legislators limited themselves to establishing a generic causal nexus between the bipartite arrangement and individual behaviour, and avoided the key effort of making explicit assumptions about educational decision mechanisms at the level of the agent.[16]

In particular it was not made clear which of the possible forces – values, cultural capital, or economic calculation – pushed more working-class children to the technical schools. From the way in which the reform was implemented and from parliamentary speeches it seems possible to gather that on the whole the reformers were more aware of cultural than economic mechanisms and that they had two main arguments in mind.

[15] In the end, after a long fight, Latin was left only in the third year, and there as an optional subject.

[16] Such a state of affairs bears quite striking similarities to the debate over the introduction of comprehensive schools in the UK, not only for the line of argument which was broadly used to support it, but also because 'the argument for a common school was rarely put in an articulated or testable form' (Musgrave 1972: 99; cf. Westergaard & Little 1970: 69).

Table 2.3. *Pupils by type of middle school and by father's occupation in 1957*

	scuola media	avviamento professionale
professionals & white-collar workers	49.0	16.4
self-employed	27.3	30.7
working-class	21.3	50.0
others	2.4	2.9
all	100.0	100.0

Source: ISTAT 1959: 43

Firstly, there was the fact that enforcing such an important decision, very difficult to reverse, at the early age of 11 left the children more exposed than at 14 to the reproductive force of the cultural resources of their families;[17] furthermore, once they were channelled into two quite different courses of education – whose influences and institutional possibilities were consistent with two distinct levels of aspiration – the discriminatory forces linked with family background would have become even more difficult to curb. Thus working-class children, who were much more represented in the *scuola di avviamento professionale* (see table 2.3), were bound to end up mainly in working-class jobs. In other words the first problem was that of eliminating an institutional arrangement which could work as a trap. But had this argument been the only one, it would probably have been enough only to lift the barriers at the end of the *scuola di avviamento professionale* rather than abolishing the school itself.

There was in fact a second argument more generally concerned with abolishing separate cultures to promote social cohesion and class integration, and improving the chances of developing talents and aspirations. It was thought that by exposing *all* pupils to similar stimuli and by attaching to the middle school a function of broad vocational guidance the forces pushing from the back could have been partly corrected in favour of fairer opportunities. As in the UK 'it was hoped that more of the able children from the working class who now left school early would be encouraged to stay on longer and attain the jobs for which their talent made them capable' (Musgrave 1972: 99). Using the

---

[17] This is an argument considered to be almost obvious by Halsey & Floud (1961: 84).

language of the previous chapter we could say that what the 1962 reform aimed at was to act at the level of *preference-forming*, by exposing the children to different causal influences, more apt to broaden their views and to foster their occupational potentialities.[18]

What the reformers seemed not particularly aware of was the different weight of economic constraints confronted by families according to their position in the social structure and the extent to which the shorter educational route was more frequently selected by working-class families (table 2.3) for just this reason, and not necessarily through lack of awareness, 'traditional' behaviour, or depressed level of aspirations: more explicitly it is very plausible to believe that working-class families were more inclined to send their children to the *scuola di avviamento professionale* not only because of cultural reproduction or terror of Latin, but also because the relative risk and cost of the training-oriented middle school were much lower than those for the *scuola media*. The former opened a way to the labour market with a minimum of qualifications in the space of three years, whereas the latter, once entered, bound the pupils who wanted a formal occupational qualification to continue their education for several additional years. Thus the 1962 Act passed without any attention being paid to the economic side of the problem of equal opportunities and no form of pecuniary aid was provided.

The slight attention which in Italy is devoted to the private economic aspects of educational decisions, especially at the lower levels of education, has been widely documented by Padoa Schioppa (1974) with respect to the sixties. In the seventies the situation was not much improved: if we take, for instance, direct money transfers to households as one possible indicator, we can see that virtually all transfers to households for educational purposes in 1977 were devoted to supporting university students (table 2.4).[19] As a consequence the economic burden of sending children to school – mainly in terms of opportunity costs – has remained predominantly a matter of concern for families.

[18]   The Act also paid some attention to a more concrete level and a remarkable effort was made to bring the new middle school to all communities with over 3,000 inhabitants: 'the number of communities with a middle school rose from 3834 in 1961–63 to 5031 in 1965–66 and that of communities with over 3000 inhabitants with no middle school fell from 528 in 1961–62 to 84 in 1965–66' (OECD 1969: 99).

[19]   This indicator excludes family allowances and includes only grants and financial aid directly intended for education.

Table 2.4. *Distribution of transfers to households by level of education in four European countries in 1977*

	W. Germany	France	UK	Italy
pre-primary & primary	—	—	—	—
secondary	37.0	65.3	—	0.7
tertiary	63.0	24.4	93.1	95.9
non-itemized	—	10.3	6.9	3.4
all	100.0	100.0	100.0	100.0

Source: EUROSTAT 1980: 240–1

But there is a further point which was neglected by the middle school reform. One of the general reasons which was given for the creation of the new middle school was that it could better satisfy the fast-growing demand for education that was expressed especially by the lower classes. If we bear this argument in mind, it is quite baffling to observe that the reform took place at a period when this new demand was showing itself mainly through faster growth precisely in the school that was to be abolished: right at the beginning of the economic boom in Italy, in 1959–60, the number of pupils enrolled in the *scuola di avviamento professionale* exceeded the number of pupils enrolled in the other type of middle school.

Whether through the force of inertia or because of some economic calculation – the latter is somewhat more convincing in view of the striking coincidence with the economic boom – the new generation of pupils were relatively more in favour of the middle school, which was capable of training in market-oriented skills. What they got instead was just the opposite. Sometimes institutions do not appear to adjust to a change in demand in the obvious direction.

The lack of annual secondary data, combining enrolment rates at various levels with class origins, has made difficult any careful test of the net effect of the 1962 Act in terms of better opportunities for all, and the literature available on this question is based either on limited and slender evidence or on no evidence at all, being rather ideological in character.[20] Some insight can be gained from looking at schooling trends as they are

[20] For a bibliography see Fadiga Zanatta (1978: 418). Only a social mobility study with some retrospective capacity – like the Oxford Mobility Study (Goldthorpe *et al.* 1980) – could allow an assessment.

given by aggregate educational statistics and, indirectly, by looking at what has been found in similar circumstances in other countries.

Attempts to explain the historical trend displayed by the growth of participation in compulsory education have been very few and have related the increase in school attendance to the increased material prosperity of Italian families, mainly viewing education as a consumer item (De Meo 1970 and Colasanti, Mebane & Bonolis 1976, especially ch. 4). Some have also pointed to the institutional modifications introduced by the 1962 reform (Barbagli 1974). The reform, however, took place after the major increase in attendance rates had occurred and it is probably better seen as a response to that increase rather than vice versa.

To sustain this view we need to consider the continuation rates between elementary school and middle school, which, unlike attendance rates, can be calculated for each year and which, like attendance rates, can be regarded as a measure of the propensity to stay longer at school. They express the ratio of pupils leaving elementary school in a given year and enrolling in middle school the following year to all pupils leaving elementary school. The major increase in the continuation rate from elementary school to middle school took place between 1956 and 1964, a period which almost entirely overlaps with the Italian economic boom (1958–63); in this span of time the proportion of pupils passing into high school went in fact from 55% to 88%. In the earliest postwar period (1946–58) there was very little increase and in the period following 1964 the pace of growth declined.[21] The Act, therefore, which was actually implemented in 1963, can hardly claim to be the origin of the massive increase in education.

On the other hand, after the reform, the proportion of pupils successfully reaching the final certificate increased, i.e. the proportion of pupils dropping out or being kept down diminished. This would appear to be consistent with a diminished selectivity and higher aspirations than before. Yet, in order to see whether these aspirations were really

---

[21]   The continuation rate in this period went from 88% to 96%. (The continuation rates I have calculated are taken from ISTAT 1947–78 and ISTAT 1966–80 and are calculated by subtracting the repeaters from the numerator, that is by considering only pupils enrolled in the first year of middle school for the first time.) It must be said, however, that if we measure the growth of the continuation rate in terms of the proportional reduction in the number not passing, we obtain $\frac{34}{46} = 74\%$ for the first period and $\frac{8}{12} = 67\%$ in the second. This is not a striking difference, especially if we consider that progress must get harder as the 100% continuation rate is approached.

increased, we must consider what happened after middle school, i.e. we must consider the subsequent continuation rate, that between middle school and high school. This rate, in fact, diminished its pace of growth after the Act, suggesting that, if the reform did raise the level of aspirations at all it was by a very modest amount, even though, to be sure, one would need to look at the continuation rate broken down by class of origin. On the whole the pattern could perhaps better be interpreted as a response to labour market than to institutional modifications (see section 4.2). In fact, 1964 is also a very important turning-point because the boom by then was over and people had at the same time less money to send children to school and fewer job opportunities to make it worthwhile taking them out of school before the final certificate.

If we draw on the international literature we will find that there is evidence that institutional reforms tend to have little effect in improving the economic equality of educational opportunities (Jencks 1972b, Boudon 1974). Recently Halsey, Heath & Ridge (1980) have found that comprehensive education 'will do little to increase (or reduce) equality of opportunity between social classes' (p. 173). They have also found, though, that 'on the other hand it may well reduce the predictability of educational careers' (p. 173). This is because 'if we take boys of *identical* social origins and intelligence, the ones sent to more prestigious secondary schools ended up with substantially longer school careers' (p. 172).[22]

In conclusion, the abolition of the technical branch of middle school might well have had a similar effect in 'mixing things up' and in alleviating what for some was working as a trap, enforced through the early decision and consequent channelling. Moreover it was probably a positive step for broad social and cultural reasons (Ferrarotti 1967). It remains unknown, however, how many extra working-class children were effectively helped by the new middle school and how many instead – though perhaps less ignorant and less 'technically biased' than before – found themselves simply 'shifted' by three years, with the same unsatisfied needs to reach an occupational qualification of some use and to find a job as quickly as possible. There are no *a priori* grounds for believing the former, those who benefited, to be more numerous than the latter.

Perhaps the best summary of the likely effects of the reform was given

[22] The influence of the type of school attended is explored in section 4.1.

by the president of the industrialists' association (Confederazione Generale dell'Industria Italiana, which is the most important private employers' union), who expressed a rather different view in favour of loosening the boundaries between the two types of middle school. The argument he used is worth the effort of translation, since it shows with rare clarity, how, besides the official view of better opportunities for all, a more down-to-earth, 'manipulative' approach was also present. He said:

> In my judgement it is far more important to have at our disposal young people who *have the feeling* they chose their occupation, being aware of its essential features and differences with respect to other occupations, rather than people ineluctably channelled towards a given job, who feel they were condemned to it with no possibility to compare it with others and believe that any other job would be easier, more pleasant and rewarding. . .It is necessary at least until 15 years of age to give the feeling of freedom of choice: only in this way attitudes come out, and enthusiastic, hence good workers, are created. (My italics: the passage is quoted by Barbagli 1974: 450–1)

The president of the industrialists' association seemed more aware than the legislators that the result of relaxing the differences between the two types of middle school would have been more psychological than factual, more a matter of 'giving the feeling' of freedom of choice rather than delivering the freedom of choice itself, somehow implying that the real selective mechanisms were in another realm, not easily changeable by institutional reforms. More generally, it remains unknown whether the reform really hit on the basic mechanisms that govern educational decisions or whether it missed them. It is to such mechanisms that the rest of this work will be devoted.

2.2 Choices after compulsory education

As we have seen in section 2.1, since the mid seventies nearly all pupils have stayed at school until 14 years of age and most of them manage to get the final certificate and to qualify for secondary education. As a consequence, it is impossible to observe any relevant variance in educational behaviour before the end of middle school. To observe any variance we have to focus the attention on the post-compulsory stage of education, where it is the system itself that allows a variety of choices. It is precisely these choices – the focus of this section – which represent the *dependent variables* of my analysis.[23]

More specifically, after compulsory education there are two main bifurcation points which are both defined by institutional arrangements and refer to the choice between staying on or leaving the educational system. The first choice concerns whether to stay on and enter high school; the second choice, which is met around the age of 18 to 19, on successfully completing high school, concerns whether to go on to university. These two choices, however, do not adequately represent the entire set of main decisions which pupils have to make. In fact, a considerable number of children leave neither before nor after but during high school. For example, in 1975, 21% of the total number of pupils who left school in that year made their exit through the 'fire escape', so to speak, rather than through the main gate (CENSIS 1977). Thus the choice between leaving or staying on during high school must also be considered, bringing the basic sequence of decisions to be analysed up to three binary choice nodes (see figure 2.1).

2.2.1 Dropping out

Before going further, a few words are needed in order to clarify the nature of the decision to leave the educational system during high school as opposed to leaving before beginning or after completing the course. When the act of leaving school takes the form of dropping out at non-institutionalized points, the reasons for doubting whether educational decisions are properly decisions at all are often considered to be

Figure 2.1 *The educational decisions*

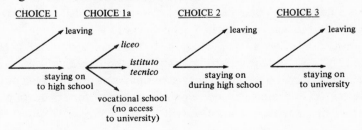

---

[23] The absence of variance would make impossible any effort to 'reach the causes' of educational decisions. Survey analysis must rely on differences in the behaviour concerned across significant groups in the population.

strengthened. In Italy, those who leave in such a manner are formally left empty-handed, since for most purposes, such as employment and admission to higher education, only the final certificate counts. The majority of those who drop out from high school leave during the early years, but even those who leave after four or five years will only have the middle school certificate as a credential. Therefore, from a common-sense perspective, the years spent at high school are considered as wasted. Also the act of abandoning school is viewed in the literature mainly as the negative consequence of the school selection mechanisms which push pupils out, mainly by keeping them down: dropping out tends to be thought of as a constrained act rather than a decision (Balbo & Chiaretti 1972; Dei & Rossi 1978; Padoa Schioppa 1974: 243).

There is indeed quite a high correlation between failure at school and the probability of dropping out, a finding which lends some support to this view. (In one of the surveys analysed here, 71% of dropouts had at least one failure as opposed to an average of 44% over the whole sample.) There are, however, certain considerations which prevent one from concluding that dropping out is not a decision at all. First there is the fact that the correlation between repeating and dropping out is far from perfect and that more than one-quarter of those who left during high school had never been kept down. Moreover, only half of them declared that they had left as a consequence of a failure. Secondly, the correlation between dropping out and having been kept down does not necessarily mean that the latter produces the former. Thirdly, as far as I am aware, no study of Italy has ever attempted to check the rather crucial issue of whether additional years of secondary education without attainment of the final certificate are really a waste of time, by verifying whether dropouts fare better or worse in terms of jobs and earnings than those pupils who did not enter high school. Clearly, if evidence were to be found similar to that gathered in other countries – where, in terms of rate of returns, even a few years of college are by no means a waste (cf. Becker 1975: 171; Layard and Psacharopoulos 1974) – the idea that dropouts are only constrained by severe selective mechanisms would have to be reconsidered, and some grounds would be provided for advocating the existence of an attractive force as well.[24]

[24] Evidence from the international literature mainly refers to higher education rather than to secondary school and suggests that an incomplete university education is by no means a complete economic waste (cf. Becker 1975: 171 and Layard & Psacharopoulos 1974). Usually this is attributed to the fact that more education is useful in itself because it

At any rate, even if such evidence were to be found, the decision to interrupt a course of study would still, to some extent, represent a change of mind and a negative decision, certainly different from the decision faced at the beginning of the course. In a sense, it could be argued that it is even more of a decision, precisely because it does not take place at the institutionalized times. Perhaps the most plausible view is that there are children who enter high school uncertain of their ability to complete their chosen course successfully, but who wish to attempt it. In the Italian institutional context it is hard to imagine anyone planning in advance to take only, for instance, three years of a five-year course. If one starts, it is because one has some hope, however feeble, of obtaining the final certificate. Even if, *ex post*, people can find out that those years were not entirely wasted, for a wide variety of public as well as private jobs high school credentials are an essential requirement for being able to apply. The decision to leave before the end of the course probably comes as a result of new insight and information acquired while at school. It may be in the form of poor school reports or of new labour market opportunities, or, finally, of a dislike of formal schooling (cf. Lazear 1976). It is under such circumstances that individuals can be seen as changing their minds or, at least, as solving negatively their initial uncertainty about whether they have the required capacity, or whether continuing to go to school is really worth their while.[25]

raises skills and productivity. Certainly, as shown by Layard and Psacharopoulos, the fact that dropouts get better earnings comes as quite a shock to the alternative view of education as a screening device for employers, because the latter is quite obviously linked with certificates rather than with unfinished courses of study. This assumption, however, would require more severe testing: for instance, it should be considered whether the positive effect accrues from additional job-searching carried out during school years rather than from the school years themselves. This could be a so-far unexplored implication of the school 'parking models', in the sense that if people go to school because they do not find a satisfactory job, it would be consistent to shop around while 'parking'. However, to jump to the conclusion that additional school years in themselves make the difference would be like concluding that it is the time one keeps one's car parked in a shopping centre that explains the better quality of one's purchases, so overlooking the searching activity. In a job market like the Italian, where the distribution of information is uneven and the value of connections – especially if combined with educational credentials – is rather high, the activity of job searching is bound to be of considerable importance.

[25] Indirectly, this fits quite well with the evidence presented by Willis and Rosen (1979). They show that skills are unlikely to have a hierarchical structure whereby, on average, those who reached a higher level of education and became, say, economically successful lawyers would also have been economically successful plumbers had they not gone to college. When deciding about their education, people would therefore take into account their perceived 'comparative advantage'. It seems plausible that, for many, the knowledge of what they would be good at is not given *a priori*, but needs some tentative experience before it is gained.

To summarize, the decision process which takes place in the non-compulsory Italian educational system – as much as in most other systems (cf. Boudon 1974:75) – can be generally viewed as a series of binary decisions where the options are 'stay on at school' as opposed to 'leave'. In particular, the basic sequence of decisions up to the beginning of university that ought to be considered includes *three basic binary choice nodes* (figure 2.1), all of which involve the question whether to leave or to continue one's educational career:[26] the first concerns the decision which is taken after middle school as to whether to stay on for high school rather than leave; the second represents the decision either to drop out before finishing high school or reach the final diploma;[27] finally, the third represents the decision whether to stop or go to university and is taken after the successful end of high school. Obviously, reaching a decision point beyond the first branching point is conditional upon having chosen to stay on at the previous points, and therefore the sequence of the three decisions is a *hierarchical structure*. These three binary choice nodes constitute the focus of the analysis which will be developed in the next two chapters.

2.2.2 Alternatives in high school

However, to give an exhaustive representation of the educational choice process it is necessary to go further. In fact, from the point of view of those who continue their education the first and the third choices are in reality more complicated than binary decisions, for they respectively involve a decision among different branches of high school and among university faculties. In this book, in addition to considering the three binary decision nodes described above, I shall analyse only the choice of the branch of high school, and not consider the specific options available at university.[28] In the analysis the choice of the high school branch will

[26] In this book I shall not consider the event of dropping out from university, which logically would represent the fourth relevant branching point of an educational career. On this subject in the Italian context see De Francesco & Trivellato (1977).

[27] The second choice can take place at any time between the beginning and the end of high school and in principle could therefore be treated as a sequence of several binary choices (drop out 'versus' stay on) according to some time units (terms or years, for instance). In this work I shall treat it as just one choice, assuming that it is irrelevant with respect to the mechanisms that govern the choice when it actually occurs.

[28] The analysis of the choice of university faculty would require a specific study and need to be based on fuller and different data from those used in this book.

Table 2.5. *Attributes of the three types of Italian high schools*

	length in years	open to university	specific job training	labour market destinations
vocational schools	3	No	Yes	manual skilled/routine
istituti tecnici	15	Yes	Yes	non-manual
licei	5	Yes	No	non-manual/professional

be represented as *hierarchically subsequent* to the first binary decision, 'staying on vs leaving' (see figure 2.1, choice 1a). Such a choice offers three main alternatives: vocational schools, *licei*, and *istituti tecnici*.[29] Since the three alternatives differ substantively among each other on a number of attributes which make the choice non-trivial with respect to both higher education and occupational prospects (table 2.5), it is important to go into some detail.

Vocational schools provide training for skilled manual operations and for routine non-manual ones. Most courses last for three years and with very few exceptions are dead-end schools with respect to access to university. Since their courses are shorter than those of the high schools, vocational schools require a smaller sacrifice in terms of deferment of labour market entry and consequently of costs, both direct and in the form of forgone earnings. At the same time, though, they prevent people from going into higher education[30] and involve therefore a high degree of pre-commitment relative to the expected length of one's educational career.

The second type of high school is called *liceo* and is meant to prepare for university entrance rather than providing training for any particular job.[31] To decide to enrol in a *liceo* involves a greater degree of commitment towards the longest possible educational career and being prepared for a long-term deferment of full labour market entry. *Licei* are

[29] The three alternatives open to those who decide to stay on at high school have undergone relatively little change, as far as the main organizational features are concerned, since 1923.

[30] Those who want to do so have to pass the usual high school examination, which of course requires a very different training.

[31] There are two main sub-types of *licei*. The first, called *liceo classico*, which is more oriented towards arts subjects, used to be the traditional and privileged route to university education, the sole high school to allow access to any university faculty without exception. The second sub-branch, the *liceo scientifico*, which is more oriented towards science subjects, was created in 1923 and has had only two main restrictions with respect to university faculty access (Law and Philosophy), which have now been lifted.

not perceived as self-contained, but as a way through to further education.

The third type of high school, *istituto tecnico*,[32] reproduces – alongside vocational schools and in contrast to the *liceo* – the same division between 'culture' and 'technique' which characterized the pre-1962 Act middle schools. They are supposed to train for non-manual skilled occupations and are divided into several sub-branches which are completely separate from each other (they include technical jobs in various industrial sectors, services and agriculture, accountancy, and so on). With respect to vocational schools they differ not only in the subjects taught, but in two other major respects: firstly they last five years instead of three, and secondly all barriers that once prevented pupils from these schools from going to university have been lifted, partially in 1961 and fully in 1969. These characteristics make the *istituti tecnici* a sort of intermediate between the other two types of school: with vocational schools they retain the attribute of being devoted to job training while with the *licei* they share the openness to further education. For these reasons they can be considered as the schools that minimize the risk involved in changing one's mind, in the sense that they require the least degree of pre-commitment either towards university, as *liceo* demands, or towards the labour market, as do vocational schools.

Access to university is regulated in the following manner: when pupils choose either *istituti tecnici* or *licei*, at the end of the fifth year they take a final examination which, when passed, gives a certificate of legal external validity and allows the pupils to register in any university faculty they wish, without any further entry examination. In this respect the Italian educational system would appear to be extremely *open* in that it establishes no necessary connections between what one does at secondary school and the subject which may be read at university. At the same time it must be stressed that for a number of reasons the Italian educational system is also a strongly *channelled* as opposed to a branched or flexible system. Firstly, it is very difficult to switch from one type of school to another once one has begun; secondly, the decision that pupils can take concerns only the type of school, and once the school has been

---

[32] The major exception is the *istituto magistrale*, the high school that trains elementary school teachers. For the purpose of my work it is not necessary to treat this separately from the *istituto tecnico*. Both, in fact, are labour market oriented high schools and provide access to university.

Table 2.6. *Percentage of high school pupils by type of school*

	1948–9	1958–9	1968–9	1978–9
vocational school	5.9	12.1	14.6	17.9
istituto tecnico	47.0	58.0	59.2	56.9
liceo	47.1	29.9	26.2	25.2
all	100.0	100.0	100.0	100.0

Source: until 1968–9 ISTAT 1969; after, CENSIS 1980

selected there is no room for selecting subjects: within each type of high school the syllabus is the same for everyone all over the country and it is centrally decided; in other words the pupil faces a *lump choice*, either to take all subjects or to take none and go to another school. Thirdly, if an individual drops out before the final diploma he will be a failure; intermediate examinations are intended only to qualify pupils for the next year and have no credential value.

There are two further points which must be considered relative to the role of the three main branches of secondary schools: the first is how pupils distribute themselves across the branches and the second is how they have responded to the major institutional modification, namely the reopening of university access for *istituti tecnici*.

Since the sixties the majority of pupils have been concentrated in the *istituti tecnici* (56.9% in 1978–9; see table 2.6); more generally the trend since the war has been towards an increase in the proportion at both *istituti tecnici* and vocational schools, and a corresponding decrease at *licei*. Here we find at a higher level of schooling the same relatively higher propensity to go to more job-oriented schools which we met earlier in the middle school before the 1962 Act. This trend has been explained by the increased proportion of working-class children staying on at school and by the fact that working-class children are more prone to follow the route offered by *istituti tecnici* (Corbetta 1975). Yet in this case, as much as in the case of middle school, there is no clear assessment of why working-class children should be more likely to go to technical schools rather than to more academic schools. One of the basic questions as to whether it depends on values or on economic calculations and constraints remains unanswered.

Together with the 1962 Act, which introduced comprehensive education, the liberalization of university access has been the major institutional change in the postwar Italian educational sytem, and it was carried out for very similar reasons (Barbagli 1974: 454–64), that is to avoid working-class children, who are relatively more numerous in the *istituti tecnici*, being 'trapped' at the end of high school with no possibility of going to university, and more generally to lessen the gap between the two types of high school.[33]

The measure was successful and despite the labour market orientation of *istituti tecnici*, a large number of pupils graduating from these schools responded positively to the reopening of university access: the year after the first liberalization of 1961, 40% of those eligible went to university. Even leaving out of consideration the several student protests in favour of opening access to university (see Barbagli 1974:454–64) these data show quite clearly that the act of liberalizing access was itself a response to a massively felt demand 'from below', which was in turn partly motivated by the employment difficulties met by this particular group of school-leavers.[34] In the following years the continuation rate from *istituti tecnici* to university went up constantly to reach its peak in 1971 (75%), before declining again slowly but steadily. The proportion of students going to university from the *istituti tecnici* never, however,

---

[33] The decision to liberalize university access was also presented as an anticipation of the reform of high school which had been long debated, though not yet introduced. For the different proposals for reform and a wide bibliography see Fadiga Zanatta (1978:211ff).

From an historical viewpoint, liberalizing access to university represented a return to origins. The early Italian educational system (created by the *Legge Casati*, 1860–1) was in fact in many respects more open and advanced than that which was introduced by the Fascist regime in 1923. (For an interesting viewpoint on the relatively advanced features of the Casati Act, see Barbagli 1974: ch. 3). Among other things the early Italian educational system, though branched into two main streams of classical and technical education, allowed pupils from the latter to register in some university faculties for which the subjects they had done at school prepared them (e.g. engineering). The 1923 Act, by introducing many screening procedures and streams at middle school levels and by strengthening the selection barriers, instead created a much more closed and channelled system whose heritage has been strongly felt. Furthermore it abolished completely the possibility of going to university for those pupils who were not from the *licei* and it has taken until the sixties to reliberalize access.

[34] There is no clear evidence that such was indeed the case, though much of the literature and the political reasoning put this view forward. A circumstance which somewhat contradicts this explanation is that in the South, where the unemployment problems are normally higher, the pressure from below to reopen university access was not as marked as it was in the North of the country, where there is evidence that pupils who have graduated from the *istituti tecnici* have not experienced particularly marked unemployment problems (cf. Capriolo, Luccitelli & Pratesi 1980).

reaches the percentage going from *licei*, which has traditionally been close to 100%.

It is interesting to observe that although the liberalization had such a positive and massive response at a direct level, it did not provoke an indirect response on the side of those enrolling in the first year of high school. It might be expected that in view of the new possibilities offered to pupils graduating from *istituti tecnici* by the liberalization, more individuals would prefer this type of school to the *licei*. Since the latter was formerly the only type of school to offer a direct way to university, it would be reasonable to expect that some students would go to the *licei* essentially in order to gain the qualification enabling them to enter later into higher education. As a consequence some, under the new circumstances, would prefer the *istituti tecnici*, which became less restrictive than they had been and at the same time provided an intermediate job qualification. On the contrary, in the years that followed the partial and total liberalization, there was no marked shift of first-year enrolment towards the *istituti tecnici*. Thus it seems that despite the relevant alteration to the feasible set introduced by the liberalization, pupils did not alter their behaviour when deciding which school to go to. The absence of any evident change in behaviour is indirectly suggestive of what might be the motives inducing some pupils to register in the *licei*.

Firstly it may be that all those pupils who decide to go to *liceo* make such a decision mainly in conformity with tradition and class values. Secondly, and in part similarly, pupils may opt for *liceo* only when they like the subjects and attribute a considerable value to the status associated with this type of school; in other words they may all choose *liceo* for its own sake. In both cases, therefore, a change in the opportunity set will not affect the behaviour.[35] Thirdly, those who choose *liceo* might in advance be reasonably confident that they will not stop at the end of the school and will go to college. In this case the alteration introduced by the liberalization in the feasible set will not really affect the perceived risk attached to the choice of *liceo*.

All three reasons could in principle be compatible with each other, either in the sense that individuals going to *liceo* may each have a different reason or in the sense that within the same individual there

---

[35] Unless of course the change in the relevant options is such as to make unfeasible the course of action selected for traditional reasons. Cf. Becker (1976: ch. 8) and Elster (1979: 138).

coexists more than one reason. In any case, each of the three reasons could be sufficient to explain the absence of an indirect response to the institutional modification. But to pursue this matter further would lead us already into the core of the decision mechanisms which are analysed in the two following chapters.

2.2.3 Educational decisions as discrete choices

The educational decisions described above can be analysed as a set of discrete choices. As we have seen in the introduction, the analysis in terms of discrete choices represents a considerable advance. Yet the structure which is given to the educational choices in this book is still rudimentary. Although in fact more realistic with respect to the process of decision than in its representation as a dependent variable using the number of years of education, it is far from being necessarily a faithful representation of the process of choice as it takes place in the minds of the subjects and it should be considered as closer to a representation of notional alternatives than to actual ones. There remain, in fact, some unresolved problems, which it is important to point out, if only very briefly.

First there is the problem of considering which are the relevant alternatives that ought to be considered. For instance, in the rest of this work it will be assumed that the option 'leaving' means mainly 'going to work'; but in treating the option 'leaving' as just one alternative, residual with respect to 'staying on', there is the risk of grouping together significantly different alternatives. There are, it is true, quite good reasons in favour of making such an assumption, for work is the most trodden alternative path to school. Still, in principle, the option 'leaving' could equally well mean 'travelling around the world' or 'getting married'; the information I use, however, places a constraint on the alternatives I can analyse, for if subjects were travelling they could not have been interviewed and if they got married as an alternative to work, they could not have been sampled among unemployed young people.

Second there is the problem that when there are more than two alternatives they can be represented in *trees* that may take a variety of *hierarchical structures* depending on what one thinks (or knows) about how the choice looks from the subject's point of view. This type of problem does not arise when considering the sequence of the three binary choices 'staying on vs leaving', because their hierarchical structure is institutionally predefined: if one wants to go to university one must have been to high school first.

If we take instead the first choice by itself, including in it the choice of the branch high school, we have four final possible options, namely 'leaving' plus the three branches of high school; these four options can be represented by a variety of different trees, all of which make some assumptions with regard to how people reach one of the final options (figure 2.2). The structure of the tree I have selected (figure 2.1 choice 1 and choice 1a) assumes that the choice of whether to leave or to stay on at school is independent of and logically prior to the choice of which type of school to go to. In other words it assumes that people do not compare directly option 'leave' with any one of the three types of school taken separately, but that in the first step of the decision, the three types of school form one unique relevant alternative which is opposed to that of 'leave'.

It must be said, however, that the assumption which 'my' tree represents could also be inappropriate in some cases, for it is in fact reasonable to imagine other hierarchical structures: to imagine, for instance, subjects who, had not a three-year course like that offered by vocational schools been available, would not have stayed on. If such

Figure 2.2 *Plausible decision trees*

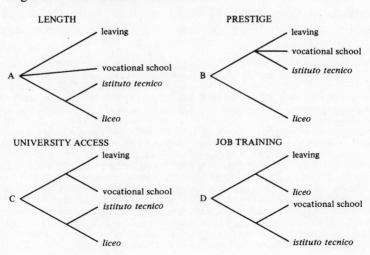

were the case the first step ('staying on vs leaving') would not be independent of the alternatives available at the second step, and the structure of the tree should be represented differently, organizing its branches on the basis of the *school length* of each alternative, for example; length, in fact, would be the most relevant attribute considered for the choice (figure 2, tree A). Similarly it is easy to imagine someone – of upper-class origin, for instance – viewing the choice mainly in terms of *prestige* of the school and for whom *liceo* is the only alternative which really makes a difference (figure 2.2, tree B); it is also plausible to imagine other trees which would express a choice primarily based on *access to university* (figure 2.2, tree C) or on a *job training* oriented school (figure 2.2, tree D).[36]

With respect to all possible tree structures, the one I decided to analyse can be seen as implying weaker and less binding assumptions as to which process leads to the choice; it also satisfies some of the requirements of the statistical model – the logit model – I shall use to analyse the choices. Above all, it seems reasonable to believe that a large number of people consider staying on at school or university as opposed to leaving before considering which type of school or which faculty to go to. Generally, in the psychological literature, there is evidence that 'when faced with many alternatives (e.g. job offers, houses, cars) people appear to eliminate various subsets of alternatives sequentially according to some hierarchical structure, rather than scanning all options in an exhaustive manner' (Tversky & Sattath 1979: 542–3). More particularly, Tversky and Sattath (1979: 548), in an example of a decision where it seems

---

[36] Of the two possible methods of finding out which is (or are) the 'true tree(s)' of decision, neither was available. The first method would have required direct questioning of subjects about which attribute(s) they evaluated when making their decisions; but using surveys which were planned for other purposes creates a gap between the information one would like and the information available. The second method – that of inferring from actual behaviour – would have required 'social experiments', i.e. altering attributes of different courses of education, controlling others and observing responses, that are obviously unfeasible. By social experiment I mean, for instance, that, in order to test whether 'length' is the attribute that matters most in the choice of the three-year course offered by vocational schools as opposed to the five-year course of the other high schools, one should alter the length of the vocational school course and bring it up to five years, while leaving everything else unchanged. Only if such changes were not followed by any evident response and the proportion of pupils going to vocational schools remained the same could the hypothesis that length matters be ruled out. Above I adopted a similar procedure when I discussed the lack of response that followed the opening of access to university for *istituti tecnici* on the part of pupils of *licei*. Reforms can often be considered as 'social experiments' (Gilbert & Mosteller 1972; Campbell 1979).

particularly appropriate to assume a 'hierarchical elimination model', mention a case rather similar to that considered here: 'a student' – they say – 'who has to decide what to do after graduation, for example, is more likely to consider the alternatives in a hierarchical manner. That is, first decide whether to go to graduate school, travel or take a job, and only then evaluate in detail the relevant alternatives, e.g. graduate schools, travel plans, or job opportunities.'[37] Nonetheless there is no specific evidence that can be helpful in the case of educational choices as to which particular structure might be considered as universal and whether such a structure exists.

2.3 Conclusions

The Italian educational system operates in a variety of ways in defining, circumscribing, and indirectly influencing individual behaviour. Firstly, it keeps all pupils at school in one unique comprehensive course until they are 14 years old. Secondly, it sets the standards required to qualify for further educational stages. Today, at compulsory level, everyone manages to reach the final certificate and dropping out is a circumscribed and declining phenomenon; yet, obtaining the certificate after having experienced one or more failures – in terms of years 'repeated' – is still a widespread occurrence at any level of school. This raises the important question of how failures affect pupils in their future educational decisions.

Thirdly, the educational system that exists in Italy, by imposing a choice after compulsory education, 'streams' the children who stay on into three different channels, that of vocational schools – which leads straight to the labour market and closes the possibilities of going to university – and those of *licei* and *istituti tecnici*. Only the children who meet the standards required in the latter two will become qualified for university education.

But there are also ways in which the educational system fails to influence behaviour. For instance, by no longer enforcing a choice at the age of 11, it diminishes the influence of early channelling on future

---

[37] Other authors (Hughes 1980) suggest the same type of hierarchical framework for the analysis of migration decisions, and, more generally, this tree structure is suggested as an acceptable way of simplifying many consumers' decisions (Deaton & Muellbauer 1980: 122).

decisions, and by imposing a unique, centrally defined syllabus controls one of the factors which could in principle be expected to play a major role in explaining inter-school differences in subsequent educational decisions.[38] Similarly, by not taking certain steps to favour a growth in participation in education – for example by providing little or no pecuniary aid – the Italian educational system leaves up to extra-institutional mechanisms much of the 'work' of selecting pupils.

In conclusion, the Italian educational system defines a set of relevant decisions which will be analysed in the two following chapters as (1) a set of three, hierarchically ordered, binary choice nodes, all involving the decision of whether to leave or continue one's education and as (2) a multinomial choice with three alternatives, each of which represents a particular branch of high school.

---

[38] How inter-school differences are actually able to explain educational destinations is a much-debated issue. Recently, for the UK, where the inter-school variance is at the opposite extreme to the centralized Italian system, Rutter *et al.* (1979) have attempted to prove the extent to which different schools may heavily affect pupils' academic attainment. Their results have been criticized by Heath & Clifford (1980). With respect to the United States the evidence seems to support the conclusion that school differences play very little part in explaining educational attainments (Jencks 1972a; Smith 1972). However, more recently, Barr and Dreeben (1983) have convincingly argued that these studies, by assigning the properties of each school (or class) to all students who attend it, remove 'the possibility of finding out whether what happens organizationally inside the school varies and then influences achievement' (p. 165). Moreover, they present evidence that the crucial variance in school productivity is within schools and even classes rather than between schools.

3 Were they pushed?

In the first chapter I developed the idea that people tend to act purposefully in the sense that they know something of what they want, and can in principle be expected to compare alternative courses of action and evaluate them according to both their perceived probability of success and their preferences. Yet their actions are also shaped by external constraints which narrow down their feasible set of alternatives and, at the same time and independently of the abstract feasibility of alternatives, cognitive constraints, inertial forces, and other non-rational mechanisms can to some extent limit the purposefulness of their actions. What we need now is to articulate these ideas with respect to the educational choices of individuals and to connect them to a more manageable set of concepts less resistant to empirical testing.

Although it will not be possible to establish a perfect correspondence between the three theoretical approaches and the empirical analysis, each independent variable will be tentatively referred to these approaches. The exposition of the results will be organized in two parts, developed respectively in this and in the following chapter. The present chapter is devoted to forces which can be seen as predominantly *pushing*, to those forces, that is, which either constrain action directly (structuralist view) or through limiting subjects' awareness (pushed-from-behind view). The analysis will focus on variables such as parents' education, family income, and father's occupation, which constitute the cultural and economic resources at the disposal of children.

The next chapter is devoted to considering forces which may be seen as predominantly *pulling*, forces, that is, which tend to refer to an intentional agent, capable of adapting intelligently to circumstances and to the perceived probability of success, as well as of planning his life according to personal preferences. The role of pulling forces will be analysed through the effects on educational decisions of variables such as past academic achievement, objective labour market conditions, individuals' time perspective, and job preferences.

The exposition of the results is approximately ordered in such a way as to entail an increasing number of *degrees of freedom* for the subjects: it follows a line that runs from constraints at one end to planning one's life at the other, passing through non-intentional forces and intelligent adaptation to circumstances. This does not imply that at the level of the action which is shaped by constraints the subject will be merely treated as a passive entity; here too I shall assume that we are dealing with an intentional and thoughtful agent, capable of acting also on the basis of expected future constraints, rather than being mechanically pushed at the moment of their actual appearance.

Having explained the general framework of the analysis which will follow, and before turning to consider the empirical results, I must introduce a few methodological clarifications. First, I shall remind the reader of the empirical sources – two sample surveys – which will enable me to carry out the analysis. The first survey, which I shall use only in the next chapter, is based on a sample of 1,031 high school pupils interviewed in Turin in 1977. It will be particularly useful in analysing pupils' post-high school intentions. The second survey – which represents my major source – contains data from 1,739 questionnaires filled in by subjects of 14–29 years of age who were officially registered as unemployed young people in Piemonte a year before being interviewed in 1978. Through this sample it will be possible to analyse all the important steps in individuals' educational careers.

The former survey does not present any particular problem for the analysis of educational decisions (see Appendix 1). By contrast, the latter sample, which was drawn from an already 'selected' population, could present some problem of bias in the estimation of the coefficients of the logit models. In particular, there is the possibility that highly educated young people from a very privileged social background were under-represented in the sample, because they had no reason to register in the youth unemployment lists. This could lead to a limited underestimation of the effects on educational choices of the various measures of socio-economic background which are considered in this book. In Appendix 2 I show that this possible bias should not affect the validity of the results, because these particular unemployment lists had a fairly universal appeal to school- and university-leavers from virtually any socio-economic background. Moreover, making a virtue out of necessity, we should look with even greater confidence at the various effects of social background which the coefficients actually show, for *a fortiori* we know that they are certainly not lower than we have been able to estimate.[1]

The second methodological point which needs to be made is that in this work it is assumed that among my subjects the supply of school places was not a constraint, either in general, i.e. with regard to the possibility of staying on, or with respect to the three branches of high school. All those who wanted are assumed to have have been able to find a place at school and in the branch they desired. This assumption is grounded in the logic of the Italian educational system, which has been that of giving a place to all those qualified for it.[2]

Thirdly, something has to be said to make clear which models I am going to consider. As the reader already knows from the introduction, the analysis will be based on a set of *logit models* (see section 3.1). Given the set of discrete educational choices which have been defined in the previous chapter, one would need no less than four basic models, one multinomial for the choice of the type of school, and three binary models, corresponding to the three binary choices with the alternatives 'staying on vs leaving'.[3] However, given the presence of a large number of interactions, I have estimated two sets of models, separating subjects of working-class origin from subjects coming from the other classes (which for convenience I shall call the 'middle class').[4] This brings the basic

---

[1] The detailed description of the two sample surveys along with a treatment of the problems they present for the estimation of the models can be found in Appendixes 1 and 2 respectively. A more specific possible bias concerning sex is considered in section 4.1. Other possible biases due to age and cohort effects are also dealt with in Appendix 2.

[2] Furthermore, it is assumed that school places are available in the town of residence and that therefore differences in transport costs can be overlooked. The latter assumption would normally be unreasonable, but the nature of my data – which were collected exclusively in the urban environment of the same region – makes it plausible.

[3] Since the three probabilities are hierarchically ordered, two of them must be read as conditional probabilities. In the rest of the work when I refer to the probability of staying on while at high school or to that of staying on at university, it will always be implicit that these are probabilities conditional upon the previous educational choice. This hierarchical form, however, does not alter the fact that each probability is assumed to have a logistic form and its parameters can be estimated separately by specifying independent models which analyse only the individuals in the sample actually reaching that particular choice.

[4] The adoption of models separated by class should also limit the influence of the selection bias mentioned above only to the middle-class models, given that there is no reason to believe that the working-class subjects in the unemployment lists were unrepresentative of the population to any degree. Cf. Appendix 2.

number of models up to eight, one set of four models for each class. The inter-class differences in behaviour will constitute a major focus of the analysis.[5]

In conclusion, a substantive remark: the subject of decision that will be assumed here is the family rather than the individual. This assumption is based on the fact that the family – as the primary socio-economic unit – is the subject which transmits most of the cultural as well as economic resources to the children and which decides on their allocation among alternative uses, including education.[6] Seldom do young individuals have control over family resources, and even if the final decision is left to them, the parents must still be willing to support the children longer; in other words, a kind of basic *altruism* on the side of parents is required.[7]

This chapter, which introduces predominantly pushing forces, is organized in the following way. In the first section there is a brief description of the logit model. In the second section the well-known class inequality in educational participation is articulated in its major economic and cultural components, in an attempt to understand the relevance of different pushing mechanisms by looking at the effects of parents' education, family income, and father's occupation. In the third section the analysis is conducted along more exploratory lines, considering the net effects on educational decisions of family migration

[5] I also estimated two sets of models by sex, but, since no significant interaction was found between sex and the other independent variables, these models are not discussed in the text. In addition, in the next chapter I shall consider a few other models, concerning exclusively the choice of whether to stay on at university, for the purpose of testing for the effect of particular variables.

[6] On the issue of who actually makes the decision, fairly old data (ISTAT 1959) tell us that 45.6% of middle-school-leavers decided by themselves whether to continue their education, whereas the majority decided either jointly with their family (41.8%) or had their family decide for them (10.1%; 2.5% did not answer). The proportion of family unilateral decisions goes up considerably to a level between 36 and 40% when the intended jobs are in the father's or the family business.

[7] Unfortunately, I could not test for this hypothesis, because in neither sample was there a variable that could be interpreted as expressing the parents' degree of altruism. However, a rather striking example of the importance of the family's economic generosity is indirectly provided by German law, which goes so far as to regulate the potential conflict between children and parents; more specifically, it allows children whose parents refuse to pay for their university education to take them to court in order to force them to do so. The idea that there are two fundamental parental attitudes or values, one of altruism and the other of lack of altruism towards offspring, which affect educational investment, has been developed by Ishikawa (1975), whose work constitutes an interesting way of merging a 'sociological' approach which highlights the importance of values with an 'economic' approach of rational maximization and of suggesting that different utility functions can be derived from these different values (on this see also Becker 1981a).

experience and the father's age. Migration will be explored in its cultural as well as economic implications, whereas the father's retirement age is taken to signify constraints to come.

3.1 The logit model

For the analysis of the survey data, I shall employ a non-linear model, the so-called *logit model*, a multivariate technique of analysis which allows the estimation of the effects of a set of independent variables upon the probability of making a given educational choice, maintaining the discreteness of the decision approximately as subjects encounter it in reality. The effects of all variables are considered simultaneously, thus the estimated coefficients associated with each variable measure the effect of the latter *net* of the effects of all other variables on the probability of making a given choice.

Given that this technique of analysis has been developed quite recently and, especially among sociologists, is not widely known, I shall introduce it, if very briefly, in this section. The reader who is acquainted with the logit model can go directly to the next section.[8]

The logit model is based upon the logistic cumulative distribution. In comparison to the more common linear distribution, the main advantage is that the shape of the logistic distribution produces sounder predictions, especially when the probability is closer to its extremes. An illustrated example may be helpful. In figure 3.1, two lines are plotted: the continuous line shows the shape of the cumulative logistic distribution on which the logit is based, while the dotted line shows the shape of a linear probability distribution; the vertical axis represents the probability of staying on after compulsory school, and the horizontal axis an independent variable x, which, to make the example more concrete, we can imagine as the family income. The two curves can be seen as approximating the relationship between income and the chances of staying on at school. From the graph it can be seen that as the probability

[8] There already exists a large body of literature on discrete choice models in general and on logit models in particular (see the review by McFadden 1980), mainly in economics but also in psychology and biometrics. In economics the pioneering work at both the theoretical and empirical level jointly is probably that of Domencich and McFadden (1975). For a description of the logit model accessible to 'amateurs' see Hanushek and Jackson (1977) and Pindyck and Rubinfeld (1981: 2nd edn, ch. 10). The logit model has also been used a few times for the analysis of educational choices: Miller and Radner (1970); Fuller, Manski and Wise (1980, unpublished, quoted by McFadden 1980).

gets closer to its mid point (0.50) the slope of the logit distribution becomes steeper both in absolute terms and relative to the linear distribution. This means that the logit model tends to be more sensitive than the linear model when the probability level is far away from both extremes (i.e. around 0.50) and that the same change in income produces a greater effect on probability in the logit than in the linear model. Instead, when the probability gets closer to the extremes, an increase in income produces the opposite results, and the logistic distribution becomes less sensitive than the linear. (In graphic terms the slope of the logit curve becomes less steep than that of the linear model.)

In the case of educational choices it is reasonable to expect that a person who is already very likely to go to school would be less affected by a change in income than a person who has only a 0.50 probability of going to school. This expectation can best be approximated by the logit model, whereas the linear model would assume that, whatever the probability magnitude, the effect is the same.

We need now to introduce the mathematics of the model. A logistic function implies that the probability for an individual i characterized by a vector X_i of the independent variables may be written as:

$$P_i = exp(a + bX_i)/1 + exp(a + bX_i) \qquad (1)$$

where b is a vector of coefficients to be estimated (in this study the coefficients are estimated by the method of maximum likelihood).

Figure 3.1 *Logistic and linear probability distributions*

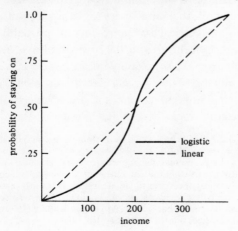

Table 3.1. *Probability changes produced by four coefficients at two levels of the probability*

Values of the coefficients	Probability levels	
	0.50	0.90
0.04	0.01	0.004
0.40	0.10	0.03
1.00	0.23	0.06
3.00	0.45	0.09

The results of the calculation that interest us in this study are not so much the probabilities, but rather the coefficients – the *b* in the equation. Unfortunately, though, the meaning of the coefficients cannot be interpreted directly as it can in the linear model. More precisely, the same quantitative effect on the probability cannot always be attributed to the value of a given coefficient, because, as a consequence of the logit curve, the effect of the same coefficient assumes a very different magnitude in terms of probability changes depending on the point of the distribution at which the probability is located.

Table 3.1 illustrates the relationship between probability changes and values of the coefficients. The values shown in the table represent the probability changes produced by four different coefficients in a case where the independent variable is a dummy taking value 1 or 0.[9] More precisely, for each coefficient they represent the changes associated with

---

[9] To obtain the probability associated with an individual with a given set of characteristics one should apply the estimated coefficients to actual values of the independent variables and simply calculate the probability according to equation (1). There are two ways to calculate the changes in probability associated with a given change in the independent variables and they depend on whether the independent variable is continuous – like age – or dummy – like sex. In the former case one should calculate the marginal change, i.e. the derivative of P_i with respect to X_i, which is equal to:

$$d\mathbf{P}_i/dX_i = b_i*[P_i(1 - P_i)]$$

(For a demonstration see Pindyck & Rubinfeld 1981:299.) The marginal change tells us the rate of change (slope) at a particular point (p_i, X_i).

In the case of a dummy variable, where the problem is that of calculating the change in probability when the variable 'switches' from 0 to 1 – e.g. when passing from a subject who has never been failed at school to a subject, otherwise similar, who has been failed – one should calculate the two overall probabilities for both types of individual, one with the given dummy variable set to 0 and the other with the dummy variable set to 1. The difference between the two probabilities expresses the change.

two different levels of the probability, 0.50 and 0.90. The values of the coefficients are chosen in such a way as to represent the type of values that are actually obtained in my models and to cover approximately the range that the values of the coefficients of dummy independent variables normally take. This can give the reader an idea of the extent to which the magnitude varies depending on the level of the probability itself.

In spite of the interpretative difficulty, the coefficients do express the effect of the independent variable upon the probability and they represent the basic qualitative results of the estimation. First of all, they tell us whether an effect is there, and whether it is positive or negative. Next, they can be compared with each other: for instance, it is possible to say whether the effect of a failure at school is as (or more or less) effective as (than) belonging to a given social class.[10] Finally, they also give some unscaled idea of the strength of the effect.

To make this point clearer, it is probably helpful to transform equation (1) into the following equation:

$$\log P_i/1 - P_i = a + bX_i \qquad (2)$$

Equation (2) shows that the logit model can be expressed as a model which is linear with respect to the natural logarithm of the odds of choosing, say, 'staying on' rather than 'leaving'. The log of the odds can be seen as measuring a generic proneness to stay on and the coefficients (b) as linearly and additively influencing such proneness.[11]

So far I have introduced the binary logit model, but, as the reader

[10]   Of course one can only compare with each other either dummy variables or variables which have the same scale.

[11]   For the purpose of testing the fitting of the model I have used the *log likelihood ratio* test:

$$LLR = 2[L_{max} - L_0]$$

where L_0 is the value of the likelihood function when all independent variables other than the constant are constrained to 0, and L_{max} is the value of the same function when all variables are left free to vary. Their difference tells us whether introducing the independent variables significantly improves the value of the likelihood function. This measure also allows us to test the difference between models with different independent variables. Suppose we estimate model A with 3 variables, parents' income and education, sex plus the constant; then we want to see whether another model B, with school reports added, produces any significant improvement. The answer to this question can come from the following measure:

$$LLR = 2[L_{maxB} - L_{maxA}]$$

which considers the difference of the two values of the likelihood function at their maximum in both models. The LLR approximates the chi-squared distribution.

knows already, the choice of which type of high school to go to has three alternatives; therefore we must briefly introduce the *multinomial* version of the logit model. The multinomial logit model can be written as a set of three separate equations, each of which represents one of the three possible pairs and involves three sets of corresponding coefficients. The equations read as follows:

$$\log \text{prob }(1)/\text{prob }(3) = a_{13} + b_{13}X_i$$
$$\log \text{prob }(2)/\text{prob }(3) = a_{23} + b_{23}X_i$$
$$\log \text{prob }(1)/\text{prob }(2) = a_{12} + b_{12}X_i$$

where

1 = *liceo*
2 = *istituto tecnico*
3 = vocational school

As can be seen from the equations specifying the multinomial model, the odds of choosing, say, *liceo* relative to vocational school are independent of the presence of alternatives other than *liceo* and vocational school. In other words estimating values in a multinomial logit model is equivalent to arriving at estimates for as many binary logit models as there are pairs of alternatives.[12]

3.2 Mechanisms of educational inequality: major hypotheses

It is widely recognized that social differences in educational attainment are broad and pervasive: children from working-class backgrounds receive on average less education than children from higher socio-

[12] This property is known as the *independence of irrelevant alternatives* and is considered a disadvantage of the multinomial logit model; this is one of the reasons why some would prefer the multinomial probit analysis, which does not present this disadvantage (Hausman & Wise 1978). However, computational reasons have led others (McFadden 1980; Hughes 1980) to look for ways to modify the multinomial logit model in order to mitigate the disadvantage of the assumption. One of these ways suggests the use of a hierarchical structure – like the one I have assumed – which consists of splitting the first four-options choice into two steps, the first step made of a binary choice with the options 'staying on vs leaving', and the second concerning the choice among the three branches of high school. In this way the problems raised by the independence of the irrelevant alternatives can be avoided. In fact in the first step the two alternatives are exhaustive of all possible behaviours and therefore the problem does not arise; in the second step it is reasonable to assume that the relative odds of choosing *liceo* rather than vocational schools – conditional, of course, on a prior decision to stay on at school – are independent of the presence of *istituto tecnico*.

Table 3.2. *'Survivors' at each level of education by social class of origin*

	working class	self-employed	non-manual	upper class
level of education:				
compulsory education	100.0	100.0	100.0	100.0
beyond compulsory education	82.9	83.1	93.0	97.5
high school	63.0	73.3	90.2	93.9
beyond high school	19.9	27.5	46.5	75.6

Source: youth unemployment sample (1,631 cases)

economic origins.[13] Italy is no exception (Balbo & Chiaretti 1972, Padoa Schioppa 1974, Corbetta 1975, Trivellato 1978), nor is Piemonte, the north-west region where the surveys I shall use were carried out.

From the data of the youth unemployment sample such differences can be seen clearly: table 3.2 shows the 'survivors' at each educational level by four social classes of origin and we can see for instance that an upper-class child has four times as high a probability of reaching higher education as his working-class counterpart. Inter-class differences apply also to the choice of the type of school: a working-class child, for instance, is more than six times less likely than an upper-class child to go to *liceo* (table 3.3).

Yet, as has often been observed (Craft 1970, Lane 1972, Murphy 1981), such differences do not tell us anything about the mechanisms which produce them and are merely suggestive of the existence of some degree of social inequality in educational opportunities or preferences and of the fact that social origins bear upon schooling behaviour. Moreover, the correlation is far from perfect and the reproductive force that would seem to run from social origins to educational attainment is never so strong as to prevent 'deviant' behaviour from occurring in all social classes.[14]

However, the presumption that constraining elements are at work is reinforced when these differences are taken into account, so much so that

[13] For a recent although critical review of the literature on inter-class differences in educational attainment see Murphy (1981).

[14] In a review of mostly North American literature Leibowitz (1977) shows that the quota of 'explained' variance in completed years of schooling ranges between 10% and 47% when various family background measures are taken into account; in other words, from 53 to 90% of the variance in educational attainment is to be accounted for by factors other than socio-economic background.

Table 3.3. *Percentage distribution of pupils by educational route and social class of origin*

	working class	self-employed	non-manual	upper class
leave	37.0	27.1	9.8	9.3
vocational schools	22.8	20.6	17.9	4.9
istituti tecnici	28.8	35.2	41.2	16.3
licei	11.4	17.1	31.1	69.5
all	100.0	100.0	100.0	100.0

Source: youth unemployment sample (1,631 cases)

many authors have considered as irrelevant the more general question concerning whether people are 'pushed' or rather choose their education, and have straightforwardly concentrated on analysing pushing mechanisms. For these authors there is no question that children are pushed in a particular educational direction; for them the crucial problem is only to find out how this happens.

One objection that could be raised against putting the question so bluntly[15] is that even in the absence of compelling inegalitarian forces it could be a matter of inter-class differences in educational preferences, which – as with all preferences – should traditionally not be disputed. The counter-objection is that even if the latter were the case, it would still be difficult to refrain from disputing preferences and asking how it is possible to find such a consistency between constraints and preferences; in other words, how it is possible that those who are most likely to be exposed to inegalitarian forces should also be those who have the least preference for education. In short it could be questioned whether preferences are truly 'genuine', i.e. independent of social background.

In order to tackle these questions properly we have to discuss the major explanations which have been put forward to make sense of the nature of the inegalitarian forces. These explanations can be usefully reorganized by distinguishing cultural causation from economic causation and by distinguishing further whether causation acts at the level of opportunities or at the level of preferences. As exemplified in table 3.4, this reorganization of the major mechanisms of educational inequality

[15] This objection has in fact been raised by Murphy (1981), whose article is discussed below.

Table 3.4. *Possible mechanisms of educational inequality*

	opportunities	preferences
economic causation	resources to pay for one's education, to wait for an interesting job etc.	'over-adaptation to the possible', risk-aversion etc.
cultural causation	'cultural capital' (capacity for abstraction, language manipulation etc.)	low aspiration levels ('This is not for us'), cognitive constraints

yields four possible outcomes. The first column of the table expresses the effects of economic and cultural causation as possible *constraints* on educational opportunities, affecting respectively the capacity to afford one's education and the ability to meet the intellectual standards of school culture. The second column expresses the indirect effects of economic and cultural causation, as possible *behind-the-back* forces, which can shape preferences and aspirations; causation in the latter column can act in a variety of ways, not easy to distinguish with survey data, which can involve on the one hand a tendency to over-adaptation to constraints and to risk-aversion, and on the other, sub-cultural values – for example attributing a greater formative value to an early working experience than to a long career in formal education – and cognitive constraints, inhibiting the emergence of a preference for education.

In this section I shall discuss these four possible mechanisms and try to assess their role, by measuring simultaneously – i.e. using statistical control – the effects of three traditional dimensions of social inequality: parents' education, family income, and father's occupation. The underlying idea of this test is that although dimensions of inequality are to some degree inter-correlated, each of them carries a specific meaning which it may be helpful to pinpoint and analyse separately from the others. The test for the effect of these variables on the probability of staying on at school and of choosing a particular type of school can be applied – through the youth unemployment survey – to the whole set of choices which were described in the previous chapter. In the logit models used for the test there are – besides father's occupation, parents' education and family income – other variables simultaneously specified which will be discussed in later sections. There are, to be precise, five dummy variables singling out subjects as follows:

(1) father was retired
(2) subject had migrated to Piemonte
(3) father had migrated to Piemonte
(4) subject had been kept down in school
(5) subject is female.[16]

All results will be presented in separate tables where only the coefficients under discussion are shown, but the reader should be aware of the fact that each coefficient belongs to a separate model and that the effects which will be referred to are *always* net of the effects of all other variables.[17] It should therefore be kept in mind that when we discuss, for example, the effect of father's occupation upon the probability of continuing in school or university, that effect is net of those of family income, school achievement, parents' education and the rest.

3.2.1 Cultural constraints and culturally determined aspirations

Among the possible explanations of inequality in educational attainment, a major hypothesis is that of differences in the possession of cultural capital, first advanced by Bourdieu and Passeron (see Bourdieu 1966; Bourdieu and Passeron 1964, 1977). The chief contention is that children from families with a low level of formal education are very likely to lack those abilities which are transmitted in the family, as well as positively selected by the educational systems of Western countries. According to this view, the lack of cultural resources of the family acts as a constraint preventing most children of working-class background from attaining educational success.[18] In particular, the dominant culture, transmitted through the educational system, would require a capacity for abstraction, language manipulation, and formal thought which can

---

[16] Exclusively for the third choice, i.e. that relative to university, I could also test for additional variables which will all be discussed in the next chapter. In particular, I could test for the type of school attended and, on a more restricted set of the youth unemployment sample, the effects of labour market conditions and of job preferences on the decision about university. Furthermore, the high school pupils sample gave me the opportunity to test the effects of some additional variables concerning school achievement and preferences.

[17] The set of logit models from which the coefficients shown in the text are taken is presented in full in Appendix 4.

[18] This hypothesis has been developed also by Bernstein (1977) with respect to language abilities in different social classes.

Table 3.5. *The effects of parents' education (years): logit coefficients*

	CHOICE: staying on at school vs leaving		
	after compulsory education	during high school	after high school
models for the working class:			
coefficients	0.03	0.01	0.09*(1)
	(N = 920)	(N = 681)	(N = 379)
models for the middle class:			
coefficients	0.02	0.24*	0.05*
	(N = 686)	(N = 636)	(N = 476)

Coefficients marked with an asterisk are statistically significant at or below 0.05% probability of error
Source: youth unemployment sample (Appendix 4, Models A)

be acquired only by subjects already endowed with the adequate system of predispositions, as it can only be received from educated parents (Bourdieu 1977). The lack of these resources would be fundamental, even more fundamental than the lack of economic resources, in explaining lack of educational success and the consequent reproduction of inequality in the social structure.

Our results do not seem to support this hypothesis as a generalized explanation of educational destination. This conclusion is based on the use of parents' education, measured by the total number of years of education of both parents, as an indicator of the family's cultural resources.[19] Agreement with our conclusion of course depends on whether one accepts parents' education, and the way it is measured, as an adequate indicator of cultural capital. We have found that parents' education plays a remarkably small role in explaining educational choices.[20] In the working-class models (see table 3.5), it has virtually no effect on the first choice (whether to enter high school) or on the second (whether to stay on when already in high school). Only for the third choice (whether to go to university) does it have a positive effect. It is with regard to the second choice in particular that one would expect the

[19] I preferred this measure to the separated measures because the parents' levels of education are highly correlated (0.70 is the simple correlation coefficient) and it would have been statistically risky to measure the effects of both simultaneously because of multicollinearity. Moreover, maintaining the distinction would not have been meaningful in relation to the hypotheses of this study.

[20] Cf. Colasanti, Mebane & Bonolis (1976), who provide some evidence of a decline over a period of time of the relevance of cultural factors (pp. 97ff).

relative lack of cultural capital to be most strongly discriminatory (by pushing pupils out of school). The fact that this does not seem to happen is somewhat surprising, for it is precisely here that those pupils who lack both the ability to absorb the standard school culture and the capacity for perceiving their inadequacy in advance could be expected to meet the greatest difficulties.

Two objections could be raised against taking the lack of any relevant effect of parents' education in the working-class models as a finding that weakens the cultural capital hypothesis. First one might suspect that the effects of parents' education might pass through some other variable, particularly school achievement. In order to test for the latter possibility, I estimated the whole set of logit equations without the dummy variables singling out kept-down children, which is the only indicator of school achievement present in the equations; the coefficients for parents' education did not change, thereby suggesting that parents' education can be assumed to have an effect independent of school achievement.

Secondly, it could be argued that within the set of working-class parents there could not be much difference in educational terms and that therefore it would be more than natural to expect a negligible effect. According to this explanation, the effect of cultural resources would pass, as it were, through the class as a whole, and our assumption that parents' level of education is the best indicator for this variable would not hold. An indication which supports this objection is that in the middle-class models (table 3.5), where subjects with more heterogeneous social backgrounds are grouped together, the effect of parents' education is very strong, with the precise effect of preventing pupils from being pushed out of high school. (In the middle- as well as in the working-class models, parents' level of education has no effect on the first choice and some effect on the third choice, i.e. increasing the probability of going to university.)

However, there are indications that this objection could, at least in part, be unfounded; although in fact around a lower mean – 10 years as against 16 – the standard deviation of parents' education is high enough within the working class (5.2 vs 7.3 years for the middle class) to allow an effect to appear if it did exist. There is a further circumstance to be considered: in the working-class models too, parents' education is indeed effective, though only with regard to the choice of whether to go to university. Thus it could be asked why, if the effect of cultural resources were really 'absorbed' by the class as a whole, this should occur in the case of the two first choices only.

This result is rather counter-intuitive: one would in fact expect that the longer the education already successfully received, the lower would be the negative effect produced by poorly educated parents and the greater the autonomy of the pupils. Perhaps a more likely explanation of the fact that in working-class families parents' education seems to affect only the choice concerning university could be that the effect of this variable operates mainly through preferences and aspirations. In other words, here parents' education could measure a different mechanism, namely the indirect effect of the cultural capital on preferences, rather than its constraining effect on opportunities (see Beaton 1975: 391 for some evidence in this respect). Moreover, the third choice, unlike the second, is made before starting the course of study, and therefore if the explanation were that of cultural capital, it should be assumed that it would not work directly as a constraint, but through expectations and anticipation of constraints to come. The process should resemble a sort of Socratic 'knowledge of ignorance' which would lead to self-discrimination.[21]

In the next chapter I shall consider – exclusively for the choice of university – another set of models derived from the high school pupils survey, where job preferences are also specified among the independent variables. In these models, the effect of parents' education disappears altogether, strongly suggesting that once preferences and aspirations are taken into account the hypothetical direct effect of cultural constraints vanishes. This conclusion is supported also by the coefficients of the logit models applied to the choice of the three types of high school. Here the level of parents' education has a considerable effect, especially by strongly increasing the probability of going to *liceo* rather than to *istituto tecnico* or to vocational school (table 3.6). Its effects are felt in both classes, and the coefficients of the middle-class model are similar to those of the working-class model.

These findings have two implications: firstly, they further reinforce the idea that parents' education, *even within the working class itself*, is a meaningful variable whose effects are very likely to refer to some specific

---

[21] Some evidence of self-discrimination is provided by Kahl (1961) for the USA. He observed that families who took their children out of the educational system after high school, while rejecting the idea of sending them to college, often justified it by saying 'we are not bright in school'.

Table 3.6. *The effect of parents' education (years): logit coefficients (models with three alternatives)*

	CHOICE: type of school		
	liceo vs istituto tecnico	*liceo* vs vocational school	*istituto tecnico* vs vocational school
model for the working class (N = 583): coefficients	0.14*	0.17*	0.03
model for the middle class (N = 596): coefficients	0.09*	0.13*	0.03*

Source: youth unemployment sample (Appendix 4, Models A)

mechanism not adequately expressed by family income and father's occupation. Secondly, they suggest that, by being positively correlated with the choice of the most academically oriented branch of high school, the amount of cultural resources acts through the preferences and the aspirations of the subjects and of their families.

As Halsey, Heath and Ridge (1980) have pointed out, the concept of cultural capital 'is useful as an umbrella term for a set of mechanisms through which families influence the formal educational experience of their children' (p. 88). Although their findings, based on British data, cannot be directly compared with my findings, because of differences in the educational systems and in the measurement techniques, the test of the 'cultural capital' hypothesis they carried out shows interesting points of convergence with the test presented here. Halsey, Heath and Ridge (1980) found (1) 'a large volume of upward intergenerational education-al mobility' and an overwhelming presence in state selective schools of 'first generation novitiates into the "national cultural heritage"' (p. 88); (2) a decline of the relative chances for selective secondary schooling of those from educated backgrounds; and (3) small inter-class differences in examination success as distinct from length of schooling. Their final comment seems to be supported by my findings: 'Bourdieu's postulated mechanism – the acquisition of the dominant culture of capitalist societies which is effectively accessible only to middle class children – is of no great importance' (p. 146). However, before drawing any firm conclusion, we need to go further and consider the other two dimensions of social inequality which we have specified in the logit models, i.e. family income and social class.

3.2.2 Economic constraints

The other major hypothesis that has been put forward, particularly by economists, in order to explain educational behaviour is that of economic constraints. In the sociological literature, a major contribution is that of Boudon (1974), who elaborated this hypothesis in contrast with the hypothesis of cultural capital and that of differential class values. According to this view, education, which in most countries must be financed by family resources, involves direct costs (books, fees, transport) as well as forgone earnings. Hence, it is natural to expect education to be partially dependent on the pecuniary resources that individuals and their families have at their disposal. Thus the greater the wealth of the family, the higher the chances for the pupil or student of staying longer in school. In this section I shall try to test for this hypothesis.[22] But before discussing the results of the logit models, it is worthwhile considering the theoretical implications.

Starting from the fact that education can be considered as an investment commodity, economists – especially those who follow the human capital approach – have often contended that, if the two following conditions hold, the relationship between family resources and children's education becomes irrelevant: if (1) education was acquired mainly for its investment value, for its capacity, that is, to bring pecuniary returns, and if, at the same time, (2) borrowing money for educational purposes was feasible and easy, then we could expect economically rational individuals to make educational choices irrespective of their income, but only in view of future expected rewards. Sometimes economists have been very extreme in making these assumptions and rather forgetful of any determinant of educational choices other than expected rates of return. But generally they have been ready to acknowledge that, despite the theoretical soundness of the whole argument, the latter condition often does not hold (Becker 1975: 79–80), for there are capital market difficulties which mean that, even if education were governed merely by expected rates of return, still 'wealthier families would tend to invest more [in education] than poorer ones', for these would have to have recourse to 'internal financing', i.e.

---

[22] For a test of the 'consumption hypothesis' with time series in Italy see Colasanti, Mebane & Bonolis (1976, especially ch. 3).

household resources (Becker 1975: 79). The tendency that seems to prevail now is that of considering education simultaneously as an investment and as a consumption commodity.[23]

A different objection, which has been raised by sociologists, against the relationship between family economic resources and children's education holds that in Western countries *per capita* income has gone up so much that, especially since the Second World War, it has no longer constituted an important constraint to those who really want education for their children. Poverty is seen as the sole relevant economic aspect and income, with respect to education, is imagined as a binary variable: either it acts as a barrier or is no constraint at all. It follows that for families in Western countries, where poverty is thought to have disappeared, the main determinants of educational choices should be sought among aspirations or sub-cultural values (e.g. Craft 1970, Floud 1970).[24] This set of convictions has led a number of sociologists to disregard economic constraints on educational decisions and to consider as relevant only what comes 'beyond' sheer material circumstances.[25]

These assumptions seem rather simplistic: it is certainly plausible to suggest that, beyond a certain threshold, income does not affect decisions and that the higher the income the lower the marginal effect on the probability of staying on at school. Yet it would be very optimistic to argue that the large majority of families living in industrialized countries had actually crossed that threshold; if perhaps low income no longer represents a constraint, it does not follow that we should therefore consider it altogether irrelevant. At the same level of preferences, of ability, and of probability of success, families with lower income can be

---

[23] See for instance Padoa Schioppa (1974), Lazear (1976), Michael (1975), Pissarides (1981b) and Becker himself in the second edition of his standard text on human capital (1975: 67–9). Recent evidence shows not only that every family simultaneously considers education as an investment and as a consumption commodity, but that different families tend to stress either the consumption or the investment side of education, depending on the context in which they live: according to Park (1980) education is sought as an investment commodity by 'traditional' families and as a consumption commodity by 'modern' families; according to Post (1985), a relevant distinction with corresponding effects would also be between 'centre' and 'periphery'.

[24] Banks (1976: 71–2) seems to share the same view, even though she points out in passing that according to the Crowther Report 'the proportion of young people mentioning the desire to leave school declined as father's income increased'.

[25] In educational sociology probably the most notable exception is Boudon (1974). However, most of the students of social stratification are also unsympathetic to this anti-economic view (e.g. Stewart, Prandy & Blackburn 1980).

expected to yield sooner and take their children out of school earlier.[26] In this light there is no need to look for an explanation in terms of differential aspirations when we observe that children from a middle-class background obtain more education than children born into a working-class family.[27] Even if they had the same preferences and ambitions, the relative costs of fulfilling them would be different and would exert different pressures. Undoubtedly many working-class families nowadays send their children to school for longer periods, but this does not contradict the statement that economic resources count and that those families which do so need at the same time to make heavier sacrifices and to have relatively stronger ambitions.

In this context the view of the economists is more helpful, and it is to it that I shall mainly refer here.[28] In short, it considers education as a commodity which simultaneously satisfies consumption needs and produces pecuniary returns. Hence, just as with any consumer commodity, it is acquired in greater quantities the lower its price or the wealthier the subjects who acquire it; and, as an investment commodity, it is assumed to be relatively more attractive the higher the expected rate of return. In the latter sense, the treatment of education is postponed until the next chapter; education as consumption will be considered here.

The measure of family affluence used in the logit models in order to test the hypothesis of economic constraints is per child income. I preferred this measure to total income because education has *per capita* costs and has to be bought for each child, unlike housing and cars, whose costs are less dependent on how many members there are in a family. Furthermore, I also preferred this measure to *per capita* income following the suggestion – originated by Becker (1981b) – that if a family plans a given amount of education for one child it must also plan the same amount for all other children, for the reason that one can plan 'to

[26] Recent evidence in Britain indicates that pupils' staying on rate depends – among other things – on per capita income (Pissarides 1981b). Other recent evidence on a positive relationship between school leaving and low economic resources is provided by Gordon (1980). The evidence concerning Italy on the relationship between income and education is rather scanty and is not based on survey data (cf. Barbagli 1974 and the next chapter for a discussion of the evidence presented by that author).

[27] The view that aspirations are what matters most was, for instance, expressed by the Plowden Report (1967), though referring to achievement rather than to decision-making. With the same data from the Report, Acland (1980) shows that a different interpretation, more focused on circumstances than on parental attitudes, comes out when a more careful scrutiny is made.

[28] As well as to Keller & Zavalloni (1964) and Boudon (1974).

Table 3.7. *The effect of per child income(*): logit coefficients*

	CHOICE: staying on at school vs leaving		
	after compulsory education	during high school	after high school
models for the working class: coefficients	0.91* (N = 920)	0.49* (N = 681)	0.18 (N = 379)
models for the middle class: coefficients	0.44* (N = 686)	0.26* (N = 636)	− 0.04 (N = 476)

Source: youth unemployment sample (Appendix 4, Models A)

own both an expensive and inexpensive car, but is unlikely to plan on having both expensive and inexpensive children' (p. 106). As a consequence, children's *capita* are likely to reverberate with greater force on educational decisions than adults'.[29]

Finally, I regressed the logarithm rather than the actual per child income because the logarithm can represent the decreasing marginal effect of the variable upon the decision. In other words it represents the expectation that the same income change is more effective at lower levels than at higher levels of income.[30]

In general the coefficients strongly support the crucial role of economic constraints. In particular, with regard to the set of the three binary choices 'staying on vs leaving', there are two major results (table 3.7), namely that (a) per child income is more important earlier on, especially at the first choice, the one taken immediately after the end of

[29] In constructing per child income I also weighted younger and older children differently by attributing a factor of 2 to children below 14 years of age. The reason for this lies in an attempt to allow for the fact that, on average, younger children represent a greater economic burden on the family, not so much in current as in future terms, for they can be expected to leave home and enter the labour market later than older children.

I have also carried out tests using three other measures – *per capita* income, per child income not weighted, and per child income including only children below the age of 14 – in addition to that presented in the text, and the differences did not prove particularly marked. The results of these further tests are shown in detail in Appendix 3.

[30] The models on which I based the analysis of this section have been estimated with all independent variables; the effect of per child income is therefore controlled for by father's occupation, parents' years of education, father's retirement age, migration experiences, school achievement, type of school attended, and sex (see chapter 4). The model concerning the middle classes has two additional variables controlling for the type of middle class: middle-class self-employed, and upper class; the left-out group is the middle-class dependent workers (see below).

Table 3.8. *The effects of per child income(*): logit coefficients (models with three alternatives)*

	CHOICE: type of school		
	liceo vs *istituto tecnico*	*liceo* vs vocational school	*istituto tecnico* vs vocational school
model for the working class (N = 583): coefficients	−0.09	0.38*	0.47*
model for the middle class (N = 596): coefficients	0.27	0.86*	0.59*

Source: youth unemployment sample (Appendix 4, Models A)

compulsory school, and that (b) working-class subjects are more responsive to income than middle-class subjects, again especially at the first choice.[31]

With regard to the choice of the type of school, there are also two major results (table 3.8); the first, and more important, is that, regardless of class, a higher per child income discriminates in favour of the longer high schools, namely *liceo* and *istituto tecnico*, and against vocational school. The second is that economic resources seem here more important for the middle class than for the working class, particularly when the pair of alternatives is *liceo* and vocational school.

The first important result – namely that per child income is of key importance in the first post-compulsory choice and that its relevance declines alongside the level of education at which the choice is taken – could be explained by the fact that the longer the education lying ahead the greater its cost and the more important the role of economic constraints. When deciding about the possibility of attending high school the burden of economic constraints is greatest. At the same time, when pupils reach the threshold of university they are more likely to be potentially more independent from family economic resources and capable of taking up work if necessary. This circumstance could further

[31] The difference is statistically significant according to the following test:

$$\text{Test} = bX - bZ/[var(bX) + var(bZ)]^{1/2}$$

where X and Z are the two variables whose coefficients – 'b' – need to be compared. In general I have considered only significant differences between coefficients in different models.

explain why the effect of income declines in relation to the decision to go to university.[32]

That length of education is an attribute of major importance is also indirectly suggested by the results concerning the choice of the type of school: while, in fact, parents' education encourages only the choice of *liceo*, per child income encourages both *liceo* and *istituto tecnico* and negatively influences only the choice of the shortest route, namely vocational school.

While these findings generally support Boudon's claim that economic forces are probably more powerful than cultural constraints in determining educational choices, they also invalidate his further claim that the effects of economic constraints, which he calls 'secondary effects' as distinct from 'primary effects' due to cultural factors, tend to remain constant throughout all educational levels and that, through a multiplicative effect, they decrease the chances of 'survival' of working-class children at later stages of their educational careers (cf. Boudon 1974: 79–83). From our results, on the contrary, it would appear as if economic constraints played a decreasing role the higher the educational stage already reached by the working-class child. It would appear as if economic constraints act as a binding element before high school and are, in this sense, more 'primary' than cultural constraints.

Once again we find a striking convergence with the results of the Oxford study (Halsey, Heath and Ridge 1980), which found 'an enormous drop-out of working class boys at the minimum school-leaving age, but the longer a working class pupil survives within the school system the more closely do his chances of surviving yet further approximate to the service and intermediate class pupils' chances' (p. 130).

The second major fact to emerge from the results is that working-class subjects are more sensitive to income at the first two binary choices, whereas middle-class subjects would appear to be more sensitive to income when deciding about the type of school to opt for. A possible explanation of this difference is that the marginal effect of an additional unit of per child income is greater when income is smaller. Hence middle-

---

[32] A further reason could be found in the presence of selection effects: those most affected by economic constraints are not at risk for any later decision because they have left earlier.

class families, which have on average higher incomes, should be relatively less sensitive. However, the inter-class difference in average per child income is not so marked as to suggest an explanation simply in terms of the differential impact of income changes at different levels of income.[33] Moreover, middle-class families too accommodate their choice to their financial constraints by selecting, relatively more frequently than working-class families, the shorter route when less wealthy. In other words, when finances are scarce, working-class families take their children directly out of school while middle-class families have them sent to high school anyway, even if to the less demanding branches.

This could suggest a different explanation of the differential responsiveness, namely that even at the same level of income, working-class families tend to be more sensitive, for they are more uncertain about education and do not consider it as an unconditionally attractive good. The differential responsiveness could be due to differential class values or other *behind-the-back* mechanisms which I shall discuss below.

These findings leave unresolved a problem of substantive and methodological importance. There is the risk that in measuring the effect of per child income on education we may have incurred a problem of circularity, for the current level of per child income could, to some extent at least, be influenced by the very educational decisions it is supposed to constrain. While from the point of view of the child parents' income is very much a binding constraint, especially at younger ages, from the point of view of the family, per child income depends also on two prior decisions: how many children to have and which type and extent of labour market participation to pursue. Of course, there are components of both that are not decisions at all: labour market participation, needless to say, depends on a wide range of factors, determined regardless of families' will and efforts; fertility decisions too, which are eligible to depend entirely on parents' choice, could well be made, if at all,

---

[33] At the first choice the average natural log of per child (weighted) income is 5.85 for the middle class and 5.58 for the working class and the corresponding standard deviations are 0.64 and 0.68. However, the absence of a marked difference in the average middle- and working-class per child incomes – on which the latter hypothesis indirectly relies – must be taken *cum grano salis*, for it could be the result of an underestimation in reporting the exact family income, more frequent in the middle class than in the working class. People in general, and Italians in particular, are considered to be rather reticent in declaring their true income. If there is such a tendency it could be more marked in those families where income does not come exclusively from employment and where therefore hiding its true amount is important for tax evasion. The effects in the middle-class models could therefore be underestimated.

irrespective of the costs of the amount of education which may become desirable later on.[34]

Yet, both fertility and labour market behaviour involve some degree of freedom for families. Among the many determinants of fertility it is conceivable that rational parents when deciding to have children somehow take account of the expected (and desired) length of education and of its cost; and, as a consequence, parents more concerned with the 'quality' of their children are on average to be expected to reduce their 'quantity' (Becker 1981b).[35] Similarly, the extent of labour market extra effort by family members (second job, overtime, mother's work) may also be influenced by the costs of the desired amount of children's education.

Here, it is not possible to measure the 'true' net effect of per child income on education, its effect, that is, net of family planning and labour market behaviour, which can themselves be influenced by the expected education for the children. We are therefore left in doubt as to how much of the effect we measured with the logit models is really the product of unavoidable economic constraints.[36] What we have been able to measure are the economic constraints, as they exist in the present conditions of the family, as the combined result of constraints and decisions met by its members in the past.

This doubt notwithstanding we can briefly summarize the findings

[34] Some evidence that a fair proportion of pregnancies tend to occur rather than to be planned is provided by a recent survey carried out in England and Wales, according to which '48% of the pregnancies leading to the survey babies were either unintended, accidental, initially regretted or wrongly spaced' (Cartwright 1976: 32).

[35] Simon (1977), for instance, asserts that: 'numerous surveys in poor and rich countries have shown that the cost of education is an important consideration to parents when deciding how many children to have' (p. 387). In general, a large body of literature in historical demography suggests that neither getting married nor having children has ever been a natural process to be left untouched by economic calculation, or an exclusive attribute of industrial societies. To pick just one piece of evidence from the region where my surveys are based, in the town of Susa farmers used to marry only one of their sons while leaving the others unmarried, in order to limit the size of the population making pressure on their land (Livi Bacci 1977). For further evidence of the fact that expected children's cost affects fertility see Hawthorn (1970), Andorka (1978), and Easterlin (1978).

[36] As a solution to this problem, Becker (1981b: 111) suggests simultaneous or reduced form equations: 'for example, the education (or other measure of quality) of a child could be related to the education of his parents, the number of his siblings, and other variables, while the number of children is related to the education of parents, the education of children, and other variables'. However, to pursue the test of the effects of income on education along these lines would have involved empirical data and an amount of work both far beyond the scope of this book.

presented so far. On the whole, the influence of economic resources appears to be more pervasive than that of cultural resources. The former play a crucial role in the early educational choices, particularly within the working class. The lack of cultural capital, as measured by parents' education, seems to work mainly against middle-class children, and tends to push them out of high school before the end of the five-year course. Parents' education has a positive effect upon the probability of going to *liceo* and later to university. It is dubious, however, whether the effect measures cultural resources in the sense of a constraint or rather culturally determined preferences and aspirations.

3.2.3 The effect of class and over-adaptation to the possible

There still remains a measure of inequality to be considered, namely father's occupation, which represents the traditional means of defining social class of origin, but whose effects in this case will be analysed *net* of those of family income and parents' education.[37]

Since for each choice two models were run – one for working-class and one for middle-class subjects – the effects of class as measured by father's occupation must be detected by looking at the constant terms of the models separated by class. The constant, in fact, indicates the underlying force by means of which a member of the class to which the model refers is attracted by or, indeed, pushed towards a given alternative, independently of all other conditions specified in the model itself.

With regard to the models referring to classes other than the working class (which for convenience I have called middle-class models) there is a further problem to be taken care of. Since they form a rather heterogeneous aggregate, I have introduced two extra dummy variables, singling out whether the subject is (1) from that section of the middle classes constituted by self-employed workers (artisans, shop-keepers, farmers) or (2) from the upper class (entrepreneurs, professionals). The left-out group, whose effect is incorporated in the constant of the middle-class models, includes all subjects who are dependent non-manual workers.

[37] Class or origin is here defined only by father's occupation. Quite correctly many authors would regard the absence of mother's occupation from the definition as problematic, yet, in Italy, comparatively few mothers have an occupation (approximately 20% in the youth unemployment sample). It would therefore have been of little help to try to define social class by taking both parents' occupation into account.

Table 3.9. *The effects of social class of origin: logit coefficients*

	CHOICE: staying on at school vs leaving		
	after compulsory education	during high school	after high school
models for the working class:			
constants	−3.52*	0.76	−2.78*
	(N = 920)	(N = 681)	(N = 379)
models for the middle class:			
coefficients for the self-employed	−1.22*	0.84*	0.04
coefficients for the upper class	0.31	−1.73*	0.32
constants	1.48	−1.73*	−0.64
	(N = 686)	(N = 636)	(N = 476)

Source: youth unemployment sample (Appendix 4, Models A)

Two major points emerge from the whole set of findings. If we assume that the effect of economic resources is adequately controlled for by per child income and that of cultural resources is adequately expressed by parents' education, the principal fact to emerge is that father's occupation still has an effect. In other words, it would seem as if the mechanisms associated with social differences in educational choices could not be – as is often suggested – limited to either cultural or economic discrimination. The fact that school achievement is also crudely controlled for reinforces the conclusion that some mechanism revolves specifically around father's occupation.

Thus, the simple fact of being a working-class child makes a net negative difference with respect to the probability of entering high school (table 3.9) and also of entering university. This additional difference is independent of the level of per child family income, of the level of parents' education, and of school achievement and, more generally, of all the variables which are specified in the models. In contrast, middle-class children – excluding children of self-employed workers, who are the least privileged within the middle-class models – do not undergo any marked selection either at 14 or at 19 (see table 3.9).

The second important finding worth mentioning is that there are several signs of the existence of a 'natural selection' type of process, whereby the group which underwent a more severe selection at one stage is more likely to 'survive' through the next. Thus at the intermediate choice, which is the least conventional one, the interesting fact is that working-class children especially[38] do not appear to suffer from any form of selection beyond that produced by economic constraints; but they do again at the third choice. At the opposite extreme, upper-class children do not undergo any selection at the first and third choices, but, relative to the other groups in the middle-class models, they become particularly prone to leaving high school before the end.

In the previous chapter I showed that the choice of leaving after the beginning of high school is quite different from that of leaving before or after. It is an experience which is commonly regarded as a failure or, at the very least, as a substantial change of plan. Why, then, should the fact of having a father in an upper-class occupation have a negative net effect increasing the probability of failure or change of plans?

The reason probably is that while working-class subjects seem to be risk-averse to an extent which takes the tendency dictated by economic constraint to extremes, upper-class families tend to send their children to high school almost automatically, independently of their probability of success and often independently of their true inclinations. Obtaining at least a high school diploma is felt to be a norm, a mandatory accomplishment. It is only when confronted with their behaviour in high school that upper-class parents eventually come to realize their children's inability or unwillingness to continue. One remarkable consequence of this pattern could be that the pushing forces tend to work upwards (i.e. compelling children to stay on) as well as downwards even though most authors have been stressing only the latter.

Such a possibility is strengthened if we take into account the coefficients of the models referring to the choice of the branch of high school (table 3.10). Being the child of an upper-class family, even if family income and parents' education are controlled for, still increases – and very strongly – the probability of being sent to *liceo*, while in all other classes the tendency is to avoid this type of school in favour of the less demanding *istituto tecnico* and vocational school. The *liceo* seems to possess a rather irresistible *status* appeal which makes the upper classes choose it independently of any other considerations.

The pattern of effects measured by parents' education, which has been discussed above, is consistent with this pattern and suggests that some kind of over-ambition is present in the middle class at large and not

[38] Being the child of a self-employed worker also makes a net negative difference relative to the other middle classes at the first choice; in the remaining two choices there are no significant differences.

Table 3.10. *The effects of social class of origin: logit coefficients (models with three alternatives)*

	CHOICE: type of school		
	liceo vs *istituto tecnico*	*liceo* vs vocational school	*istituto tecnico* vs vocational school
model for the working class (N = 583):			
constants	− 1.87	− 3.07*	− 1.21
model for the middle class (N = 596): coefficients for the self-			
employed	0.19	0.49	0.30
coefficients for the upper class	1.09	2.23*	1.14
constants	− 3.38*	− 5.52*	− 2.14*

Source: youth unemployment sample (Appendix 4, Models A)

simply in the upper class. If we look at the second choice in the middle-class models, we see that parents' education is a key variable in increasing the likelihood of finishing high school successfully; this circumstance suggests that the middle-class subjects are very bold in trying to make their way through high school, but are likely to succeed only when supported by an adequate level of parents' education, while they are likely to fail when, other things being equal, the desire for a high school diploma is coupled exclusively with ambition.

On the contrary, in the working-class models, parents' education has virtually no effect: it increases neither the probability of going to high school nor, for those who do so, the probability of staying on, successfully, until the end. The reason for this is probably that working-class subjects meet a very severe selection barrier at the first educational choice, partly, as we have seen, because of the impact of economic resources and partly because of some mechanism linked with the very fact of being from a working-class background. The process of selection, by filtering in only the highly promising working-class children, acts as a shelter against subsequent risk of failures.

Since the hypotheses concerning cultural capital and economic constraints do not seem exhaustive as explanations of the mechanisms associated with social differences in educational behaviour, is there a theory which can make sense of the pattern of net effects associated with father's occupation? Is there, in other words, a convincing theoretical framework which can make sense of the tendency of middle-class parents to send their children to school even at a greater relative risk of failure and which can, at the same time, account for the greater caution shown among the working class, where families send their children to school only when fairly certain that they can successfully complete the course?

A useful way of reformulating the major differences between existing theoretical approaches which can constitute an answer to these questions is to separate the views which posit the existence of an over-adjustment of class behaviour to material and cultural circumstances – i.e. an adjustment which takes to the extreme the pushing forces in a *behind-the-back* type of process – from those which instead suggest that class differences in educational choices result from an adequate adaptation, rational in a passive sort of way, to objective possibilities and constraints.

To the first type belongs a well-known article by Hyman (1966), which suggests the presence of an 'extremizing' class behaviour, behaviour, that is, which brings to a non-objectively justified extreme the adaptation to actual constraints:

> Opportunity in the society is differential; higher education or specialized training, which might provide access to a high position, must be bought with money – the very commodity that the lower classes lack. Such objective factors help maintain the existing structure. But there are other factors of a more subtle psychological nature which have not been illuminated and which may also work to perpetuate the existing order. It is our assumption that an intervening variable mediating the relationship between low position and lack of upward mobility is a system of beliefs and values within the lower classes which in turn reduces the very voluntary action which would ameliorate their low position. (p. 488)

We find a striking, if more sophisticated, counterpart in a rather different field. Paul Veyne (1976) suggests that the obedience of the populace to the power of the notables in ancient Greece was not the direct result of power and coercion, but involved also a mental process of legitimation which did not simply realign behaviour to the actual balance of forces, but carried the feeling of submission to a non-objectively justified extreme.[39] Moreover, Veyne holds that this process is of a

---

[39] Veyne explicitly acknowledges the adoption of Festinger's theory of cognitive dissonance. Taking one's own submission to extremes has sometimes been the object of

generalized and pervasive nature and belongs to the process of legitimation in many different historical circumstances.[40]

To return to educational choices, Hyman received a critical reply from Keller and Zavalloni (1964), who argued against the presence of over-adaptation on the part of the lower classes. In particular, they said that the presence of less absolutely ambitious goals among working-class subjects, shown by Hyman, does not entail ambition being lower in relative terms also. In the words of Boudon (1974), who gave a more general status to Keller and Zavalloni's approach, 'it simply means that the distance they have to travel to reach a given social status will be different from the distance covered by middle class youngsters . . . reaching a given educational level or a given status means being exposed to costs and benefits that are going to differ according to social background' (p. 23). The explanation of inter-class differences is therefore not so much a matter of differential values and beliefs as the result of differential costs which, at the same level of ambition, give rise to different outcomes. Boudon explicitly acknowledges that his approach is to a large extent derived from economic analysis.[41]

The latter view is theoretically as well as empirically convincing. As we have seen, subjects adjust to their economic constraints and, as we shall see in the next chapter, they adjust to labour market opportunities. In other words, they take sensibly into account the costs and the benefits of education. There are, however, both empirical and theoretical reasons to believe that the process of adjustment – especially to economic constraints – is taken to the extreme, as Hyman suggested. However, while Hyman saw this process as working only downwards in the lower classes our findings suggest that it works also in the opposite direction in the middle classes.

comic literature. *The Good Soldier Sweick* by Jaroslav Hašek, for instance, shows how an appalling degree of obedience can be more disruptive than overt revolutionary action, even though the author leaves us in doubt as to whether Sweick is behaving in such a manner on purpose or through sheer stupidity. This, however, suggests that extreme submission could, in certain circumstances, be the product of rational choice.

[40] Obedience too, of course, has been presented in terms of rational adaptive behaviour by the contractualist and utilitarian tradition since Hobbes and, incidentally, Veyne's argument is explicitly put forward against the 'bel optimisme des théoriciens du contrat social' (1976, p. 311). These considerations were generated by Elster (1980, 1983); I am grateful to Geoffrey Hawthorn for having brought this to my attention.

[41] It is precisely on the grounds of the economic approach of human behaviour that a generalized version of rational adjustment to costs and benefits is found. Generalized in that it aims at going beyond the purely economic sphere to explain a wide range of behaviour from marriage to criminal acts (Becker 1976).

The *empirical* reasons can be inferred from the pattern of results discussed above. Although we cannot categorically exclude the possibility that such a pattern is the product of unmeasured differential opportunities associated with social class and which can make education less rewarding for working-class children, it seems more plausible to interpret it as the result of different mechanisms (cf. the conclusions below). First let us look at the behaviour of the upper- and middle-class children who appear to be attempting to make their way through high school *over* the threshold that likelihood of success indicates as advisable. If in fact it were just a process of rational adaptation, we should expect the probability of success to be as high in the middle class as in the working class. The mirror image of this process, namely working-class pupils under-adapting in the sense of entering high school less frequently than probability of success would advise, cannot be directly inferred because the fact that once they have entered high school they are – *ceteris paribus* – virtually certain to obtain the diploma could be the result of the circumstance that all those who did not enter high school would have been unsuccessful. In other words, for all we know, it could be the result of optimal adaptation rather than of under-adaptation. Still, it is undoubtedly plausible to presume that this is not the case and that working-class behaviour reflects in the reverse direction the behaviour of the middle and upper classes.

Secondly, consistent with this view that the working class tends to over-adapt to material circumstances there is a further piece of evidence, namely that subjects belonging to this group – as we have seen – appear to be twice as responsive to income changes as middle-class subjects. When income is low, working-class parents take their children out of school, whereas middle-class parents have them sent to the less demanding branches of high school.

To make clear the *theoretical* reasons in favour of the view positing the existence of over-adaptation processes we need to follow a somewhat oblique route. According to Murphy (1981), there seem to be two possible logical alternatives to explain class disparity in educational attainment: we can suppose either (1) that the demand for education is universal and that forces of some sort or another push individuals from the lower classes out of school earlier than they would really have liked, or (2) that for some reason more individuals from the lower classes actually prefer less education. Since – in Murphy's view – there is no hard evidence against the latter possibility, i.e. that inter-class differences are the result of choice, the former possibility, i.e. that inter-class differences are the result of pushing and discriminatory forces, relies upon an unwarranted inference.[42]

If we try to view the problem more realistically, however, we can see where the crucial question lies, namely not so much in the alternative between a frustrated universal demand and differential values and aspirations as in whether such aspirations can be regarded as genuine, i.e. formed independently of inegalitarian forces. In this way the alternative, despite its logic, no longer appears as such. Murphy, quite correctly, perceives that there is an unresolved problem relative to subjects' intentions, which are often shortcircuited by authors, and that one ought to be more careful in attributing to constraints what may be the result of preferences; yet he fails to grasp the fact that the crucial problem is precisely whether subjects shortcircuit themselves (cf. Mahon 1985). In educational studies, it is all too often taken for granted that differential aspiration is mechanically produced by inegalitarian forces while, on the other hand, it remains to be explained why educational values and aspirations should be distributed in a socially uneven manner so strikingly consistent with the uneven distribution of constraints.

Beyond the material constraints which make access to education difficult for some, a possible explanation of inter-class disparity is to be found in what could go under the umbrella term of *inertial forces*, which can take the form of sub-cultural values, adaptive preferences, or other subtle psychological mechanisms. Here inertia must be understood in the sense of a force that selects one educational option (1) independently of the intrinsic rewards attached to the educational alternatives and to the expected probability of success, and (2) consistently, or rather over-consistently, with one's own social class of origin, regardless of the fact that inertia works downwards in the working class and upwards in the middle class.

The question is, where does this inertia come from? Here we leave the survey data, which can provide no answer for the world of speculation. Nonetheless, four explanations may be considered in an attempt to see,

---

[42] For instance he strongly criticizes authors such as Bourdieu and Passeron, Boudon, and Halsey, Heath and Ridge for mistaking class disparity for class inequality, purporting to explain statistical differences as the product of inegalitarian forces. According to Murphy (1981) these writers try to overcome this logical impasse by realigning 'the evaluation with the explanation by taking differential aspiration to be itself a consequence of inequality' (p. 189).

theoretically at least, how plausible an answer they can provide, bearing in mind that the explanatory mechanism may differ depending on which social class we consider.

Elster (1983) – while discussing adaptive preferences in general – suggests a rather interesting possibility, which revolves around a set of psychological mechanisms:

> Adaptive preferences do not lend themselves to fine tuning . . . One will either try too much or too little . . . This tendency, in turn, may be explained by 'lack of toleration for ambiguity', by 'stereo-typical thinking', or 'primitive mentality' which, failing to distinguish between external and internal negation, assumes that when not everything is possible, nothing is . . . The poor might over-evaluate the present over and above the extent to which this is rational for them to do so as a result of their poverty. (p. 118)

Although Elster refers this mechanism to 'the poor', it could probably be applied to 'the rich' too, who could go to the opposite extreme and try too much, rather than too little, as a result of their wealth.

A second possibility – resulting from a different mechanism, but leading to the same incapacity to evaluate correctly one's present action with respect to one's future conditions – may be to posit the existence of cognitive constraints. At a very low level of culture, that is, subjects might be impeded from seeing the advantage in acquiring more education, mainly because their capacity to generalize and draw inferences could be reduced, along with their ability to associate present action with future outcomes. It differs in this respect from the mechanism of adaptive preferences suggested by Elster, which could explain the presence of inertial forces working both upwards and downwards. Cognitive constraints could only account for the latter. Some evidence will be presented in the next chapter when I discuss differential responsiveness to labour market conditions, where it appears that having a very poorly educated father makes subjects much more insensitive to objective labour market prospects.

Evidence in favour of inertia as the result of cognitive constraints is also provided by Schwarzweller (1967), who found that (1) half of the young people in his sample who opted out after elementary school took their decision automatically without asking themselves what exactly they were doing; and, more importantly, that (2) as many as one-third of those who left later regretted their 'decision', saying that they were unaware of the chain of circumstances linked to that crucial step. In this sense, however, inertial forces are probably active only at the lowest extreme of cultural deprivation, and, as we shall see in the next chapter, they are likely to underlie the effects of social class only with respect to the first choice.

The third hypothesis is provided by Lane (1972), and is relative to the *income career* of parents, especially of the father. Like the hypothesis of cognitive constraints it could only explain the inertial forces in the working class. In general, it suggests 'that economic experience, usually the pattern of income over time, or *income career* is of crucial importance' for explaining educational choices (p. 257). Lane holds that the way in which income is earned and especially has been earned in the past influences the view of future actions and situations by producing *models of the world*, models, that is, which involve some basic assumptions with regard to the ways in which socio-economic forces operate. Lane's intention is to offer an account of the value approach to educational choices, criticizing its vagueness and causal circularity with respect to explaining where the values come from and how they spread. Yet, Lane does not for this reason move closer to a future-oriented and intentional view of social actors, but rather tries to found values upon the basis of past income experience. Thus, for instance, if an individual's income stream 'is frequently disrupted by short-time working or redundancy then he will tend to see uncertainty as an attribute of the economic system. If his income stream has no future then he will tend to generalize this characteristic to the economic system *in toto*' (p. 260).

The crucial psychological mechanism seems to be that people draw inferences from their past experience about their future, and tend to generalize *independently* of whether such a generalization is objectively plausible and truly applicable to the future or is merely based on a private, singular, unrepresentative experience: 'Where past experience leads men *to believe* that life is unstable, insecure, and unpredictable, they will tend to see investment in the future as being highly unlikely to give reasonably certain results' (Lane 1972: 264, my italics). Essentially, this hypothesis presupposes a particular mechanism of economic causation which acts *behind the backs* of agents and, regardless of the alternatives they objectively face, influences their preferences through their beliefs.

Given that working-class fathers are more likely than middle-class ones to have experienced a fragmented income career, Lane's hypothesis could account for the presence of inertial forces within the working class.

This view, although interesting and seminal, presents some problems. The income career is presented as a rather passive experience which happens to subjects independently of what they 'are'. If we find any correlation between an uncertain income career and a view of the world as an insecure and risky place we cannot infer that the view necessarily follows the experience rather than being the other way round. Here I am not simply putting forward the chicken-and-egg objection, i.e. that the view could equally well precede the experience, but rather that view and experience may be kept together by a mechanism resembling the *self-fulfilling prophecy*: thus, if a father is not sending his children to school as a result of the uncertainties attached to such a choice, then, on average, his children will get worse jobs and, on average, they will be more exposed to the risk of unemployment and to an insecure working life.

Furthermore, Lane does not make clear by virtue of which particular socio-psychological process people should have a 'tendency to generalize *in toto*' their experiences. If their pessimistic 'view of the world' were a rational response to the future, we would not really need any additional hypothesis, such as Lane's income career. Hence, the really interesting question is about the way in which *incorrect* generalizations and *over-reactions* come about (cf. Nisbett and Ross 1980). Unless one wants to assume straightforward foolishness, there are two alternatives to explain the occurrence of wrong inferential processes as a consequence of a fragmented income career. The first is to assume that subjects are so secluded from the rest of the world that they simply lack the chance of making any comparison before drawing their own inferences. Although there are signs that it may be of marginal importance (section 4.2.1), this explanation seems rather implausible in industrialized societies as a generalized element of educational inequality: in principle, I cannot see why an insecure manual worker could not generalize about his son's future and education on the basis of, say, his doctor's experiences rather than his own personal experience, drawing the opposite conclusion to Lane's, i.e. that more education may lead out of manual work and insecurity.[43]

---

[43] Intuitively, I would say that in postwar Italy it is the latter type of inference rather than the former which has had the upper hand (cf. Barbagli 1974, especially the introduction, and Colasanti, Mebane & Bonolis 1976, especially ch. 3). Oddly enough this

The second way to account for ill-grounded inferences is to assume, rather than the lack of appropriate information, the existence of some psychological mechanism which would distort information and make the subject *blind*, or, at least, one-eyed. There are several possibilities in this respect: for instance, one could think of the reduction of cognitive dissonance (Festinger 1957), which could make a frustrated father deny that his particular income career misfortunes were anything but general and assert that therefore everybody else, his children included, should expect them. Besides, experiences such as long stretches of unemployment could be expected to create a more cautious attitude to life through a mechanism similar to that suggested by Popper (1963) with respect to neurosis. The state would be that of

a resistance to demands for the modification and adjustment of certain schematic interpretations and responses. This resistance in its turn may perhaps be explained in some cases as due to an injury or shock, resulting in fear and in an increased need for assurance or certainty, analogous to the way in which an injury to a limb makes us afraid to move it so that it becomes stiff. (p. 49)

Lane's hypothesis, once suitably reformulated and more firmly based on socio-psychological models, could represent a theoretically plausible explanation of the over-cautious educational behaviour of the working class. However, as we shall see in the next section, to the limited extent to which I could test for it, this hypothesis does not seem to be empirically confirmed.

Finally, a fourth hypothesis which could work better in explaining inertial forces in the middle and upper classes rather than in the working class may be found in the notion of *reference group*.[44] The general

inference may in reality turn out to be wrong and be based on the *fallacy of composition*, whereby one assumes that if something is possible for some then it is possible for all. The result is that education becomes like a race where everybody runs as fast as they can only to remain in the same place (Elster 1978; Boudon 1977; Hirsch 1977; cf. also section 4.2 below).

[44] For the notion of reference group see Runciman (1972). In this context the notion is used in the sense of a 'normative reference group' and in a rather loose fashion, which is nonetheless consistent with the definition given by one of its original proponents: 'the reference "group" need not to be a group at all; it may be a single person or even an abstract idea . . . Reference group behaviour can be applied to a son whose driving impulse is to emulate his father or to a lapsed Catholic blaspheming in order to emphasise his rejection of the Church, just as much as to a *bourgeois gentilhomme* imitating the habits and attitudes of the aristocracy' (pp. 12–13). For a discussion of reference group as a way to accommodate aspirations to actual position see Runciman again, especially pp. 31ff.

assumption is that within one's reference group – for example relatives, peers, community – there exist common automatic responses (norms) which result from a limited process of social comparison, whereby one would tend to consider as relevant only the standards of the other people in the group. A working-class child, for instance, could decide to leave school as a result of his peers' influence, most of whom are not staying on at school; or an upper-class child could be seen to be under extra pressure to stay on at high school at all costs, as a consequence of his being systematically exposed to and surrounded by professionals and managers, who would represent for him and his parents the only model to imitate.[45]

There is a major difficulty in applying the notion of reference group to the explanation of the presence of inertial forces in the educational choices of working-class subjects, which is similar to the problem of explaining incorrect inferences as the result of cognitive constraints. It is related to the phenomenon called 'empathy' or 'psychic mobility' – i.e. the capacity to picture oneself in another person's situation (see Colasanti, Mebane & Bonolis 1976, especially ch. 3). Social psychologists have dwelt extensively on it and related it specifically to modernization (Lerner 1958, Cottle & Klineberg 1974).[46] Some have even seen in the spreading of 'psychic mobility' a *sine qua non* of modern economic development (Durkheim, of course, and more recently Schramm 1964:

---

[45] From both such examples, supporters of the rational adjustment version could claim that it would be too hasty to consider such behaviour as inertial because everything depends on how many variables we specify in the utility function underlying the decision process. Hence, if we specify also 'psychic costs', action that could have appeared in some way inertial, irrational, pushed from behind and the like if only ordinary educational costs are used could once again be explained as the optimal fruit of rational adaptation. Thus, for example, the working-class child could be seen as responding to the 'costs' that his eventual 'deviant' behaviour would provoke in terms of his peers' friendship, or the upper-class child could be seen as responding to the 'costs' in term of shame and reputation that his leaving school early could cause to him and his parents. This claim, however, would seem to be a rather sterile way of dealing with the problem, because – logically – there is always the possibility of imagining a utility function, *ad hoc*, which can 'explain' almost any form of behaviour as rational. Once the fuzzy notion of 'psychic costs' is introduced, the rational choice approach can never be proved wrong (cf. Elster 1979: 156 and the conclusion below).

[46] It is interesting to note that 'psychic mobility' is also one of the major techniques for social investigation (among recent work see Boudon 1979). Significantly, it was first – I believe – suggested by Thomas Hobbes' *Leviathan*: 'for a similitude of the thoughts and passions of one man, to the thoughts and passions of another, whosoever looketh into himself, and considereth what he doth when he does *think, opine, reason, hope, feare* & C, and upon what grounds: he shall thereby read and know, what are the thoughts and passions of all other men, upon the like occasions' (Hobbes 1980:82).

131). Furthermore, there is evidence that when a process of modernization occurs 'psychic mobility', rather than leading to humble adjustment,
tends to spread exaggerated hopes for the future, whereby the money and
successes some are seen to acquire are believed to become universally
accessible.[47] More generally, there is evidence indicating that very few
unskilled manual workers would encourage their sons to do their jobs
(see Stewart & Blackburn 1975).

Those ideas would seem to be opposed to applying the notion of
reference group to the explanation of inertial forces in the working class.
Perhaps it would be more plausible to hold that if a comparison with a
limited reference group takes place at all, it is itself the result either of a
response to the frustration produced by the non-fulfilment of hopes for
social mobility[48] or of the presence of cognitive constraints. By contrast,
the notion of reference group could make more sense of the inertial forces
present in the upper class, for those in the latter group, unlike the
working class, have no reason to compare themselves with society at
large, but only with those limited groups which they perceive as similar or
whose higher achievement attracts their imitation. It is among the upper
class that a high school diploma, possibly from the *liceo*, and a university
degree can be felt as mandatory achievements and pursued at all costs,
even when the probability of success may be extremely low.

3.2.4 Summary

We can now conclude and summarize the findings with respect to the
major causes of educational inequality. A set of pushing mechanisms
seems to be acting upon educational destinations: economic constraints
and inertial forces are probably the strongest. The former operate at the
external level and hit working-class children very hard, particularly with
respect to the early educational choices. The latter seem to work through
mechanisms that act *behind the backs* of subjects, and push in two
opposite directions: upwardly, for middle- and upper-class children who
will continue their education over and above their actual probability of

---

[47] See Klineberg (1971), who found that among young people in Tunisia, modernization meant widespread high and unrealistic expectations. See also Hirschman (1973), who
treats this process in terms of 'tunnel effect' and makes of it a major mechanism which can
prevent revolutions.

[48] The disappointment does not necessarily need to be that of the last generation, but its
effect may be passed over through advice or rules of caution or crystallized in habit.

success, and downwardly, by keeping out of high school more working-class children than economic constraints would indicate.

The hypothesis that cultural capital plays a major role in influencing educational decisions does not seem to be supported by our data; the cultural resources of the family seem important mainly in determining whether middle-class ambition to obtain a high school diploma will be successful. In this respect, the level of cultural resources does not work so much by pushing out of school those working-class children who lack the ability to absorb formal education, but rather by helping to keep in school those middle- and upper-class children who lack the same ability, but whose parents are sufficiently equipped with formal education. The crucial issue concerning inegalitarian forces – paradoxically – could be not so much how many potentially talented children from a working-class background are disadvantaged because of the lack of formal education of their parents, but rather how many children from the higher classes manage to obtain a high school diploma *only* because of the cultural resources of their families. One could still suspect that reducing the weight of economic constraints for the benefit of working-class children would prove insufficient for, in this case, more children would get through the early selection stages, but would later encounter difficulties imputable to lack of family cultural resources. Yet, as things stand now, even if both cultural and economic constraints are present, only the latter are *binding* on working-class children.

Parents' education, however, plays a positive role in both class models by enhancing the probability of going to university both directly and through the influence on the choice of *liceo*. This effect is probably a direct consequence not so much of an advantage in terms of cultural resources as of the more subtle influence of parental education upon the families' and children's aspirations and preferences.

3.3 The mechanisms of educational inequality: further hypotheses

The analysis of pushing forces presented so far mainly refers to the influence of a set of conditions as they exist at the time of the educational choices. The possible influence of important conditions and events met in the past or expected in the future is not adequately captured by the variables we have discussed. In this section I shall try to lead the analysis along more exploratory lines and consider the effects on educational choices of two variables – family migration experiences and father's age – which are both specified in the logit models and can bring more evidence to clarify the mechanisms that could produce educational inequality.

3.3.1 The role of migration

I shall start by considering the experience of migration, which even if it took place some time in the past, could still embody a set of pushing forces relevant to educational decisions. In the postwar period Italy has seen a large number of internal migrations, especially from the rural areas of the South to the industrial cities of the North-West. Piemonte – the region where my surveys were carried out – was one of the major areas of attraction for Southern migrants.[49] Nearly five out of ten respondents of the youth unemployment sample had either migrated to Piemonte themselves or had fathers who had done so.[50] Most of the migrants – though they were not necessarily the poorest of their community – came from rather poor areas of the country, which often had a subsistence economy.[51] By and large the migratory phenomenon has not been of the kind known in advanced industrial societies where people move around in search of the best opportunities, always feeling themselves to be more or less within their own society.[52] Migrating from the South has often been perceived as a major and risky step in life, leaving behind the traditional society with its stable kin relationships to move into a rather alien part of Italy, and has involved – apart from the sheer disruption effect – social as well as cultural problems of adaptation in the areas of destination.[53] Intuitively, it would appear plausible,

[49] For an account in English of the migration of Southerners to Turin see Fofi (1970).

[50] I include only distant migrations, that is from South, Central and North-East Italy; I do not consider migration from the bordering regions of the North-West of the country.

[51] Interesting work has been done by Arlacchi (1980) and Piselli (1981). One of the interesting parts of their analysis of migration shows – contrary to a view commonly held in Italy – that migrants need at least some money to be able to migrate, but also that, besides direct economic resources, they need a certain type of extended family structure which acts as an insurance and at the same time as a money lender (cf. the remarks of Becker (1981a) on the 'altruistic' family). Areas of the South of Italy where this type of family did not exist had very little long-distance migration.

[52] See the account of urban migrants given for instance by Blau & Duncan (1967: 255ff).

[53] Visconti's masterpiece *Rocco and his brothers* probably still remains the best account of some of such traits of postwar internal migrations. For a different viewpoint stressing more the 'anticipatory socialization' see Alberoni (1970).

Table 3.11. *The effect of being a migrant and of having a migrant father:*
logit coefficients

	CHOICE: staying on at school vs leaving		
	after compulsory education	during high school	after high school
models for the working class:			
coefficients for migrant subject	−0.32	−1.21*	0.55
coefficients for migrant father	−0.30	−1.47*	0.20
	(N = 920)	(N = 681)	(N = 379)
models for the middle class:			
coefficients for migrant subject	−1.45*	−0.28	−0.68*
coefficients for migrant father	−0.95*	−0.18	0.43
	(N = 686)	(N = 636)	(N = 476)

Source: youth unemployment sample (Appendix 4, Models A)

therefore, to expect that the experience of migration could have negative consequences on children's education.

In order to test whether this is true, two dummy variables were introduced into the logit models: (1) if the subject himself was born outside and then migrated to Piemonte and (2) if the subject's father was born elsewhere and then migrated, while the subject was born and brought up in Piemonte.[54] The distinction between the two variables is rather important. In the first group there are respondents whose families must have settled in Piemonte only some time after their birth and have been resident for only a relatively short while; for example, if the subject is 15 years old then his family – although not necessarily his father – must have migrated no more than 15 years ago. In the second group there are subjects whose families must have migrated to Piemonte before they were born and which therefore have been in the region for no less than 14 years (the minimum age of subjects was, in fact, 14). Separating recent from less recent migration allows us to get some idea of whether a longer period of settlement makes a difference, reducing the expected disadvantage. In general the migration we are considering is made up of settlers and not of short-term migrants.

The coefficients present two major facts (table 3.11): first, migration,

[54] The large majority of migrants in both categories are from the South and the islands of Sicily and Sardinia.

Table 3.12. *Possible mechanisms of educational inequality affecting migrants' children*

	opportunities	preferences
economic causation	lack of local connections, special plans etc	fragmented income career
cultural causation	dialect spoken at home	instrumental values, traditional values

whether recent or not, does indeed make a negative net difference to the probability of staying on at school in both social classes. Secondly, migration affects the classes at different choices: the stronger negative effect to be found among the middle class is on the choice taken before high school, whereas for the working class it is on the choice taken while already at high school; in this social group, that is, the migration experience sharply increases the chances of dropping out. With respect to the third choice – leaving vs staying on to university – the negative effects of migration decline and those migrants' children who have escaped the previous selection points appear to behave little differently from everybody else.[55]

There are several factors that could in principle explain why the migration experience produces negative effects on children's education. They can be organized along the same criteria already applied at the beginning of this chapter to the general hypotheses, by distinguishing whether the effects of migration are due to economic or to cultural causes, and by distinguishing further whether the causation acts upon opportunities or preferences (see table 3.12).

First, the effect of migration could be due to differential economic opportunities or constraints not adequately measured by family income. Migrants' families could have a more limited number of contacts and consequently fewer labour market opportunities than local people with otherwise similar characteristics, hence they would probably have lower rates of return and less incentive to go to school, somewhat similarly to blacks in the United States (Becker 1975: sec IV.3). At the same time, migrants' families could have different plans. Although often separated

[55] In order to simplify the exposition I shall not present the results of the models concerning the choice of the type of school and I shall refer to them only when particularly important. The result of the effects of subject's and father's migration on the choice of the type of school can be found in Appendix 4, Models A.

from the extended family members who remained in the areas of origin, they could act with the extended family's level of welfare as reference; thus, for instance, they could want to finance the migration of weaker and older members of their family or to improve grandparents' standards of living. In this case, *per capita* income for migrants would be lower than estimated and the negative effects of migration on schooling could be the result of those further economic constraints.[56]

A second group of factors could relate to cultural constraints, such as dialect spoken at home, indirectly felt through a lower level of achievement, or directly relevant to educational choices as a result of ignorance of opportunities, and difficulties in gathering information or in coping with the bureaucratic practices required to enrol children in school.[57]

Thirdly, there could be a different type of economic effect – which we have encountered already – acting more through mental processes: the pattern of the past *income career* (Lane 1972) may be expected to be on average more unstable and problematic for migrants than for people residing in the areas of destination in the North of Italy. The experience of economic uncertainties could make migrants more cautious and less likely to send their children to school.

Finally there may be cultural effects acting through preferences and aspirations. Migrants' families are often thought to belong to a particularly instrumentally oriented section of the population, an attribute which – in conjunction with a certain dose of short-sightedness –

---

[56] A slightly different version of this hypothesis could be deduced for instance from the work of Arlacchi (1980), which refers to Italian migration to America at the beginning of this century (cf. Alberoni 1970 and Piore 1979). According to Arlacchi most Italian migrants to America were *birds of passage*, i.e. they did not want to settle down but only to make as much money as possible and then go back to Italy. As a consequence migrants had very little interest in taking part in any social mobility process in America, for their reference group remained their native community. If this idea of the birds of passage applies also to recent internal migration – as argued by Sabel (1982) – one could expect that this return-oriented view had an effect on children's education and generally decreased the family incentive to send them to school and increased that of sending them to work in order to earn money and finance their return. It is, however, very doubtful if internal migration in Italy were really intended to be transitory. Alberoni (1970), for instance, denies it altogether. Piselli 1981 expresses a more mixed view, but she points out that the transitory character of migration was dramatically more marked for the early trans-oceanic migrants. The latter were mainly heads of families who migrated alone. More recent migrants to Europe and especially to Northern Italy are instead to a large extent youths, characterized by relatively weaker bonds with their original community.

[57] For a lively phenomenological description of the educational difficulties of migrants' children, see Fofi (1976: 260ff).

may presumably increase the attraction of moving earlier into a paid job. There is some evidence, for instance, that even at similar income levels migrants are more apt to send their children to work even if they are below 14 years of age (Tagliaferri 1980).

Alternatively, several authors have considered traditional values rather than instrumental values as the source of the weak interest of migrants in education: 'and the secular habit of being concerned only with labour, of doing without school and therefore giving it little importance' (Fofi 1976: 211, my translation). Referring to the United States, Strodbeck (1961) outlined Southern Italian migrants' values as opposed to those of American Jews and explained the higher achievement of the latter in terms of the two different traditional cultures: the fatalistic, family oriented, non-productive culture of the former Southern Italian peasants would generally devalue the role of education, as opposed to the high achievement, future oriented Jewish cultures.

So far I have introduced four groups of factors which could explain the negative influence operating on the education of migrants' children: economic constraints and differential opportunities, cultural constraints, fragmented income career, and instrumental or traditional values. There is a fifth hypothesis which would instead predict that migrants, other things being equal, would be more, rather than less, prone to send their children to school. This hypothesis moves from exactly the same premises as the idea that migrants can be seen as that section of the population which is more instrumentally oriented. From these premises, however, it derives the opposite conclusions, assuming further that the instrumentalism is of a more rational nature and that people who are oriented to take risks and make a long-term investment to improve their well-being would also be more careful to make profitable investments for the future of their children, rather than being likely to send their children to work as soon as possible for the aim of earning money here and now.[58]

The pattern of empirical results can, to some extent, be helpful in selecting among this wide array of hypotheses, at least by indicating the more plausible ones. I shall start from the last-mentioned, the only one

[58] This hypothesis is generally linked with the human capital literature. For instance, Bowles (1970) explains blacks' lower responsiveness, in terms of migration, to expected rates of return as a consequence of their being more risk-averse and entertaining higher rates of time preferences (see also Mann 1973: 45–6).

which would predict a positive effect. Migration has in the logit model a negative effect, and it would seem therefore that this hypothesis should be rejected. Yet there is a possible objection: in the logit models there is no direct measure of the labour market opportunities for migrants' children, hence if they were lower than those for local children, it would still be possible that, if opportunities are controlled for, local families would prove to be less prone to invest in education than migrants. According to this argument, the negative effect of migration would simply be due to the fact that, on average, migrants have worse opportunities than non-migrants, which makes it relatively less worthwhile for them to invest in education.

There is, however, one major circumstance in the results which weakens this objection, and that is that working-class migrants' children have virtually the same chances as all other working-class children to continue to high school, while it is only during high school that they meet the major difficulties. If it were a matter of opportunities, one could ask why they stayed on in the first instance. This circumstance reinforces the conclusion that the negative effect is unlikely to be made spurious by the presence of differential opportunities; at the same time, it also excludes the possibility of the negative effect being the product of further economic constraints or lower labour market opportunities.

This pattern has even more far-reaching implications and would suggest that all those hypotheses which hold that for one reason or another it is a disposition to education that migrants lack – because of uncertain income career, or because of traditional or instrumental values – should be rejected. If in fact it were the case that education for migrants was less attractive either because of a desire to enter into a paid job sooner or because of an over-cautious view of the world, or because of a traditional disregard for formal learning, one would have expected the negative effect of migration to occur soon after compulsory school. On the contrary working-class migrants' children do try to make their way through high school just as much as children of non-migrant working-class families, even though more of them eventually fail to do so.

The hypothesis which would seem to gain support is that of cultural constraints, which could explain why so many migrants' children drop out of high school. The cultural difficulties met by migrants' children, which seem independent of whether migration is recent or not, might not be expressed by parents' education because they could derive from specific difficulties which become effective only in the new area of residence, such as the fact that migrants' families often speak dialect almost exclusively. Here it could be that the cultural difficulties are so marked as to prevent working-class migrants even from perceiving their existence in advance, and this could explain the fact that they start going to high school as much as working-class non-migrants. These subjects, therefore, would tend to go ahead until the cultural difficulties make themselves directly felt. This is the first empirical sign which could lend some support to the 'cultural capital' hypothesis. Although, as we have seen, it cannot claim to constitute a generalized explanation of the mechanisms of inequality, it could nonetheless hit the most culturally deprived section of the working class.

It is not clear, however, if the same explanation could hold also for middle-class migrants' children, who follow a different pattern, and tend to leave before the beginning of high school but, once they have begun, are as likely to reach the end of it as any other middle-class child. In this respect it could be helpful to go back to the discussion of the previous section concerning the effects of social class as defined by father's occupation. There we found the reverse pattern: to belong to the working class in general means a negative effect at the first choice, that concerning the choice of high school, which eventually disappears after the beginning of high school; by contrast, middle-class subjects find it very easy to stay on after compulsory education, but are comparatively more likely to drop out during high school.

Here, instead, we find that migration would seem to compensate partly for those tendencies: middle-class migrants, in fact, are not as automatically likely as their non-migrant counterparts to send their children to school, and they generally seem to be relatively more prepared to take them out of school immediately after the end of middle school. At the same time, the behaviour of the migrant working class matches the behaviour of the working class in general in a totally reversed manner: at the first post-compulsory choice they do not show any relevant difference with respect to the rest of the working class, yet, unlike the latter, they are very likely to drop out when already at high school. It is as if in the middle class being a migrant introduced an element of caution lacking in the rest of this social group, while in the working class it introduced an abnormal boldness. The middle-class migrants' children would tend to stay on at school only when highly promising, as is suggested by the absence of any negative effect at the second choice and, moreover, by the fact that, if they stay on, they more frequently choose the more demanding schools (see Appendix 4: Models A).

It seems unlikely that the pattern relative to the middle class can be settled by the hypotheses concerning a lower proneness to education – income career, instrumental orientation, and traditional values – for, to assume that middle-class migrants are relatively less prone than middle-class non-migrants to stay on at high school on these grounds, one ought to explain why the corresponding difference does not emerge between working-class migrants and working-class non-migrants. But this would seem to be a rather difficult task, for why should middle-class migrants as compared to middle-class non-migrants be expected *a priori* to have a more uncertain income career or hold more tightly to traditional values while, on the other hand, all these differences do not apply to working-class migrants with respect to working-class non-migrants?

A more plausible explanation for the behaviour of the middle-class migrants could result from some combination of the remaining hypotheses. The greater caution of middle-class migrants relative to the middle-class non-migrants could perhaps be due to wider differential economic opportunities between the two groups than between the same groups in the working class. In other words, except for specific cultural difficulties, the migrant and non-migrant groups of the working class could be in more similar situations relative to economic opportunities and constraints than migrant and non-migrant groups of the middle class. Against this hypothesis, however, there is evidence from previous work carried out on the youth unemployment sample which showed that, both in terms of employment chances and earnings, local subjects do not fare any better than migrants (cf. Colombino, Gambetta & Rondi 1981).

An alternative possibility could be that middle-class migrants are generally less sensitive to the normative pressure of sending children to school at all costs felt by the local middle class. Consistent with this interpretation there is the fact that less recent middle-class migrants are not as unlikely as recent ones to keep their children away from high school; thus, as most of the migration literature would suggest, it could be that families of more distant migration tend to become increasingly, if slowly, similar to local families. This difference between recent and less recent migration, however, does not apply to the working class, whose children suffer from the same probability of dropping out, regardless of the period in which the family migrated. Perhaps cultural difficulties are less likely to disappear quickly, while opportunities or adaptation to the norms of the local middle class could improve more rapidly.

3.3.2 Expected economic constraints

In concluding this chapter, and before turning to explore the pulling forces of educational decisions, we can still concentrate on the pushing forces, but at the same time come closer to the notion of intentional action by considering the effect of constraints to come, which, rather than affecting decisions directly by their presence, exercise their influence through expectations about the future.

As we have seen in chapter 1, there are sound theoretical reasons to believe that individuals' decisions are influenced by the present view of their future. If the temporal perspective includes income, it follows that the present expectation of future income could be influential and that the measure of income used in the previous section could be incomplete, for it does not incorporate this expectation. What we need here is to measure the effect of an event which can be understood to influence the image of the family's future capacity to produce income or, alternatively, to reduce expenditure. Events like a mortgage nearly paid up, an expected career advancement or, on the other hand, the risk of being made redundant could respectively enhance or depress the expected income and – through such expectation – the chances of sending children to school for longer periods.

The data in the youth unemployment survey offered the possibility of considering one particular variable which can be seen in this light, namely the age of the father and, more precisely, whether the father is over 64. The coefficients produced by introducing this dummy variable into the logit models are remarkable (table 3.13): other things being equal (including per child income), having a father older than 64 decreases drastically the probability of staying on at school, with an intensity similar to that of having been kept down (see section 4.1). This occurs particularly in the choice of whether to go to high school (-0.98 for the working class and -1.30 for the middle class) and in that of whether to complete high school (-1.61 and -1.19 respectively); in

Table 3.13. *The effects of having a father over 64: logit coefficients*

	CHOICE: staying on at school vs leaving		
	after compulsory education	during high school	after high school
models for the working class: coefficients	−0.98* (N = 920)	−1.61* (N = 681)	0.06 (N = 379)
models for the middle class: coefficients	−1.30* (N = 686)	−1.19 (N = 636)	−0.71 (N = 476)

Source: youth unemployment sample (Appendix 4, Models A)

both cases regardless of class.[59] In the decision about university the effect becomes either negligible (0.08 among working-class subjects) or statistically non-significant (−0.71 among middle-class subjects).[60]

What emerges as particularly interesting is that the father's retirement age can have such an effect on the first two post-compulsory decisions. The fact that the effect – and this is similar to what happens to per child income – is less marked at the choice concerning higher education could be a consequence of the fact that by this time subjects tend to be potentially more independent from family economic resources.

At a somewhat superficial level the interpretation of these results is straightforward. The age-threshold of 65 is an important turning-point in life, and is a time when people either retire or are not far from retirement. There are objective reasons why subjects could connect this event to lower potential income and greater financial worries: a person who retires – although he may face a decrease in expenses such as laundry and transport – usually expects to face a declining trend in his earnings; moreover, he approaches an age where he becomes more likely to need his children to act as a form of insurance.

At the same time, the event of retirement is also linked with subjective

[59] The models also gain considerably in terms of fitting, i.e. introducing the dummy on father's age significantly increases the log likelihood ratio.

[60] The results concerning the choice of the type of school are not as satisfactory, essentially because of the low statistical significance. They show, however, very large coefficients which are consistent with the hypothesis that expected economic constraints have a discouraging effect on education: in the working class a retired father pushes children both away from longer high schools and towards vocational schools, whereas in the middle class the effect would seem to favour the *liceo* (cf. Appendix 4, Models A).

feelings of fear and insecurity which may accentuate the financial worries and enhance the urge to see one's children 'settled down'. On the whole, this variable, independently of the current level of family economic resources, expresses a set of factors which could prevent families from sending their children to school for longer periods, in order to hasten their entry into the labour market. The interpretation of the negative effect of the paternal age threshold could therefore be limited to a given combination of rational and perhaps less rational fears. But it can also be pushed considerably forward, at least on speculative grounds.

Finding oneself with a child of school age when one is already approaching old age is not an externally determined event. The relationship between father's age and educational decisions is in fact by and large equivalent to the relationship between father's age and child's age, which, in turn, means *fertility timing*: if a child faces the choice of high school when his father is already over 64, this means that by this stage he is only 14 and that he was born when his father was no younger than 50.

In this light we could raise the following objection: if the retirement effect shows that people are capable of responding to their future expected constraints, why did they not respond in a future oriented manner earlier and not have the extra child?

There are four possible answers to this question:

(1) the parents wanted the child, but they were – at that time at least – either unaware of or not preoccupied with his education
(2) they wanted the child, and they were aware of the importance of his education, but they underestimated the relevance that their financial worries would have assumed by the time the child had reached his first educational choice after compulsory education
(3) they had an unwanted pregnancy which for some reason – moral values, health problems, lack of proper abortion opportunities – could not be interrupted
(4) they had an unexpected pregnancy which either could not be interrupted, as in (3), or became eventually accepted as in (1).

In the first case, when parents wanted the child, we have to distinguish whether or not they knew what the consequences were going to be. It is plausible that the desire for a child, even at a relatively advanced paternal age, may consciously outweigh the worry of being unable to provide for his education properly. If this is the case the decision may be regarded as rational, insofar as this means acting according to one's desires in full knowledge of the consequences. If instead they were not aware of the importance of education the question that comes to mind is why should unawareness be more frequently present among older than among younger parents? Why, in other words, if the true cause of the negative effect of the variable on educational attainment is unawareness, should this become apparent merely through older parents?

One answer could be that there are cohort effects and that one is more likely to find a higher preference for education among younger parents. The fact, however, that parents' education is controlled for somewhat weakens this argument. A more convincing explanation is that of assuming, as it were, a constant quota of unawareness across all ages and to assume further that for some families such unawareness is removed with the approaching of school age; but – and this is the relevant consideration – the effects of unawareness can be removed only insofar as the constraint of retirement is absent, independently of whether or not the fertility timing was the product of conscious choice: a retired father can become aware of the importance of education for his young child, but by that time it may be too late.

The latter answer brings us to the second case (underestimation of future constraints or worries), which is perhaps the more interesting. It implies that expectations as well as the actions that follow from them are not independent of the temporal horizon which is held by subjects at any given time; in simple terms, people could be more 'optimistic' when looking at things from a distance than when actually near them. Action may be based on expectations, but the closer the expected event the greater the activating power of the expectation.

This does not necessarily mean that they did not act rationally at the time of the child's birth: the more 'optimistic' view could well be the rational one, namely that which properly corresponds to their expected level of resources, and the over-reaction could be that occurring later, when closer to the crucial age. In any case, however, under these circumstances time would not be irrelevant, as it should be for the perfect maximizer of the standard utilitarian view.

Earlier writers – especially economists – were very well aware of this problem and devoted considerable attention to it, quite unmatched by modern writers. According to Ainslie (1975) they generally shared the view of Jevons (1911):

To secure a maximum of benefit in life, all future events, all future pleasures and pains, should act upon us with the same force as if they were present, allowance being made for their uncertainty. The factor expressing remoteness should, in short, always be unity, so that the time should have no influence. But no human mind is constituted in such a perfect way: a future feeling is always less influential than a present one. (Quoted by Ainslie 1975:464)

In more recent times we find a counterpoint to this argument in the criticism that Bernard Williams (1976) offers of Rawls' theory of justice, suggesting that the capacity for planning one's own life independently of temporal considerations assumes a person with no real character and without a project to hold his life realistically together.

The third possibility, i.e. that of an unwanted pregnancy, could be in some respects independent of parental awareness: discounting the stochastic element in pregnancy (namely that unexpected pregnancies can happen to anyone), if the reasons that prevented the interruption of the pregnancy were sufficiently compelling – whether moral or practical – then the constraint due to paternal age would have come about anyway.

The data are not of direct help to us in this higher-order level of considerations. Undoubtedly, however, if the lower educational chances of retired fathers' children were merely hiding straightforward parents' lack of thought, we would expect the age effect to occur only *before* high school. But since this holds true *during* high school as well, it becomes more difficult to claim educational distraction or inertia on the side of the parents, because one way or another they would already have sent their children to high school. It would also be difficult to claim perfect rationality, because if the parents were – since the child's birth – aware that they would have problems in sending him to school, they would have avoided the painful experience of sending him to school only to withdraw him unsuccessfully later.

In conclusion, the most likely explanation would seem to lie in some form of underestimation of future constraints: the retirement age is probably regarded when looked at from several years earlier as still a long way ahead and the worries associated with it are still too small to be responded to; the expectation will nonetheless become a source of action a few years later.

3.3.3 Summary

I have shown that migration has a negative effect on the probability of staying on at school and that this is probably due to two different sets of reasons which depend on the social class of migrants. Working-class migrants' children probably face specific cultural constraints, which heavily affect the probability of successfully finishing high school as well as offering the capacity to foresee this. In contrast, middle-class migrants' children who stay on find no more difficulties than their non-migrant counterparts. For them, the tough selection point is before the beginning of high school, which might be due to their family being less affected by local middle-class norms. The working-class migrants' mechanism would definitely seem to be a predominantly pushing force, whereas the greater tendency of children of middle-class migrants to leave after middle school – which declines if migration is less recent – may be the result of a less clear-cut set of forces.

Finally, the analysis of father's age has shown the considerable importance of expected economic constraints, which, even at the same level of family income, markedly affect children's educational opportunities. However, it seems likely that subjects, rather than planning their present decisions on the basis of events which are far ahead, respond to constraints which are expected in the fairly near future.

4 Or did they jump?

I shall now turn to the *pulling forces* of educational decisions. In chapter 1, two distinct versions of the pulled-from-the-front type of action were identified. The first tends to stress the adaptive features of rational choice and treats preferences as irrelevant. The only 'preference' which counts is a kind of built-in mechanism which makes people act according to the goal of 'the more the better', where the more is largely taken to refer to material goods and well-being. Differences in behaviour are accounted for by differences in the probability of success of a given course of action relative to other alternatives. In this chapter, I shall analyse the key notion of probability of success as referring to those circumstances through which subjects form an idea (1) of how likely it is going to be for them to reach successfully a given level of education and (2) of how relatively rewarding that level of education will be in terms of material benefits. With respect to (1) this notion will be dealt with in the first section of this chapter, where I shall consider the effects of past academic achievement, for example school reports and type of school attended on future educational decisions; with respect to (2) it will be dealt with in the second section, where I shall try to measure subjects' response to labour market objective circumstances.

The second version of rationality posits an intentional actor capable of behaving according to his preferences, and such preferences are not necessarily seen as coinciding with those of economic maximization. This view is developed in the section 4.3, where I shall look at the relationship between educational decisions and subjects' temporal perspective and job preferences.

These two views of rational agents, rather than being treated as two contradictory theoretical approaches, are better seen as identifying two real orders of purposefulness which are sometimes simultaneously present in the actors themselves and sometimes in conflict with one another, as is well exemplified by the following: 'When he told his headmaster he wanted to teach art, he was advised to take a degree in some other subject by way of insurance' (Obituary of Kingsmen, King's College Annual Report 1981). Subjects, sometimes, have to choose the mechanism of their choice: they can decide on the basis of their preferences, independently of risks and costs, or alternatively, and sometimes painfully, take the latter as being the crucial focus of their choice.

4.1 Adjusting to past achievement

It is straightforward to think of ability as a key component of educational attainment. The crucial question which will be addressed in this section is how ability exercises its force on educational choices, rather than where it comes from. In fact, irrespective of how a given level of ability is formed – of whether, that is, it is predominantly the product of genetic or environmental factors – once there it can be expected to exert its influence both directly, by meeting (or failing to meet) educational standards, and indirectly, by affecting one's self-evaluation.

Given these premises, it is striking to observe from the available evidence how little, after all, measures of ability like IQ appear to affect educational attainment, once an adequate number of control variables is taken into account (McLelland 1973: 3; Banks 1976: 21; Halsey, Heath & Ridge 1980: 163). One way to react to this evidence is to reject or at least to minimize the role of ability in explaining educational choices; the other is to suggest that the ability which counts is not necessarily that captured by IQ tests, but something different. I shall take the latter route, basically by assuming that the ability which counts most is that perceived through a number of *signals*, whose overlap with one's 'natural' level of ability does not need to be strong. My contention is that these signals are socially constructed through interaction with others and through interaction with various institutional systems of selection, both of which can distort, enhance, channel, or curb natural ability.

For our purposes the question of how these signals are produced is not irrelevant; in particular, the suspicion that they could be related to dimensions of inequality is strong and could lead us to think that ability-signals merely filter cultural or other disadvantages. If such were the case it would be better to treat the effects of these signals as a predominantly pushing force rather than – as they are taken to be here – as a sign that subjects are capable of making intelligent decisions by responding adaptively to these signals. However, the evidence from my sample surveys presents very low correlation coefficients between class or parents' education and the signals of ability I shall use in this section, thus allowing us to proceed reassured into the analysis.[1]

There are several reasons to believe that academic achievement is one of the most important ability-signals. Both common sense and a large body of empirical evidence[2] support this expectation and suggest that the level of past achievement is positively related to the probability of both staying on at school and following more demanding educational routes. The mechanisms through which the past level of performance could exert its influence are essentially two, both of which act upon the level of attractiveness associated with education.

The first revolves around psychological processes. The level of past performance acts as a proxy for personal ability and exerts an influence on subjects' self-evaluation: when lower than expected, for instance, it fosters the belief that they are not suitable for a demanding educational career and, at the same time, increases fear of future failures, thereby enhancing the perceived risk entailed by continuing one's education. There is evidence that the perceived probability of success at a future task depends on the degree of success in past performances of that task and that the higher the level of success the higher will be the effort put into future performance (Lewin et al. 1944, Diggory 1966, Feather 1966b, Atkinson 1964). Moreover, the effects of the probability of success upon decisions have been shown to be particularly marked when the choice really binds the person to act upon it – as is the case for educational choices – rather than when it is just a 'laboratory bet' where subjects know they are not going to lose much, if anything at all (Feather 1966a: 45).

Two requirements must be met for the past level of performance to

---

[1] The simple correlation coefficient between a dummy variable indicating whether the pupil had to repeat one or more years and the number of parents' years of education is only -0.13 (youth unemployment sample). The simple correlation coefficient between a dummy singling out subjects with good or very good school reports and, again, parents' years of education is as low as -0.06 (high school pupils sample).

[2] See Boudon (1974: 24ff), who reviews and discusses some of the more relevant literature on this point; and also Banks & Finlayson (1973) and Banks (1976: 79ff).

have some effect on future actions through the perceived probability of success: the first is that failures or a low level of school performance must not be related to contingent events upon which the subject had no control, such as an illness; the second is that the source which judges or ranks the level of performance must be regarded as reliable. When this requirement holds, even lies told by experimenters about subjects' performance tend to produce the same response as true statements (Diggory 1966). If generalizable to 'real world' conditions this evidence would suggest that even when pupils are ranked, streamed and selected along non-objective, class-biased or at least debatable lines, this would not necessarily matter with respect to their perception and to the consequences upon their decisions. At the same time it could lend some force to claims like that of Bourdieu and Passeron (1964: 109), who argue that particularly poorly educated parents are likely to perceive their children's failures as the product of individual fate rather than cultural discrimination. However, even if families were to understand that some kind of cultural discrimination was at the origin of their children's failures, it would not necessarily follow that they would rebel or that they would not respond to failures exactly as they do when attributing them to individual fate or ability. The expectation that similar discriminatory mechanisms can work at every level of the educational system and cause their children to fail later on could by itself be a sufficient reason to take children out of school.

But there is also a second reason, which, independently of self-evaluation and the degree of legitimacy of educational authorities, can be strong enough to affect schooling choices in the same direction. This is what we may generically call the *costs* of education and learning. There is the extreme case[3] when failure at school means to be kept behind and, as a consequence, the direct costs as well as the forgone earnings are increased: a course of five years for a kept-down child becomes a course of six or more years depending on how many times the child is failed. The increase in costs produced by a failure can turn directly into a constraint: poorer families, for instance, when confronted with a failure may find it too expensive to take defensive individual steps, like changing schools or paying for private tuition. But even when reports at school are not so bad as to result in being kept down, a higher or lower level of school performance as well as different degrees of success in different subjects

---

[3] Extreme only in the sense that it is the worst form of educational failure rather than in the sense of being a rare phenomenon, as we have documented in chapter 2.

are correlated with the 'shadow costs' of education. If one is good at something, finds it relatively easy, and takes less effort in doing it, then that particular activity should be at the same time 'cheaper' relative to others and more efficient, capable, that is, of producing a higher quantity of 'output' for any given period spent at it. Correspondingly, the incentive to 'specialize' in that activity should become greater (cf. Lazear 1976, and Willis and Rosen 1979).

Before we turn to the results a general warning must be issued. Throughout this section I shall simply assume that the direction of causality goes from school achievement to actual choices or intentions. This assumption is by no means obvious and needs to be discussed. In the case of kept-down children, the assumption seems generally justified; the temporal sequence, although not a proof, is such that it would be very tortuous to assume the opposite: the subjects in the youth unemployment sample – as we shall see below – made their educational decision *after* having been kept behind for one or more years and it would not seem very realistic to argue that some pupils, in order to be pushed to leave school later, deliberately planned to achieve a failure.[4] It is likely that such a drastic failure as that of being kept behind is closer to being the product of a low level of ability than of a low level of aspiration. The latter – it has been shown – undoubtedly influences school achievement, but more in keeping school reports low than in keeping them so low that the pupil is completely failed. Given a basic level of ability, an extra effort during the last term usually suffices to lift the pupil into the next year. However, there could still be doubts as to whether the variable which picks out pupils who declared they had good school reports and which I shall use to 'explain' their intentions might in turn be partly the result of the intentions themselves. Probably Kahl's remark on job ambitions is still the best approach, and most of the literature seems to converge on it (cf. Banks 1976: 75ff): 'It was not always clear which came first: the job ambition or the school performance. Sometimes the desire for the job did

---

[4] Such a view could, superficially, remind one of the strategy of Ulysses (Ainslie 1975, Elster 1979), which consists in altering on purpose one's feasible set by introducing constraints in the situation at time t_1, in order to be able to carry out a desired action at time t_2. It is a strategy adopted to overcome one's weakness of will, which, had these constraints not existed, would prevent the desired action from being performed. Although, as Elster (1979) has shown, these types of action are not infrequent in human behaviour, it would be too extreme to think that pupils adopted similar strategies on any scale. Moreover, school is not a siren whose chant is irresistible. This does not exclude, however, the possibility that particularly astute pupils could plan to get themselves failed to overcome the 'irresistible' aspirations of their parents; but in such cases it would not be a strategy against one's own weakness of will but against the strong wills of others.

seem to be the base for the school motivation, yet sometimes a boy who did well at school became slowly convinced that he was good enough to think of a middle class job' (1961: 358).

Using both samples I have been able to carry out several tests on the effects of past achievement on educational choices; in particular I could use four indicators which will be analysed in the following order:

(1) a dummy variable singling out whether the respondent had been *kept down* in the past one or more times
(2) a dummy variable singling out whether the subject had *good school reports*
(3) the *year or grade of high school* reached
(4) a dummy variable singling out whether the subject had attended *liceo*.

In the set of models I have been considering so far, which was taken exclusively from the youth unemployment sample, only two variables, (1) and (4), could be used. Here their effects have been controlled for by the same group of variables analysed so far (family income, parents' education, father's age and occupation, migration) and by those which are analysed in the following sections (sex for all choices, labour market conditions and preferences only for the third choice, that concerning university). The other sample, that of high school pupils, allowed me to analyse the effects of all four indicators, but only for the third choice. Unlike the youth unemployment sample, which contains information about actual choices, this sample refers to intentions. High school pupils from *licei* and *istituti tecnici*[5] were in fact asked what they intended to do after high school, whether they wanted to go on to university or stop and search for work. In this sample the effect of past achievement could be controlled for by social class of origin, sex, parents' education and job preferences.

4.1.1 The effects of failures and school reports

First of all I shall consider the effects of two dummy variables, (1) and (2), which refer respectively to failures and school reports. The results of the usual set of models taken from the youth unemployment survey are

[5] Pupils from vocational schools were not included in this sample. Pupils could also answer that they did not yet know what they were going to do, but I have excluded the undecided from the analysis. See Appendix 1 for more details.

Table 4.1. *The effects of a failure: logit coefficients*

	CHOICE: staying on at school vs leaving		
	after compulsory education	during high school	after high school
models for the working class:			
coefficients	−1.11*	−1.94*	−0.05
	(N = 920)	(N = 681)	(N = 379)
models for the middle class:			
coefficients	−1.03*	−0.74*	−0.17
	(N = 686)	(N = 636)	(N = 476)

Source: youth unemployment sample (Appendix 4, Models A)

Table 4.2. *The effects of a failure: logit coefficients (models with three alternatives)*

	CHOICE: type of school		
	liceo vs *istituto tecnico*	*liceo* vs vocational school	*istituto tecnico* vs vocational school
model for the working class:			
coefficients (N = 583)	−1.45*	−1.59*	−0.14
model for the middle class:			
coefficients (N = 576)	−0.87*	−1.22*	−0.35

Source: youth unemployment sample (Appendix 4, Models A)

presented in table 4.1. They show that having had one or more failures at school has a powerful and highly significant negative effect upon the probability of staying on at school, both at the first choice (− 1.15 for the working class and − 1.03 for the middle class) and at the second choice, where the effect is more than twice as big for the working class (− 1.94 and − 0.74).[6] The effect of a failure is also very powerful with respect to the choice of the type of school, where it neatly discriminates between *liceo* and both other high schools, obviously in the sense of pushing towards the latter (table 4.2).

[6] In the case of the second choice – that of dropping out of high school – there is no way of knowing whether the failure was in the same year as the subject left or some previous year; in the first choice, on the other hand, it is certain that the decision to leave school was not an immediate response to failure, but that failure had occurred one or more years before the decision to leave was actually taken. If they had left soon after the failure they would, in fact, not have attained the compulsory school certificate.

Table 4.3. *The effects of a failure and of good reports: logit coefficients*

| | CHOICE: staying on at university vs leaving | |
	kept down	good reports
model for the working class: coefficients (N = 344)	−0.49*	0.96*
model for the middle class: coefficients (N = 325)	−0.04	1.09*

Source: High school pupils sample (Appendix 4, Models C)

When we look at the third choice, that concerning university, the effect of a failure tends to decrease, even if the results are partially different depending on which sample we consider: among the young unemployed, being kept behind for one or more years does not seem to be effective in preventing pupils from becoming university students, whereas it does seem to have an effect on intentions in the high school pupil sample (table 4.3), where it decreases the probability of intending to go to university, if only within the working class (−0.49).

The other dummy variable, that singling out pupils with good school reports, could be tested only on the third choice in the form of high school pupils' intentions; this variable appears to have a high and statistically significant effect (table 4.3): in both social classes having good reports at school very much increases the probability of intending to go to university.

In general, all these results leave little doubt that the level of achievement has a dramatic impact upon school choices, precisely in the sense which it is theoretically sensible to expect. Moreover, they clearly indicate that its effects are independent of a wide range of socio-economic variables and, as far as the third choice is concerned, also of preferences. There are, however, two points which need to be discussed, and they are (1) the declining effect of a failure on the decision to go to university and (2) the fact that the effect of a failure varies according to social class.

It does not seem surprising that those who have successfully reached the end of high school, despite having been kept down at some point of their school career, are less affected by that failure when deciding about university: had they been affected, they would have left during high school; if they did not, it is probably because the failure was due to a particular state or accident not generalizable to the future such as an illness or a change of residence, or because, despite the failure, they are for some reason highly motivated. Furthermore, precisely the success of having been able to reach the high school diploma could have a countervailing effect on the failure suffered in the past. These reasons could also account for the difference between the two samples with respect to the effect of a failure upon the third choice: the high school pupils were manifesting an intention about university while still at high school, and thus, among those who suffered a failure and were less likely to intend to go to university, there could well be some who carry out their plan *before* rather than after the end of high school. This does not explain, however, why the difference between the two samples applies only to working-class subjects.

This interaction, whereby working-class subjects appear to be considerably more responsive to failures than middle-class subjects, appears to be very pervasive. At the second and the third choices the difference is particularly marked. Also with respect to the choice of branch of school working-class subjects show themselves to be more sensitive and when failed tend not to choose the academic route to a greater extent than middle-class subjects.

There are two possible explanations for this interaction between social class and school achievement. The first is that working-class families could be more readily discouraged in the face of a poor level of achievement because they could feel a lower capacity to control educational matters and to question schools and teachers' decisions (Kelsall & Kelsall 1971; Banks 1976: 80). By contrast, it seems sensible to assume that middle-class parents who are on average more educated are not as defenceless when faced with 'expert' opinion. This explanation, however, is somewhat weakened by the fact that parents' education is controlled for.

A more plausible explanation, which was put forward by Boudon (1974: 38), could be in terms of differential costs.[7] It suggests that the loss in *status* involved in leaving school is lower for a working-class family than for a middle-class family: if school is left, the prospects of *demotion* for the latter with respect to its point of social departure are higher than

---

[7] The model Boudon is proposing is based on Keller & Zavalloni (1964). A similar type of ladder model of mobility was also put forward by Turner (1964: 47) and has been taken up briefly by Tyler (1977: 106–7).

they are for the former. Working-class children leaving school would essentially fall from closer to the ground, whereas their middle-class counterparts would fall from higher up the social ladder, and hence when facing a failure they would generally tend to hold on tighter before leaving. In the middle class the achievement of a high school diploma could be more of a norm than an option subject to favourable conditions. In the working class, when school performance is not brilliant, it would be relatively easier to put up with the idea of leaving school, for the social sanctions would be weaker. This, of course, does not imply that when school performance is satisfactory, education is also less attractive for working-class subjects. If this were the case we could not explain why subjects from both social classes are responsive to *good* school reports with very similar intensity.

4.1.2 The effects of age and previous school choices

We can now consider the effects, exclusively on the decision about university, of the other two variables which I used to measure past achievement: the age of the pupils when they were interviewed and asked about their post-high school intentions, and the type of high school that subjects attended before reaching the choice of university.

Age in this context should be understood as an expression of how far the pupil had been able to go in educational terms when the interview took place: the higher the age, the greater the distance he had already travelled.[8] The effect of age turns out to be positively related to the intention of going to university; considering that the coefficient refers to the effect of each additional year, the influence is also rather high (0.17): suppose that a pupil at 14 were 50% likely to say he wanted to go to university; the 'same' pupil five years later would be over 70% likely to manifest such an intention. By the 'same' pupil, I mean that social class, parents' education, school reports, failures, and a set of job preferences are held constant, while only age is increased.

Such an effect, however, might partly conceal self-selection, a consequence of the fact that more of those who want to go to work than

---

[8] Age is naturally highly correlated with the year the pupils were in, and since it is controlled by the dummy variable singling out pupils who had been kept behind, it virtually coincides with it (for instance if a pupil has never been kept down, the older he is the higher the year he is in).

of those who want to go to university leave between the age of 14 and the age of 19. Thus, it could well be that what we are comparing is not the 'same' pupil, precisely on the crucial criterion of intentions.

Although I am unable to test to what extent this is the case, the dropout rates shown by secondary data in the two branches of high school leading to university are not sufficiently high to explain the effect of age simply in terms of selection. In either case, however, i.e. whether the effect is genuine or not, there would be interesting theoretical implications. If the effect is the product of self-selection it would mean that, independently of social background (social class of origin and parents' education) and school achievement (failures and reports), the intention with which high school is approached – i.e. as a preparation for work or as a preparation for university – would in itself play a role in explaining the probability of leaving between 14 and 19. In other words, if a respondent answers that after high school he wants to go to work, he is also more likely to carry out his intention before completing his high school career.

If the effect is genuine and not the result of self-selection there are three theoretical explanations which could make sense of the fact that the higher the year attended the higher the probability of intending to go to university. First, there is a simple and general explanation which points to the existence of something similar to an *addictive effect*: the more time one spends in education, the more education becomes an attractive commodity. This can be understood either in the traditional sense which implies a change of tastes in favour of education, roughly in the same sense in which Alfred Marshall thought that exposure to good music could cause preferences to shift in its favour, or in the sense more recently elaborated by Stigler & Becker (1977), where tastes are assumed to be constant and where, if we substitute education for music, we can say that 'education appreciation and consumption rise with exposure not because tastes shift in its favour but because its shadow price falls as skill and experience in the consumption of education are acquired with exposure' (p.79).[9]

Apart from the addictive effect, it is plausible to think that the rise in

---

[9] Along these lines Michael (1975) explains the positive effect of education on its consumption. However, there is evidence that educated people also have tastes which are biased in favour of education in the sense that more of them believe that education is more important. See Beaton (1975: 391 and 394).

the level of educational aspirations with the year attended corresponds to a growth of *self-confidence*: the further one has got educationally the higher one's confidence that one will be successful in the future. On this view, which is perfectly consistent with the socio-psychological literature on levels of aspiration referred to at the beginning of this section, some pupils could start off by setting themselves a low level of aspiration in order to minimize the potential degree of frustration which would be produced by an unsuccessful outcome and also because it is probably easier to increase one's level of aspiration than to lower it. The interesting aspect would be that the degree of self-confidence would simply be a function of the *passing of time* spent at school, because social origins, reports, and past failures would all be controlled for.

Finally, we could think of a different mechanism, something concerning the perspective from which educational decisions are taken: near the moment in which a decision on higher education must be made the relative benefit of going to university could appear higher than initially expected. I am not referring to a subjective but rather to some objective event. The fact that growing older is believed to expand the temporal horizon against which subjects perceive their lives and therefore increase the probability of evaluating more carefully the consequences of not going to university is in fact incorporated in another variable which is specified in the model. This variable singles out all those pupils who, when asked about their job preferences, said that it was too early to think about work, and, as we shall see in section 4.3, this has a dramatic negative influence on the probability of aiming to go to university.

The fact that this variable is controlled for suggests that age is not a proxy for the subjective time-span and that the reasons which could make some pupils change their mind as they grow older may lie in some objective change of circumstances which makes itself perceived directly *only* when university appears in closer perspective. This points to the possibility that what we are here observing is an adjustment which some individuals make to the situation brought about as an unintended effect of educational micro decisions of the type suggested by several authors (Boudon 1974, Thurow 1975, Hirsch 1977, Halsey, Heath & Ridge 1980). At first pupils would expect from education the same rewards that went to the previous generation of individuals who graduated from high school; some of them would regard these rewards as adequate and initially, no need would be felt to go on to university. Subsequently,

Table 4.4. *Post-high school intentions of high school pupils in their final year, Italy, 1973–4*

	higher education	search for a job
istituto tecnico	55.8	44.2
liceo	97.3	2.7

Source: ISTAT 1975

depending on how many other individuals have taken the decision to go to high school, the same initial expectations could turn out to be wrong, mainly because more qualified people than expected would be competing on the labour market. The perception of this initially unexpected situation could therefore grow during high school and the coefficient associated with age could be the result of pupils 'tuning' their future behaviour to the new level of competition.

The discussion concerning the effect of age could have given the reader the impression that the length of the period spent at high school is of great importance in determining pupils' intentions regarding university. Although the importance seems to be there it would be wrong to believe it to be large, because most students decide very early that they will go on to university; at the same time this impression needs to be qualified because it is in fact important not only how much time they have spent at high school but also in *which* high school pupils qualify to go to university. What we need to evaluate are the effects of the choice of the type of high school upon the decision to go to university, or in other words, to take account of the fact that the outcome of that choice becomes a condition which is likely to be considered when deciding about university.

The general evidence available from secondary sources strongly supports the view that having been to *liceo* rather than to an *istituto tecnico* makes a dramatic difference, pushing up the probability of going to university (table 4.4), but up to now no test of the effect of school net of the effects of other factors such as social background and school achievement has ever been carried out. Hence it is important to test whether the advantage that former *liceo* pupils seem to have is simply a consequence of the fact that on average they come from a higher social background and are in general more able, or whether, alternatively, the type of school in itself makes a difference.

Table 4.5. *The effect of having attended* liceo: *logit coefficients*

	CHOICE: staying on at university vs leaving	
	unemployed young people	high school pupils
models for the working class: coefficients	1.97* (N = 379)	3.45 (N = 344)
models for the middle class: coefficients	2.15* (N = 476)	3.48* (N = 325)

Source: both samples (Appendix 4, Models A and C)

The results which follow the insertion into the models of a dummy variable which singles out when subjects have attended *liceo* are striking for both samples: the coefficients and their significance are the highest scored in any of the models and the type of school attended turns out to be the best predictor of post-high school behaviour, independently of social background (table 4.5).

The main question is whether this result implies the existence of some mechanism whereby university is made more or less attractive depending on the type of school, or whether the true selection point for university is not so much in as before high school. In the latter case the type of school would simply be an indicator for abler and more motivated pupils who, since they were 14 years old, were oriented towards university and precisely for this reason may have chosen *liceo*, as opposed to those pupils who were not so sure about their future intentions and who did not want to commit themselves too strongly.

If, however, the type of school had a genuine impact, two general mechanisms could be expected to be at work. First, it could be argued that subjects' preferences and aspirations are shaped by the type of school attended; either in the weaker sense of reinforcing preferences already existing or in the stronger sense of creating preferences *ex novo*. In any case, being placed in an academic and vocationally averse environment would foster consistent aspirations and lead the great majority of pupils from *liceo* to university; correspondingly, pupils from *istituti tecnici* of otherwise similar social background and ability would become more used to the idea of working and see themselves more quickly removed from the educational system. A similar view has been held particularly in Britain where until the late sixties – through the eleven-plus examination – pupils faced a very marked educational streaming.[10]

The second mechanism could be more linked to economic factors: specializing in some trade at the *istituto tecnico* would make it relatively more convenient to enter the labour market as soon as possible, whereas studying the history of philosophy and ancient Greek at *liceo* would clearly open different labour market routes hardly accessible without a university degree.

It seems entirely plausible to suppose that both such mechanisms may be at work; however, there are reasons to believe that they act to reinforce intentions which were already there in beginning high school rather than to shape minds from scratch or form intentions anew. Above all there is the system of selection, which operates when high school is chosen, to be considered, and in this respect the Italian system differs substantially from the British. In the latter there is, or rather was, an explicit mechanism which through an entrance examination allocated children to different schools, whereas in Italy, it is left up to subjects and their families to decide which school to attend. In Britain the 'divided' system could be more easily blamed for acting as an important element independent from pupils' intentions: pupils who had high aspirations and failed the eleven-plus exam could react by lowering their aspirations, while pupils who were rather uncertain about their future could become more aware of university as a feasible option precisely because they had been accepted into grammar school. In Italy the situation is different since any type of high school is feasible for those who qualified from middle school, and no entrance examination is required. Here it is the families, and not the educational system, who judge which type of school is more convenient on the basis of how well their children went through compulsory education and from their level of performance at that stage, and, in order to be able to choose the school by themselves – particularly in the case of *liceo* – they have to have a clear intention already formed beforehand.[11]

---

[10] See, for instance, Banks (1976); also Halsey and his associates (1980) seem somewhat close to this view when stating that much of the explanation of 'differential attainment of service- and working-class children has . . . to do with the type of school attended' (pp. 143–4). They do not, however, specify exactly what they have in mind as the relevant mechanism.

[11] Cf. Banks (1976), who, referring to a wide range of evidence, concludes that 'even in the absence of early selection into a differentiated school system other measures of school achievement have a similar effect on the aspirations of pupils and their parents' (p. 81).

The available evidence supports the view that intentions about university tend to be formed early. In a national survey carried out in 1976, 68% of university students declared that they had decided that they would go to university before going to high school; of the others 9.3% decided during high school and 18% soon after it.[12] More evidence pointing in this direction comes from the high school pupils sample if we look at the proportion of subjects who, when asked about their post-high school intentions, replied that they were still undecided: *liceo* pupils appear to be very precocious in making up their minds, and among them the proportion of undecided subjects was only 15%, whereas it was 27% among *istituto tecnico* pupils.

On the whole, it would seem that for the most part the effect of the type of school on the decision about university embodies a process of selection that takes place earlier, at the end of middle school and before the branch of high school is chosen. Very likely the divided system, by reinforcing original intentions, acts as a factor of rigidity in that it does not encourage a change of mind, yet it is unlikely that it exercises an autonomous effect of any significance on pupils' intentions.[13]

In concluding it is necessary to discuss one theoretical issue. From the fact that subjects, independently of economic and cultural resources and irrespective of gender and social class, are very sensitive to their past academic performance when deciding about their future education, a relevant theoretical consequence follows. This result – as was clearly pointed out by Boudon (1974: 22ff) – restricts the validity of the *value approach* to educational decisions in the form in which it was put forward by Hyman (1966) and suggests that the presence of inertial forces cannot be generalized (see section 3.1). If pupils and their families decide on a certain amount of education merely in terms of a class-differentiated system of values, we should in principle expect to find little or no importance attached to school achievement, and consequently educa-

---

[12] Padoa Schioppa (1974: 233); 4.1% decided one or two years after finishing high school and 0.6% did not answer. This type of evidence could be affected by consistency in recall (Moss & Goldstein 1979).

[13] A further result ought to be pointed out: the type of school seems to produce a higher effect on intentions, that is in the sample of high school pupils, than it does on actual choices, that is in the youth unemployment sample. It is very likely that some of those subjects who wanted to go straight from *liceo* to university belonged to a top social stratum and at the end of their education did not need to register in the unemployment list and are therefore under-represented in the sample (cf. Appendix 2). In this respect it is almost surprising to find such a marked effect.

tional decisions to be taken irrespective of prior level of success. The survey data on which Boudon based his conclusion contained only two independent variables, one measure of social background and one measure of achievement, which were related to a measure of school attainment or aspiration. In the results presented here, the joint information of both samples has allowed the use of a much larger number of control variables, thereby reinforcing Boudon's conclusion that families are capable of adjusting to their children's achievements irrespective of their social status.

It is now necessary to push the analysis a stage further and to consider the capacity to respond to the expected probability of success beyond the subject's personal sphere and with reference to the labour market. But first of all, we need a summary of the results obtained so far.

4.1.3 Summary

In this section it was shown that independently of economic and cultural resources and irrespective of gender and social class, subjects when making a decision are very sensitive to the level of their past academic performance, through which they evaluate their probability of success for the future. They respond not only to the more costly type of failure of being kept behind, but also to reports, thereby suggesting that beyond economic considerations the level of self-confidence and the ability one believes oneself to possess are of great importance. Probably as a consequence of differential sanctions and norms working-class subjects are more responsive to failures than their middle-class counterparts. The results also suggest that some pupils could be strongly influenced by the time they spend at high school either because confidence rises or because an unexpected situation is adjusted to. Finally, the type of high school chosen represents a powerful predictor of what is chosen next: not so much in the sense of being itself the main factor in post-high school decisions, but rather as the embodied sign of aspirations that were present in advance and which, when clear enough, led to the choice of the most academically oriented route. Pupils from *licei* would really have met the relevant bifurcation point when 14 and felt sufficiently confident to think of the distant plan of university as something very real; pupils from *istituti tecnici* would be either more work oriented or have felt insecure enough to prefer the less committing route which would allow them more freedom to think again about university and work at a later stage. Thus, the expected probability of success would not act simply on the choice 'staying-on vs leaving' but also on the perspective that subjects are ready to include in their present decisions: the higher the probability of success, the higher the probability of making more distant and ambitious plans.

4.2 Adjusting to labour market opportunities

There are many empirical signs that subjects, when evaluating which course of education to choose, take account of conditions in the labour market, mainly of earning and employment prospects.[14] This section is devoted to considering whether and to what extent educational choices are the result of economic calculations and investment.

Here, the hypothesis is that subjects are capable of comparing alternatives and that they are not generally acting under the pressure of causal forces. In the context of the 'economic approach to human behaviour', however, the criteria with which subjects are seen to evaluate and choose their education are often presented as mechanistic results determined by market prices, where the point is that of maximizing economic utility. This way of treating people's adjustment to economic conditions could become just another form of viewing subjects' actions as determined by causal forces; whether this holds true would depend on whether we believe that subjects can also exercise a higher-order choice and decide whether economic utility is really what they want to maximize. If we deny such a capacity and believe that a preference for 'the more the better' is a kind of built-in attribute of humans, then a

---

[14] For the most part it is the economic literature, developed around the human capital approach, that provides such evidence (see Rosen 1977) and points to the concept of expected rate of return (Becker 1975) on education as the key to explaining individuals' educational decisions. There is, however, no need to assume the existence of an intrinsic link between education, productivity, and earnings as in the standard neoclassical approach, and some authors have suggested that from the point of view of individuals' behavioural motives it is irrelevant to know whether differences in income associated with differences in education really reflect differences in productivity (Padoa Schioppa 1974: 37). It is sufficient to assume that, whatever the reason, higher levels of education 'produce' on average higher levels of income, besides of course assuming that higher levels of income are generally preferred to lower. Among other possible reasons why education and income are positively correlated there is an explanation which has recently become known as the 'screening hypothesis' (Arrow 1973). Heath (1981: 25) notes that the unacknowledged ancestor of this view is Sorokin.

mechanistic approach to action would necessarily follow; if, however, we do not *a priori* believe the economic to be the sole utility that subjects can decide to maximize we will look for empirical evidence rather than deductive confirmation, trying to test whether people really behave differently under different economic circumstances. The latter is the line I intend to follow in this section.

In the first part of this section, I shall consider two approaches to the influence of labour market conditions on educational decisions, *the parking theory* and *the human capital theory*. By looking at geographical differences in educational behaviour I shall try to assess their validity and I shall show that the former is probably an under-articulated version of the latter. I shall also discuss some evidence which suggests that, as they stand, both approaches are likely to be inadequate, in particular with respect to the presence of unintended effects, which originate from the aggregation of individual educational choices. In the second part of this section, I shall consider differences in the educational behaviour of the sexes and I shall try to interpret them as the result of differences in labour market expectations.

4.2.1 Geographical differences: the parking theory and the human capital theory

In the Italian literature on education the idea that when deciding about their schooling people respond to labour market circumstances has taken a rather peculiar form which I shall freely translate as the *parking theory*. The human capital approach, on the contrary, has received relatively little attention at both the theoretical and the empirical level.[15]

The general idea of the parking theory – which has also been applied to countries other than Italy – is that the length of children's education is an inverse function of employment opportunities and of chances of social mobility at a low level of formal education. More simply, the theory has revolved around the notion that in certain times and places pupils, in order to avoid being unemployed, decide to stay longer at school.[16]

[15] There are, however, some exceptions (Padoa Schioppa 1974, Antonelli 1980, Martinotti 1982).
[16] Within the narrow limits of a conspiratorial view of the world the basic ideas of this model were put forward by Emma & Rostan (1971): longer education was explicitly recognized by these authors as an instrument of 'The Capital' for re-equilibrating the labour market and decreasing the potential threat of youth unemployment. Along these

Among the relevant implications of the theory there is the fact that the development of education can, to some extent, be inversely correlated to economic development.[17]

The theory, as it stands, presents two related ambiguities which can be evaluated independently of the empirical evidence which has been brought in its support. The first, to which I shall return below, is that the theory never stated clearly whether pupils stay longer in school when they cannot find a job purely as an alternative to idleness or whether they also expect (or get) some benefit out of acquiring more education. In other words the theory never made it quite clear whether education is a forced option or whether it has its own, if only relative, advantages.

This brings us to the second ambiguity. The theory has usually been presented in a rather extreme way, that is as if pupils decided to prolong their education almost exclusively because of a lack of employment opportunities; this approach, in other words, aimed at providing a *structuralist* explanation of educational behaviour, in the sense of shortcircuiting the agents and of presenting their behaviour as the only really feasible option. Paradoxically, however, there is nothing in the theory itself to suggest that the accent should fall exclusively on the constraining element rather than on the intentional one: it was stressed that pupils in the South of Italy stay longer at school because they *cannot* find a job, but the symmetrical and naturally consistent inverse proposition could just as well have been stressed, i.e. that more pupils in the North *choose* to leave school because they have better opportunities. This point carries an interesting implication, namely that the

lines see also Miegge (1971) for Italy; something similar regarding the United States can be found in Braverman (1974: 439). No such functional approach is to be found in Barbagli (1973, 1974), who brought the theory to a more refined status in trying several empirical tests, and here I shall refer mainly to his work. Barbagli refers back to Ben David (1966), who puts forward somewhat similar ideas referring to international comparisons and suggesting that among the reasons Germany and France presented a higher number of students than Britain and Belgium in the first half of this century could be the absence in the former two countries of channels of mobility alternative to those provided by formal education.

[17] Here again Ben David (1966) made some comparisons at an international level showing that several underdeveloped countries (India, the Philippines and others) had in 1958 a much higher number of graduates per 10,000 of population than Britain and Germany. (The index Ben David used, however, might be misleading because he did not measure the proportion of graduates for the relevant age groups, and thereby a country with a younger population may seem to have more graduates.) One of Ben David's major contentions – that the lower the chances of social mobility without formal education the more education will tend to be prolonged – has been more recently developed for instance by Dore (1976) with respect to third-world countries.

structuralist approach cannot really stand up unless an intentional agent is simultaneously assumed. The existence of constraints could not be conceived without some notion of their absence.

These problems notwithstanding, the theory had the merit of bringing important empirical evidence to the fore. Barbagli (1974) attempted a test of the theory based on aggregate data.[18] He showed that the average provincial *per capita* income is positively correlated with the rate of attendance in the age group 11–15. He also showed that, by contrast, the continuation rate from middle school to high school is negatively correlated with *per capita* income and with other measures of provincial economic development. His conclusion was that, while at the compulsory level educational participation is undoubtedly under the positive influence of *per capita* income, at the next level, as a consequence of the greater difficulties in finding a job, the higher propensity to stay in education was to be found in poorer provinces. In short, the surprising finding associated with the theory is that people in the underdeveloped Southern regions were acquiring more education than in the industrialized North.

This test was criticized for the type of measure the author used, for the higher continuation rate found in poorer provinces could be the result of the tougher selection met in these same areas at the previous level, that is during compulsory education (Padoa Schioppa 1974: 224). In this case the apparently striking inverse correlation between economic development of a province and its contination rate could be due to the fact that those pupils who qualify from middle school in poorer areas belong to a higher average socio-economic background and/or ability class. Even though the trend in continuation rates in more recent years has partly given more force to the criticism,[19] the counter-objection put forward by

[18] Barbagli also attempted something with time series, but the results were very unsatisfactory. Some general indications that the theory could hold also over time, if only with respect to the choice of continuing to university, is provided by Colasanti, Mebane & Bonolis (1976: 76ff).

[19] In the seventies in fact the continuation rates from compulsory schooling to high school grew closer, even though there is no sign that the 'two Italies' – the rich North and the poor South – are becoming economically closer. The distance has diminished mainly because in the South the continuation rate has declined whereas in the North it has remained approximately constant: in 1970–1 the rates were 71.7% in the North and 84.5% in the South, and in 1979–80 the corresponding rates were 68.7% and 77.6% (CENSIS 1979, 1981; Benadusi & Gandiglio 1978 also comment on this fact). The decline in the proportion of Southerners enrolling in high school is probably due to the increased flow of pupils from lower socio-economic backgrounds qualifying from middle school.

Table 4.6. *Educational participation rates of young people aged 11–26 by sex, geographical area, and father's education, Italy 1967**

	males			females			total		
	N-W	C	S	N-W	C	S	N-W	C	S
illiterate	30.8	20.5	22.6	16.7	22.2	17.3	24.0	21.2	20.0
< elementary	18.3	29.3	33.7	19.2	23.8	24.9	18.7	26.8	29.6
elementary	36.6	47.4	47.9	29.6	37.4	33.6	33.0	42.4	40.4
middle school	51.3	65.3	66.7	40.4	52.7	57.0	45.3	58.8	61.9
high school	65.2	75.4	85.7	50.0	53.8	57.4	56.3	63.9	70.2
degree	87.1	94.9	96.6	69.4	75.0	72.4	77.6	84.8	84.5
all levels	36.7	47.0	44.6	31.4	38.2	33.1	34.0	42.7	38.8

*Each figure is a percentage of the total number of individuals in the corresponding cohort
Source: ISTAT 1969b

Barbagli cannot be easily cast aside: he suggested that an explanation simply in terms of social selection being uneven across geographical areas was not sufficient to account for the fact that the rates of attendance themselves[20] – and not simply the continuation rates – showed unequivocally that the poorer regions had more children over 15 at school.

In fact if we take into account a table provided by a national survey carried out in 1967 which was surprisingly ignored in this debate, we shall see that it leaves remarkably little doubt about the fact that, even when we control for socio-economic background (in this case measured by father's education) the poorer areas of the country have higher attendance rates. Table 4.6 shows the attendance rates of individuals in the age group 11–26 by sex, father's education, and three geographical areas of the country: the North-West, which is the highly industrialized and modernized region of Italy, the South, which is the poorest and least developed part, and finally the Central area, which, economically as well as geographically, falls somewhere between the two extremes. The table shows, as one would expect, that independently of sex and geographical area, the rates of attendance grow alongside father's education. It also shows, however, a series of counterintuitive and striking facts. The first is that the lowest attendance rate is found in the richest part of Italy, i.e. the

---

[20] According to Barbagli, attendance rates could not be used in the aggregate analysis because they were not available at a provincial level.

Table 4.7. *Educational participation rates of young people aged 11–26 by sex, geographical area, and age, Italy 1967**

	males			females			total		
	N-W	C	S	N-W	C	S	N-W	C	S
11–13	96.7	96.3	90.9	93.9	91.6	82.3	95.3	93.9	86.5
14–18	48.7	62.0	55.5	41.7	47.6	37.4	45.2	55.2	46.6
19–23	13.9	25.8	20.4	8.1	16.2	11.4	11.0	21.1	16.1
24–26	3.9	9.5	9.6	1.8	4.7	2.6	2.8	7.1	6.0
all	36.7	47.0	44.6	31.4	38.2	33.1	34.0	42.7	38.8

Source: ISTAT 1969b

North-West;[21] the second, even more interesting fact, is that the attendance rates are lower in North-West Italy at virtually all levels of father's education; the third result is that both previous ones hold for both sexes, though males' responsiveness to geographical area appears to be much higher. Furthermore, although overall the Centre of Italy has the highest attendance rate, it is the South where rates are generally higher when father's education is taken into account.[22]

To complete the picture we must consider table 4.7, which is similar to the one just discussed. It presents rates of attendance broken down by sex, geographical area, and age group, and highlights two relevant circumstances: the geographical difference is in favour of the South only in the age groups above 14, while for the youngest group, 11–13, the

[21] Migration patterns could bias the attendance rates by lowering them in the North and raising them in the South, because more people in the latter part of the country could decide about their school with migration in mind (cf. Craig 1984). The relationship between migration and educational choices is discussed below.
[22] This is explained by the fact that in the South there are relatively more fathers with a lower level of education. Thus if the South had the same father's education-level distribution as the rest of the country it would have a much higher rate of attendance. Incidentally, this is sufficient to reject a criticism that the parking theorists have received from various sources and notably from Padoa Schioppa (1974: 223). She argues that if the lack of job opportunities is the reason for the higher attendance rate in the South, it should also follow that the even higher participation rate of the Centre is explained by an even higher lack of opportunity in the Centre itself – which is obviously not the case. The answer to this objection is that if the level of father's education is held constant, the higher aggregate attendance rate of the Centre disappears and the parking theory still holds. For the same reason, the explanation provided by Benadusi & Gandiglio (1978), who suggested that in the Centre pupils go to school more because they receive higher benefits from education than pupils in the South, would seem to be redundant.

South comes at the bottom. This result is consistent with the test Barbagli carried out on aggregate data and means that in the South, and more generally in poorer provinces, fewer pupils reach the end of middle school, but those who do so are much more inclined to stay on to high school than their Northern peers; moreover, their propensity is such as to reverse, in absolute terms, the participation rates and make them higher in the South than in the North. Table 4.7 indicates one other important thing: the relative distance between the North-West on the one hand and the Centre and the South on the other grows with the increase in age.[23]

Even though so far I have been referring mainly to the transition from middle school to high school, the latter fact suggests that the same pattern should apply to the transition from high school to university: the continuation rates from high school to higher education in fact show exactly the same geographical differences, and – this time even controlling for a measure of father's occupation (Barbagli 1974: 377–8)[24] – high school pupils tend to go more frequently to university in the South than in the North of the country. This is a circumstance which is important to us because it is exclusively at this level of education – at the third choice, that is – that I shall be able to carry out a test on my survey data.

How to account for these facts, which overturn many commonsense expectations? Is the parking theory adequate to make sense of the whole pattern of results?

At first sight, undoubtedly, the hypothesis that would seem to gain some force in the light of this data is precisely that suggested by the parking theory in its more refined version: 'the development of education has been, at least to some extent, the product of economic backwardness and underdevelopment, of the lack of job opportunity at secondary and higher levels of education, and finally of the scarcity of alternative channels of social mobility' (Barbagli 1974: 353, my translation).

But before trying to assess whether these conclusions are to be fully supported, I shall outline some general implications which these tables

[23] The table shows also that females in the South overtake their Northern counterparts only when over 18: their disadvantage with respect to Northerners is particularly marked at the early ages (at 11–13 93.9% of females were at school in the North and 82.3% in the South), and probably for this reason their rate of attendance is slower in catching up with the North than is the rate for males.

[24] The measure used by Barbagli is loose, but it allows at least the separation of children of entrepreneurs and professionals from those of the rather meaningless aggregate of dependent workers in general: in both groups Southerners attend school more than Northerners, though in the top occupational group the distances are smaller and by the end of the sixties seem to have disappeared.

carry with regard to the fundamental theoretical alternatives discussed in this book. The first and more general implication is that educational decisions would seem to be a function not only of social background as measured by father's education, but also of the set of labour market opportunities available in the area: a piece of evidence which strongly supports the view that before selecting a course of action people evaluate the alternatives open to them. The second point is that – although pupils are responsive to circumstances at virtually all levels of father's education – the intensity of the response varies with social background (as measured by father's education) according to a rather interesting pattern. This interaction is visible from figure 4.1,[25] where it can be seen that at both extremes of the parental educational ladder the percentage distances between Southern and Northern attendance rates are considerably smaller than they are in the middle; it would appear that being the child either of an illiterate or of a university graduate father numbed the pupil's responses to labour market circumstances. Particularly at the

Figure 4.1 *Percentage differences between southern and northern participation rates in education broken down by father's education (age 11–26)*

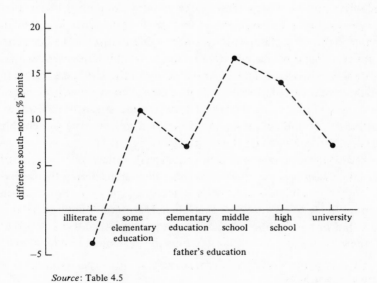

Source: Table 4.5

[25] I have plotted only the distances between South and North because those between Centre and North follow the same pattern.

level of illiteracy, the attendance rates present a negative difference in favour of Northerners.[26]

The explanation of this pattern, it would seem natural to think, is very likely to lie in two very different mechanisms: at the lowest level of parental education we can imagine the existence of *cognitive constraints* which prevent people from gathering basic information and drawing inferences even of a very elementary character; as we have seen in the previous chapter (section 3.2.3), cognitive constraints could lead subjects to acquire less education than actual opportunities would make advisable. At the highest level of father's education we can presume the existence of norms or of *lexicographic preferences*; preferences, that is, which are unrenounceable even in the face of attractive labour market opportunities and for which no realistic trade-off could fully compensate. It would be only at the lowest level that the explanation could be properly referred to *behind-the-back* forces, in the sense of forces which deny power of decision to subjects.

The third implication that we can draw from table 4.6 is opposed to an explanation of educational decisions in terms of pushing forces like *traditional values* which would have the effect of making education a less attractive option: it is difficult in fact to see how it could be argued that people living in the North-West of the country are more governed by traditional values than Southerners are; the most generous idea we can entertain in this respect is that, if the traditional forces were at all present, the effect of labour market opportunities would be even stronger, because the presence of the former would make the latter less visible in the data. In other words, to save the hypothesis relative to the presence of traditional values, one is compelled to assume the existence of an offsetting effect and therefore to allow for a greater role of sensible adjustment to labour market opportunities.

The weakness of customs and traditional values as a source of explanation becomes particularly evident when considering the behaviour of girls. At all levels of father's education, girls in the South are in fact more likely to be at school than their Northern counterparts; this means that in the traditional, family oriented and backward South of Italy there are more girls at school than in the developed North-West.[27]

---

[26] Here, we must take into account the fact that the higher rate of illiteracy in the South puts more children at risk.

[27] This certainly means that traditional values explain little. But data from the same table could suggest that, nonetheless, they play a marginal role: males are in fact more

We can turn now to the basic question: are the motives behind the higher attendance rate found in the South merely a matter of lack of employment opportunities or might there not also be a somewhat different explanation? Is it only by facing longer unemployment prospects at the end of one level of education that pupils are induced to stay on to the next, or do they also expect some positive benefits from the choice of a longer educational option?

At first sight it would not seem very plausible to assume that, independently of what they can get out of extra school years, pupils prolong their education simply because they would have few opportunities with their earlier level of education. Undoubtedly if unemployment is higher forgone earnings are lower, and if, to take an extreme case, the expected period of unemployment is as long as the course of education then forgone earnings may tend towards zero. As a consequence, if nothing else changes, the cost of education is lower and more people could be expected to stay on. However, the absence from the parking theory of any clear reference to *benefits* is of crucial importance and, at the same time, one of the elements of its incompleteness and the key to integrating this theory with the human capital model.

The question here becomes whether, independently of where one happens to live, education makes a difference in terms of labour market benefits, whether, that is, higher levels of education are associated with higher relative rewards in terms of jobs and earnings. In relative terms, it would make no difference to educational decisions if benefits as well as forgone earnings were equally reduced. By leaving this crucial point aside, the parking theory has left unclear whether, as it seems, it would also predict higher educational participation even when the relative benefits of extra education remain the same. If the theory made such a claim then

responsive to being in the South than females, and consequently the distance between the participation rates of the sexes is wider in the South (44.6% vs 33.1%) than it is in the North (36.7% vs 31.4%). This could be seen as a consequence of Southern females being more frequently expected to stay at home as good housewives rather than to go out and work. Yet, even this explanation could be challenged, by suggesting that the under-responsiveness of women in the South is not so much the direct consequence of traditional values as of the fact that, relative to men, women face lower chances of finding an occupation in the South than in the North: in other words their comparatively lower sensitivity to geographical location could be the consequence of their being objectively more disadvantaged than women in the North. Evidence that this might be the case is provided by unemployment rates: the distance between male and female rates in the North is always considerably smaller than the corresponding distance in the South (EUROSTAT 1981). Also in terms of hourly earnings Southern women are disadvantaged as compared to men (EUROSTAT 1-1979).

it could also claim to be different from the other approach, yet it would have to explain why young people lacking job opportunities and not foreseeing anything better after more education should nonetheless be inclined to get more education. If, however, the theory does not make such a prediction, then it is just an incomplete version of the standard economic approach; the only difference would be that it refers to unemployment prospects rather than to the more general notion of forgone earnings, which takes account of expected unemployment as well as earnings.

In order to test the parking theory alongside the human capital approach with my survey data, I followed the strategy of trying to see whether the decision to stay on to university is correlated with the economic situation of the sub-area of Piemonte in which the subjects live.[28] There are three reasons to believe that the local prospects of the area of residence matter, even though, of course, subjects may take into account regional and national labour market prospects when deciding about their education.

Firstly, given that migration costs are not negligible, if labour market opportunities in a particular area look good for high-school-leavers then, *ceteris paribus*, more subjects from that area than from other areas with worse opportunities should leave and decide not to go to university. Even if, in other areas of the region or the country, prospects for university graduates were better – but not sufficiently better to compensate for migration costs – local prospects should still make a marginal difference.[29]

[28] The test could not be applied to the decision to enrol in high school after leaving middle school, because no information was available relative to the conditions of the labour market when the vast majority of subjects in the sample made that choice. Moreover, to test for the effect of labour market opportunities using the same set of subjects who have been used so far in analysing the third choice presented a major problem: some of them had already graduated from university and had joined the unemployment register only after graduation; thus the labour market situation from the time they had decided to stay on to the time of the interview might well have changed and be no longer reflected by the areas as they are grouped by my indexes. The point, then, was that of keeping in the sample only those subjects who were more likely to have faced the decision of whether to go to university around the period to which the indexes referred. In order to satisfy this requirement I selected all subjects who had completed high school and, when interviewed, were not university graduates. Although some of them were already university students by the time they joined the unemployment register, they had begun their course not long before and, as a consequence, could be kept in. On this set of subjects I carried out the analysis by adopting the usual logit model.

[29] The reader should be reminded that in Italy one does not need to migrate in order to go to university; providing the student sits the examinations the attendance requirements are very loose.

Secondly, the process of searching for good opportunities is more realistically thought of as following *satisficing* rather than *maximizing* criteria. Subjects, in other words, would tend to scan their possibilities hierarchically and migration, rather than being an element of an overall maximizing plan, is likely to become a relevant option only if local labour market opportunities are generally discouraging. Thus high-school-leavers not otherwise determined to go to university will probably consider first local prospects at the level of education they have reached, and only if these look particularly unattractive will they then begin to consider the other options, i.e. local prospects if they acquire higher education, prospects elsewhere without higher education and so on. Finally, local labour markets are bound to be relevant also because information and connections, which are often indispensable resources for finding employment, are more likely to be available locally. Potential migrants cannot necessarily infer from the presence of good opportunities for residents that the latter will extend to them too.

In order to find out whether subjects respond sensibly to labour market opportunities, two different measures can be applied depending on which theory we follow. Following the parking theory, the test which should be used is some measure of employment opportunity; following instead the human capital approach, a different test – based on earning differentials between the two levels of education involved – should be used. Through the data of the youth unemployment survey, I created both indexes in the form of two dummy variables: the first index came from grouping all areas of Piemonte where the probability for high-school-leavers of finding a job was higher than average, and the second from grouping all those areas where the pecuniary advantages of going to university were low, that is, all those areas where the difference in earnings between high-school-leavers and university graduates was below average.[30] The expectation suggested by both theories would be that in either group of areas, the probability of becoming a university student should be significantly lower than elsewhere.

But are the two groups of areas really two? The empirical results of constructing the indexes were striking: the areas of the region where both conditions occurred largely coincided: in the areas where high-school-leavers had better chances of finding a job, they also, on average, seemed

---

[30] The measure I used was hourly earnings of the subjects who were employed at the time of the interview.

Table 4.8. *The effect of living in an area with better labour market opportunities for high-school-leavers: logit coefficients (model with three alternatives)*

	CHOICE: staying on at university vs leaving		
	1 vs 2	1 vs 3	2 vs 3
model for all cases: coefficients (N = 733)	0.03	−0.44*	−0.47*

alternative 1 = 'university by itself'
alternative 2 = 'university plus work'
alternative 3 = 'leaving by itself'
Source: youth unemployment sample (Appendix 4, Models B)

to enjoy earnings closer to those of graduates living in the same areas.[31] Before discussing whether the large overlap of the two indexes is consistent with some theoretical reason such that the two theories could be merged, it is essential to see whether the grouping of areas really does make some difference to subjects' decisions.

There is, however, a further obstacle we have to consider. The distinction between those who become university students and those who do not does not necessarily coincide with the distinction between those who do not work and those who do. Since several university students also have some form of employment, which can range from a full-time permanent job to odd jobs erratically performed, it is natural to expect that the type of variable whose effects we want to measure – i.e. labour market conditions – could be very sensitive to such circumstances and the discriminating line could go across 'work vs non-work' rather than 'university vs leaving'. To tackle this problem, I introduced a third alternative in the model and estimated a multinomial logit. The third alternative is constituted by those who work and go to university at the same time.[32] The other two alternatives are 'university by itself' and 'leaving by itself' (Appendix 4, Models B).

The results of the test came out as expected, irrespective of which combination of areas was used, i.e. whether those with better employ-

---

[31] The details of the method I have adopted are given in Appendix 3. Here, however, it is important to stress that the index of probability of employment could be constructed controlling for several subjects' characteristics, and therefore there is a good chance that it really measures the level of labour demand for high-school-leavers in the area.

[32] Those who had short and very temporary jobs were left out of the mixed alternative.

ment prospects, those with lower earnings differentials, or those with both (table 4.8). The coefficients refer to the latter measure where all areas singled out are kept together and show that subjects residing in those areas really are less likely to go to university than those residing elsewhere. Moreover, the dividing-line separates the option 'university' from the option 'leaving', irrespective of whether some work is combined with university. In other words, the options 'university by itself' vs 'university with some work' seem to be chosen independently of labour market conditions.[33]

So far we have seen (1) that both theories *de facto* single out virtually the same set of areas and (2) that those areas have a significant effect on post-high school choices. The latter result supports the hypothesis that subjects take sensibly into account objective labour market conditions when deciding about their education and that, independently of whether they also take supra-local prospects into consideration, local prospects make a difference. Moreover, since in the model there are a number of control variables – family income, parents' education, *liceo*, sex and preferences – we can say that the effect is independent of them.

The fact that both theories single out practically the same set of areas made it impossible to test whether simply under the pressure of unemployment pupils would have decided on more education: the areas with worse employment chances at high school level are also, in fact, those where a university degree is more attractive.[34] However, given that

---

[33] I have also run separate models by class (Models B, Appendix 4) maintaining three alternatives: middle-class subjects, when there are good labour market opportunities for high-school-leavers, prefer to go to work rather than choose the option 'university by itself'; if they choose university, they prefer to work at the same time. Working-class subjects behave differently: their choice of university, whether with or without work, seems generally less affected by labour market conditions. When there are good opportunities for high-school-leavers, they prefer to go to work only if the alternative is 'university plus work'. If they choose 'university by itself' they seem to be unaffected by labour market opportunities, for, if they do so, they do not work at the same time. A possible explanation could be that working-class subjects who go to university when they would have good chances if they left are only the very highly motivated. Support for this view can be found in the next section, where it is shown that working-class subjects need a stronger intensity of preferences to decide on university.

[34] The general evidence is undoubtedly in favour of showing that in Italy, as in many other countries, education is, on average, far from being a waste: certainly it is not in Piemonte, where it is positively and strongly associated with earnings and job quality, and negatively with length of unemployment. Cf. Colombino, Gambetta & Rondi (1981) and Bogetti (1982). With respect to Italy as a whole, evidence provided by the Bank of Italy shows the solid statistical correlation of education and earnings. But evidence from other regions, notably the South, is almost completely lacking.

the overlapping of areas is probably not a coincidence, the question could become irrelevant: if unemployment is higher, in fact, the pressure on the labour market is higher and, in principle, wages should be lower; hence, pupils who could leave the educational system after high school to enter a crowded labour market would face expected earnings which are lower, not simply because the risk of remaining idle is higher, but also because, when employed, they would face lower actual earnings.

However, if the labour market prospects for university graduates were proportionally lower there would still be no point in staying on because of higher earnings differentials. The evidence, though, shows that this is not the case: in the areas where the earnings differentials between high-school-leavers and university graduates were wider than average this was due to both possible reasons simultaneously, namely lower earnings for high-school-leavers and higher earnings for university graduates; correspondingly, in the areas where earnings differentials were more narrow, graduate earnings were lower and high-school-leavers' higher.

If we search for a plausible explanation of this pattern we shall also find that the whole mechanism of response to labour market conditions could be somewhat more complex than that put forward by both theories. If, at the time when high school pupils terminate their course of education, they find themselves in a crowded market and see graduates ahead of them faring relatively well, then more of them – we have just tested for this – would stay on. As a consequence, after a number of years, the market for graduates would tend to become more crowded and earnings should fall. At the same time, though, the degree of crowding at the previous level, i.e. at the end of high school, should become somewhat lower, thereby making it relatively more convenient to leave immediately after high school. In turn, after some years, this would decongest the labour market at the level of further education, and once again trigger off the whole cycle.[35]

If this is the case, as several authors seem to suggest,[36] neither theory

[35] An alternative explanation of this pattern could consist in the presence of structural differences in the labour demand in the two different sets of areas: there could be, in other words, areas which systematically offer better employment opportunities for high-school-leavers, and areas which offer better opportunities for university graduates. What seems unconvincing in this explanation is that the areas where opportunities are better for one group are *also* worse for the other group, while there are neither areas where they are simultaneously worse or better for both nor areas where they are better or worse only for one group. It seems hard to see how such systematic inverse correlation could be accounted for by factors concerning merely the demand for labour.

[36] See Hirsch (1977) for a general treatment and a bibliography.

would be satisfactory: the human capital approach suggests – correctly, in a way – that pupils choose to stay on because they see larger benefits ahead, but it omits to point out that when the 'ahead' becomes the present, those expectations may on average turn out to be wrong and the benefits may have become somewhat less than expected.[37] The conclusion would then, paradoxically, be reminiscent of that suggested by the parking theory, where pupils stay on 'for nothing',[38] but would follow from expectations which, to start with, looked more optimistic and which may now be the cause for some regret. To summarize, the paradox would be the following: if high-school-leavers could not see any benefit attached to a university degree fewer of them would continue their education just because they face the risk of unemployment. However, the larger the number of high-school-leavers who stay on at university on the basis of a given level of expected benefits, the lower will be the actual benefits in the end, so much so that had they known it in advance, some of them would not have gone to university at all. At the same time, had they not gone to university the actual benefits would have turned out to be higher, and so on, as in a process where no point of equilibrium can be found.

From the point of view of decision mechanisms, this whole process could be the unintended result of the so-called fallacy of composition, i.e. the belief that if one can make it, all can: thus each single individual would be perfectly justified and, in a static sense, rational in holding the expectation of larger benefits, but larger benefits would vanish if many others held such expectations at the same time and acted accordingly. This would be one of those cases where the pursuit of the most rational course of action would imply doing the right thing at the wrong moment, and vice versa.[39]

This process could perhaps adequately explain why the attendance rates in Southern Italy are systematically higher than in Northern Italy. In the former area of the country, a general lower level of labour demand

[37] In static terms there is evidence that students generally have realistic expectations (e.g. Psacharopoulos & Sanyal 1981). For a somewhat similar critique of the human capital approach see Colasanti, Mebane & Bonolis (1976), especially ch. 1.

[38] There may be other rational reasons why pupils stay on in a 'parking' fashion, notably the fact that for employers the status of 'student' may be a much better signal than that of 'unemployed'.

[39] On purely speculative grounds, we might suspect the process not to be limited to faulty timing of subjects' decisions; its consequences could be more far-reaching and the cyclical element could be associated with a cumulative effect: the fact that more people than compatible with a subject's initial expectations stay on longer when benefits look high in a

could cause a higher proportion of pupils to stay on at school longer – as the parking theory suggests; but the effects of the labour market would be indirect and depend, at the same time, on the aggregate educational behaviour, i.e. on what every individual expects everybody is going to do in educational terms. Pupils could tend to stay on more frequently, not so much because they face lower chances of finding employment as because they expect that these chances are going to be lowered even further if many others reach a level of education higher than theirs. A greater degree of competition for jobs at any one level of education confers higher relative advantage to those who achieve better educational credentials and can compete for a relatively larger number of job openings.

To expand this discussion further would take us too far away from the main thread of this book, yet the rudimentary outline given above should be sufficient to suggest that both the parking theory and also the human capital approach are in need of a rather more complex theoretical framework, particularly if we are to make sense of the striking geographical differences in educational behaviour described in this section.

4.2.2 Differences between the sexes

I shall now focus on the inter-sex differences in educational behaviour, trying to see whether they can be interpreted as the product of different labour market expectations. The standard economic assumption concerning the effect of sex is that females have generally lower forgone earnings, i.e. for them education is less costly; however, they also have lower rates of return, at least because their expected working life is shorter. In theory, this makes for an uncertain a priori prediction, since

given phase is not necessarily compensated for by the fact that more pupils leave in the next phase, when prospects look grim. In principle, the greater number of pupils going to university in one phase of the cycle should make the market for graduates progressively more crowded. Thus, at the successive cycle, the expected benefits of a university degree could be higher again, but not as high as in the same phase of the previous cycle. However, there could be a deeper unintended result compensating for the cumulative effect: depending on how elastic the demand for jobs is at the higher level of education, a certain number of university graduates could end up competing for jobs that were previously open mainly to high-school-leavers. As a consequence, the benefit of a high school diploma is pushed downwards and the relative benefit of university education becomes larger and more attractive again. This type of process, outlined by Thurow (1975) and others, is that in which 'everybody runs as fast as they can to remain in the same place'.

Table 4.9. *The effects of being a female: logit coefficients*

	CHOICE: staying on at school vs leaving		
	after compulsory education	during high school	after high school
models for the working class: coefficients	0.16 (N = 929)	0.97* (N = 681)	−0.38 (N = 379)
models for the middle class: coefficients	−0.81* (N = 686)	1.08* (N = 636)	−0.37 (N = 476)

Source: youth unemployment sample (Appendix 4, Models A)

depending on which side is more relevant, we could expect them to acquire either more or less education than males. In practice, all evidence is in favour of females having a lower incentive than males to stay on at school, for the importance of lower expected benefits should outweigh the lower forgone earnings (Becker 1975: 178). The most likely reason is that the earning differentials between the sexes, in the years which are relevant to educational decisions, are generally in favour of males to a much smaller extent than the earning differentials when considered over the whole life cycle: it is well known that women tend to work particularly before the birth of their first child, with labour force involvement tending to diverge from that of males in later years. Moreover, this very argument suggests that women may be less attracted by education not only because they work less over a lifetime, but also because they concentrate a greater part of their working effort earlier, and hence a period spent in school would in relative terms imply a heavier sacrifice.

In an attempt to test for this expectation we can consider, in the models derived from the youth unemployment sample, a dummy variable singling out female subjects.[40] The coefficients, which are shown in tables 4.9 and 4.10, indicate that at the first choice, females are less likely than males to stay on to high school, but – and this could appear puzzling – only when they have middle-class origins.[41] At the second choice, on

[40] Given the nature of the data in the youth unemployment sample, we are, if anything, likely to underestimate the differences between the sexes because the women who registered in the list and are represented in the sample are probably more oriented towards the labour market than those who did not register and can be expected to be more similar to men.

[41] Somewhat similar results are also found by Bogetti (1982: 327).

Table 4.10. *The effects of being a female: logit coefficients (models with three alternatives)*

	CHOICE: type of school		
	liceo vs *istituto tecnico*	*liceo* vs vocational school	*istituto tecnico* vs vocational school
model for the working class: coefficients (N = 583)	0.34	−1.13*	−1.47*
model for the middle class: coefficients (N = 596)	−0.25	−1.78*	−1.53*

Source: youth unemployment sample (Appendix 4, Models A)

the contrary, girls are highly advantaged and much more likely than boys to endure and reach the end of high school, irrespective of their social background. At the third choice, women from both classes appear to be slightly less attracted by university than the opposite sex. Finally, in the multinomial model on the choice of the type of school, the coefficients show a greater proneness among girls to choose the shorter route, i.e. vocational schools, with respect to both other possibilities.[42]

These results seem generally consistent with the prediction that women tend to acquire a smaller amount of education. There is one exception, though. This is the fact that girls, irrespective of their class of origin, are much more likely not to drop out of high school once they have started (table 4.9 second choice). At first sight, this would seem to contradict the hypothesis that, *ceteris paribus*, males are more attracted than females by education, but if one considers that these are subjects who had already started the high school course, it should not be difficult to see why being a girl works in the other way. Once school has been chosen, in fact, and the choice faced is whether to complete it, the cost of each extra year for girls is lower in terms of forgone earnings than it is for boys, and hence there should be a lower incentive to change one's mind with respect to the decision taken when starting high school. Unlike girls, boys would be more easily caught by the temptation of more rewarding work prospects and therefore should be more ready to leave.

[42] For sampling reasons, this effect could be overestimated (cf. Appendix 2). It ought also to be considered that women could be more prone to go to vocational schools not only because of the shorter length of these courses, but because of their content. They provide, in fact, training in trades which are regarded as 'women's work' (for instance infant school teaching and secretarial work).

Table 4.11. *Work participation of married women by social class of origin and education*

	hours of work		percentage employed	
	working class	middle class	working class	middle class
compulsory education	622 (N = 380)	656 (N = 396)	33.3	34.0
high school or more	1,409 (N = 47)	869 (N = 134)	83.3	58.2
total	710 (N = 427)	706 (N = 530)	38.9	40.2

Source: 1,000 Turin families sample

The data raise another relevant question: why, when confronted with the choice of high school, do working-class girls behave exactly as working-class boys, whereas middle-class girls are considerably less prone to stay on than their male counterparts? The answer is probably that working-class women's expectations are closer to those of men in terms of the amount of work outside the home over their lifetimes. On the basis of a third sample survey – which I have not introduced so far – it was possible to carry out a simple test of this hypothesis. This survey was carried out on a random sample of 1,000 families in Turin in 1979 (Martinotti 1982); I considered two measures of work participation of the women in the sample: one measuring the average hours of work per year and the other measuring the proportion of women who were employed at the time of the survey. Both measures are broken down by social class of origin of the women and by their educational level.

The results (table 4.11) are rather striking and show that, although on average women from both social classes tend to work the same amount, when the data are broken down by education, women of working-class origin who hold a high school diploma or higher work much more than middle-class women of the same educational level; this holds true both in terms of hours of work and in terms of participation rate. Indeed, their average – 1,409 hours of work per year – is very close to the male total and is more than one-third greater than the hours worked by middle-class women.[43] Since there are no appreciable differences in hourly earnings

[43] In industry the average for males is around 1,500 hours a year (Ministero del Lavoro, Rassegna di statistiche del lavoro 1979).

depending on social class origins, it follows that working-class women with high school or university education earn more money than middle-class women.

This evidence might indirectly support the hypothesis that the difference in expectations between girls from different social back-grounds could be at the source of their different educational choices: only for working-class women, in fact, would the prospect of high school appear almost as rewarding as for males from the same social background. Girls from this class, when contemplating their future, are more likely to hold a picture of their life which in many respects differs from that of middle-class women, and which focuses on and arises from a more intense working life. Moreover, if their expectations are shaped by future probabilities, then they should expect, on average, to marry poorer husbands and have fewer children, both of which factors are positively related to work participation.[44] Thus, the simple possibility of higher rates of return in the labour market would not be in itself sufficient to attract more women of working-class origins to high school, for, in principle, the same returns could be feasible for middle-class women as well. Educational behaviour with respect to the labour market cannot be understood only as a mechanical response to what is objectively on offer but rather as the combined result of what is objectively possible and of whether agents expect to work hard enough to make that possibility actual.

The class-related differences in the educational behaviour of women would seem to deny further ground to the claim that traditional values can constitute a generalized explanation of individual action. Why, in fact, if women were less prone to stay on at school than men because of

[44] This is based on the evidence from the survey of 1,000 Turin families. The table below shows the average annual income of husbands and the average number of children, broken down by the women's class of origin and level of education.

	Husband's income (in 10,000 lire)		No. of children	
	working class	middle class	working class	middle class
compulsory	102	112	1.62	1.72
high school (or higher)	82	144	0.91	1.39

prejudices against women's education should this apply only to middle-class women? It is difficult to see how prejudices or preferences against women's labour market participation and education relative to those of men should be comparatively less strong in the working class than in the middle class. At most, it could be argued that, for economic reasons, those in the working class are generally less able to let their values or preferences govern. In the next section I shall present further evidence in support of this conclusion.

4.2.3 Summary

The overall theoretical conclusion which can be drawn from this section is that subjects possess a certain degree of awareness of the objective labour market conditions they are facing and make their decisions taking those conditions into account. Geographical differences in educational behaviour, shown by secondary data and by the test performed on survey data, indicate that in areas where the labour market prospects associated with a given level of education are better relative to an inferior level, more subjects tend to stay on at school to reach that qualification. Evidence was also presented to show that (1) the capacity and the willingness to respond to labour market circumstances are weakened at a very low and at a very high level of father's education and that (2) there is little in favour of a view of action as governed by traditional values. Several weaknesses of the parking theory were discussed, in particular its unnecessary 'structuralist' bias and its implicit dependence on the standard economic approach to educational decisions. Some consideration was also given to the possibility of unintended consequences provoked by the aggregate effects of individual educational decisions which could frustrate 'rational' expectations, as well as explain why we find more people in education in areas with worse job prospects. Finally, inter-sex differences, while confirming that economic calculation is, among other things, at the origin of educational decisions, further indicate the important role played by class-differentiated expectations.

4.3 Intentionality, preferences, and opportunities

In the first two sections of this chapter I have shown that rationality – in its adaptive version – plays a major role in governing educational choices: the probability of success reflected by past academic achievement and by labour market prospects is taken into consideration when deciding about one's education and exerts its influence irrespective of pushing forces as well as of personal preferences. In this section, I shall consider whether subjects' intentionality influences their educational decisions, independently of pushing forces and of adaptive rationality. I shall first look at the dimension of intentionality itself, at the *temporal horizon* that underlies people's decisions, and try to assess whether a greater awareness of one's future is an important ingredient of a longer educational career. I shall then attempt to test whether higher aspirations in relation to work and earnings affect the propensity to seek a longer educational career.

4.3.1 The time perspective

The presumption of intentionality in human behaviour is based on the capacity to use the future as a determinant of action. Subjects can fear the future, perceive it as a determinant of their ambitions, or more or less try to avoid all thought of it. However, it is in a temporal perspective that persons' preferences are formed and transformed into actual intentions (see section 1.3).

The high school pupils sample offered suitable data for testing the hypothesis that the temporal horizon that subjects use when deliberating plays a central role in explaining their decisions. More precisely, my hypothesis is that the longer the time perspective invoked the greater would be one's capacity to delay rewards and make long-term investments. The consequent expectation is that the probability of aiming at university should be higher, other things being equal, when the subject takes account of a more distant future. On the basis of the responses to one question concerning the role of work in life, I was able to construct a dummy variable singling out those pupils who answered: 'I haven't yet thought about work because it is too far ahead to say',[45] on the – somewhat bold – assumption that, once controlled by age, it should essentially single out the pupils who hold an attitude more oriented towards the present.

The coefficients are reported in table 4.12 and show that a short time perspective effectively works in the predicted direction of decreasing the probability of intending to go to university. Moreover they show that the

---

[45] The answers included possibilities such as that work is 'the most important thing', 'one important thing among others', or 'just a means to survival'.

Table 4.12. *The effect of a short time-horizon and of job preferences: logit coefficients*

	CHOICE: staying on to university vs leaving			
	short time-span	interesting	good career prospects	high earnings
model for the working class: coefficients (N = 344)	− 1.77*	0.78*	0.11	1.28*
model for the middle class: coefficients (N = 325)	− 1.71*	1.38*	0.79	0.46
model for all cases: coefficients (N = 669)	− 1.86*	1.02*	0.37	0.82*

Source: high school pupils sample (Appendix 4, Models C)

effect is very large, in fact the largest associated with a dummy variable after that of the type of school. To appreciate the test the reader should be reminded that the results are controlled for by a large number of variables from age to social class, to mention only those which could be suspected to lie behind that of the perceived time-span.

It might seem surprising that to regard one's future work as 'too far away to say anything' was a response associated with a higher likelihood of leaving school earlier in order to go to work. In fact, one could believe the opposite to be true: anticipating a longer period of education ahead might justify paying little or no attention to work. That this is not the case reinforces our expectation *ex post* and suggests that a shorter educational career is not just correlated with a generically shorter time perspective, but with those potentially attractive objects that lie unseen beyond a short time horizon. In other words, a shorter temporal perspective is likely to inhibit a careful consideration of how present educational decisions can affect later working life. My evidence supports the hypothesis that among the reasons for not investing in the future is the invisibility, as it were, of the returns which could be brought about by the investment (see Ainslie 1975: 466).

An important question linked with the span of temporal horizon has its origins in the tendency, which has been very common in the socio-psychological literature, to attribute to the poor a lower capacity for deferring gratification and for making long-term investments as a result of a more frequent orientation towards the present.[46] We have already

---

[46] See Ainslie (1975) for a discussion and bibliography. Also Spilerman (1971: 104–6).

Table 4.13. *Percentage distribution
of subjects over the perceived time
perspective, broken down by social
class of origin*

	working class	middle class
time span		
short	8.2	7.8
long	91.8	92.2
all	100.0	100.0

Source: high school pupils sample

discussed this problem in the previous chapter when considering the mechanisms that could explain the pattern of additional effects linked to social class of origin (section 3.2.3). The results presented so far in this section, however, do not tell us whether there are more working-class high school pupils than middle-class pupils who regard work as a distant preoccupation. What they do tell us is that the fact of having a somewhat less precise image of the future affects negatively the probability of going to university in both classes to exactly the same extent. In order to find out whether the nature of the time horizon is associated with class we can construct a cross-tabulation (table 4.13) of the dummy referring to time perspective and the social class of origin of the pupil.

Table 4.13 provides support for the supposition that there is no relationship between class of origin and time orientation. It shows that a small and similar proportion of pupils in both classes regard work as not yet worthy of thought. The measure used for time orientation is crude, but the fact that my results are consistent with other existing evidence (cf. Ainslie 1975) allows us to regard them with some confidence. It would be wrong, however, to jump to the conclusion that class differences in young people's time horizons do not exist.

My evidence – based on the responses of high school pupils – is limited to pre-selected subjects, and precisely this fact could make the correlation invisible. Among those who did not enter high school, a higher proportion of working-class than middle-class children may have left school also because they had a shorter time perspective.[47] In this respect, the figures presented in table 4.13 do not necessarily go against the

---

[47] Moreover, a different definition of social class, obtained for instance by polarizing the upper and lower parts of the social spectrum, could yield different results.

conjectures made in the previous chapter, but simply limit their extension. The table only indicates for certain that among subjects who continued school after the first choice node, social class of origin and time horizon are not correlated. Therefore mechanisms concerning the ability to conceptualize the future can still be suspected to underlie the effects of social class on educational decisions, if only in relation to the first choice node.

4.3.2 Work and earnings preferences

We can now turn our attention to the effects of subjects' preferences, in terms of work and earnings, on educational choices: the general hypothesis is that more ambitious subjects are more likely to try and fulfil their ambitions by investing more in education, irrespective of their social background and of their probability of success as measured by past academic achievement and labour market prospects.

Both surveys could be used in this respect. The high school pupils had answered a question concerning which of the attributes of a future job they valued most highly. I singled out the subjects who gave first place to one of the following:

(1) an interesting job
(2) a job which could bring success and good career prospects
(3) high earnings

thus constructing three new dummy variables. The left-out group comprised all 'risk-averse' pupils, who answered that the main thing they wanted from a job was security.

From the youth unemployment data, I also created three variables: two scales and one continuous variable. The latter is (1) the earnings that subjects would ask for in order to accept their preferred job. The other two variables are based on a five-point scale which ranks jobs from unskilled manual labour to professional and managerial occupations. On this scale are expressed the subjects' answers to two questions; from a set of possible jobs they were asked to indicate: (2) the job they would prefer and (3) the job they would be prepared to accept. Thus, the first scale ranks subjects' top preferences, while the second ranks subjects' lowest acceptable job choice, in the sense of the job they would be prepared to accept in the absence of the preferred alternative.[48]

---

[48] For a detailed description of the whole set of variables see Appendix 3.

These variables could only be tested with respect to the third choice, and in the form of the intention of going to university among the high school pupils and of actual choice among the unemployed young people.[49] It is important to note that since only this choice was used, it meant that the group of subjects was restricted to those who had succeeded in entering high school, or had obtained the final diploma (in the case of subjects in the youth unemployment sample), that is an already selected sub-sample of children. At this level of education it is plausible to expect subjects to have a greater capacity for choosing independently of family constraints and to make their preferences count. Although these factors limit the test, it nonetheless produced results worth presenting.

The results of testing the six variables – three for each sample – are presented in tables 4.12, 4.14 and 4.15. Let us consider first the high school pupils models where social background, school reports, failures, and type of school attended are all controlled for.[50] In general the coefficients show that job and earnings preferences affect schooling decisions, independently of all other specified conditions. They also show two relevant differences in the way in which preferences work, depending on the social class of the subject: (1) preference for high earnings is the most effective for working-class pupils in making university a more attractive option; for middle-class pupils it is of negligible importance; (2) preference for an interesting job is most effective for middle-class subjects; it is also effective, but to a lesser extent, for working-class subjects.[51] On the basis of the analysis of the

[49] In the high school pupils sample, the reason for such limitation is obviously that it was the only choice which could be analysed. In the youth unemployment sample I introduced this limitation on the grounds that subjects were asked their preferences with reference to the time of the interview, and, by that time, the choices concerning high school had already been taken some time ago. Hence, it would have been wrong to use as independent variables the preferences that may have been formed later and, possibly, as a consequence rather than as a cause of the choice of high school. I therefore restricted the sample to the same set of cases used in the analysis of the effects of labour market conditions (cf. n. 28). This set includes only those who faced the choice concerning further education in the period around the time of the interview. Those who already had a university degree were not included. We should therefore be in a position to assume that preferences are not in this case the result of the very choice we want to explain.

[50] The reader should be reminded that age and sex are also controlled for and that social background is measured by father's occupation and parents' education.

[51] Ranking success and good career prospects as the most important attribute presents a negligible effect for the working class and a statistically non-significant effect for the middle class.

Table 4.14. *The effects of the wage wanted for the preferred job: logit coefficients (models with three alternatives)*

	CHOICE: staying on to university vs leaving		
	1 vs 2	1 vs 3	2 vs 3
model for the working class: coefficients (N = 343)	− 0.03*	0.01	0.04*
model for the middle class: coefficients (N = 394)	0.01	0.01	0.00

alternative 1 = 'university by itself'
alternative 2 = 'university plus work'
alternative 3 = 'leaving'
Source: youth unemployment sample (Appendix 4, Models B)

high school sample, let this be the tentative conclusion: personal preferences concerning future work do indeed make a difference by themselves – i.e. irrespective of social background and other variables – for educational choices; yet there are signs that depending on social background the same preferences tend to result in different courses of action.

The plausibility of such a conclusion is reinforced by the indications coming from the other survey. The consistency of the results from both sources – and therefore between intentions and actual choices – is indeed striking. As in the other sample, personal preferences are very effective and influence educational choices in the expected direction. What is most striking, though, is not so much that subjects act intentionally, following their preferences when deciding about education, but rather that certain preferences have a different effect depending on the class of origin of the subjects. The higher the wage requested to accept the preferred job, the higher the probability for a working-class subject of going to university. For the middle-class subject the effect is much lower and non-significant. Furthermore, somewhat similarly to what we have seen in the case of the high school pupils, a higher level of job preferences is more effective in favouring the decision to go to university for a middle-class than for a working-class pupil. The opposite appears to be true with regard to the level of the lowest acceptable job choice. It makes a difference only for working-class subjects, in the sense that the higher the position on the scale of the acceptable job, the higher the probability of going to university.

From these combined sets of results it would really seem as if the social background acted as a filter and modified the behavioural spectrum associated with the same preferences. There are two ways in which this process appears to take place. First, a greater importance attached to money – either in terms of considering it as the most relevant attribute of a job or in terms of the wage required to accept a job offer – affects educational decisions almost exclusively when manifested by working-class subjects; middle-class subjects who express such a preference seem to decide indifferently either for or against going to university. Second, among middle-class subjects, it is the level of job preferences that makes a difference with regard to the university choice, whereas for the working class it is the level of the lowest acceptable job that plays the same role in encouraging entry into post-secondary education. In other words, the more attached working-class subjects are to their preferences and the less prepared to resign themselves to inferior options, the greater the likelihood that they will pursue higher education.

To gain a clearer view of these differences we can look more closely at the results and in particular at the third option included in the model 'university plus work'. Two further points emerge. Firstly, from table 4.14 we can see that a higher threshold in the level of the requested wage positively affects not only the choice of university in general over the option 'leaving', but also that of 'university plus work' vs 'university by itself'. *Prima facie*, it would seem as if a greater keenness on earnings induced subjects to invest more in their education, but at the same time to sacrifice less time to their studies for the sake of earnings. This, however, would merely explain why university students with such preferences work at all, but not why only university students of working-class origin do. Probably, the simplest explanation is that they need money to finance the desired education.[52]

Secondly, for working-class subjects 'university by itself' is favoured over both other alternatives only by a higher level on the scale of the lowest acceptable job. A higher level in the preferred job scale, by

---

[52] If conveniently adapted to inter-class differences, the hypothesis that Levy Garboua (1976) put forward to explain the overtime increase of student-workers in France could also make sense of the data, if in a somewhat more convoluted manner: the taking up of jobs by students would be the result of the decrease in opportunities for more highly educated people, which would in turn increase the relative value of the present over the future, whence the importance of earning more money now. Similarly if working-class students were expecting lower returns they would have greater incentive to take up jobs.

Table 4.15. *The effects of the preferred and acceptable job scales: logit coefficients (models with three alternatives)*

| | CHOICE: staying on to university vs leaving | | | | | |
| | preferred | | | acceptable | | |
	1 vs 2	1 vs 3	2 vs 3	1 vs 2	1 vs 3	2 vs 3
model for the working class: coefficients (N = 343)	−0.30	0.21	0.51*	0.51*	0.43*	−0.08
model for the middle class: coefficients (N = 394)	0.23	0.68*	0.45*	−0.10	0.04	0.14

alternative 1 = 'university by itself'
alternative 2 = 'university plus work'
alternative 3 = 'leaving'
Source: youth unemployment sample (Appendix 4, Models B)

contrast, induces less committed action and has a positive effect only on the probability of producing the mixed option of 'university plus work' (table 4.15). The middle-class pattern goes contrariwise: a higher level of job preference is *always effective* in encouraging the choosing of university, irrespective of whether with or without work, whereas the level in the scale of the acceptable jobs *never* retains any importance. In summary, for a working-class child, job preferences, although not entirely ineffective, are not strong enough to produce the choice of 'university by itself'. For the latter option to prevail, an unrenounceable level of job preferences must come into play. By contrast, middle-class subjects evidently perceive their preferences as worth following and their chances of success as high enough to justify choosing university, and at the same time seem to regard the eventuality of being forced to retreat to the level of their lowest acceptable option as unrealistic. Subjects from the latter group tend to achieve what they want, and subjects from the working class, only what they want at all costs.

The first inter-class difference (i.e. that relative to the effects of a preference for higher earnings) suggests an explanation in terms of the opportunity set open to subjects of different social origins. It could be that middle-class children, on average, expected to have better opportunities of higher earnings regardless of whether they had been to university. This, in other words, would be a case where inequality is located at the level of the actions and efforts required to fulfil one's ambitions, rather than at that of direct economic constraints or socially conditioned preferences.

Could this explanation also apply to the second difference, that relative to job preferences? The case here is somewhat different and my data do not allow any precise answer to the question of whether greater boldness on the part of middle-class subjects in following their inclinations is itself the result of different objectively founded expectations, or has instead its origin in fundamental differences, for instance in the propensity to take risks, in a sense related to 'views-of-the-world' mechanisms discussed by Lane (1972). The fact that these results refer to subjects who had already chosen to remain in school after compulsory education disfavours the notion that 'pushing forces' of the latter sort are governing subjects, and favours the former explanation. For one could ask why subjects, if they were pushed by an over-cautious view of the world or by other sub-cultural values, had not left school before. Even without considering the possible availability of more useful and powerful family connections, it seems realistic to suppose that middle-class subjects expect to be comparatively better able to reach what they want, if only because they expect to be able to cope with longer periods of unemployment after their degree while waiting for the desired opportunity.[53] In this case too, therefore, the inter-class differences in the subjects' responses to the same job preferences when deciding about higher education could be the result of a class difference in the opportunity set.

In conclusion, *within* the same class, more ambitious preferences lead to more ambitious educational choices, and thus in this sense preferences exert their influence independently of social class. But *between* classes, the same preferences act in different directions and with different force. In the latter sense their effect is dependent on the opportunity set specific to each class. In chapter 3 we discussed the effect of constraints on opportunities – i.e. independently of preferences one can afford education to varying degrees – and as a possible influence, via *behind-the-back* processes, on the formation of preferences. Here, we have encountered a third type of effect in which different constraints *interact* with the same preferences and lead to different educational outcomes.

The inter-class differences in the effects of preferences considered so

---

[53] See Padoa Schioppa (1974), who shows that, if the level of education is held constant, subjects of working-class origin remain unemployed for shorter periods.

Table 4.16. *Percentage distribution*
of subjects over job preferences,
broken down by social class of origin

	working class	middle class
preferred *attribute*		
high earnings	4.6	6.0
interesting	61.5	67.0
success–career	9.3	9.8
security	24.6	17.2
all	100.0	100.0

Source: high school pupils sample

far indicate that when subjects from different social backgrounds develop the same preferences they tend to pursue them in educational terms, even if they find different opportunities for doing so. What we need to know now is the extent to which the probability itself of developing the same preferences is affected by social background, through an adaptive process. In chapter 3 we found evidence that, especially at the first choice, suggests the presence of inertial forces, and we have discussed the possibility that such forces may result from adaptive preferences: 'the poor' may develop an exaggeratedly low level of ambition and 'the rich' an exaggeratedly high level of ambition, as a result of their respective resources.

Table 4.16 presents the distribution of high school pupils from each social class according to the attribute of work they regard as the most important; there seems to be little difference in relative frequencies, and in both classes the overwhelming majority clusters around 'an interesting job'. In general, as in the case of time perspective, social class seems to have no direct effect. The only difference consistent with the idea that social class could shape preferences is with the 'risk-averse', those subjects, that is, who value security above all: in this category 24.6% of working-class subjects are clustered as opposed to 17.2% of middle-class ones. We cannot, however, draw any general conclusion from this evidence, for it is based on a preselected sample exclusively of high school pupils: therefore the correlation might only be visible if we could also include those subjects who left before high school. Although this evidence leaves us in doubt and it may still be the case that adaptive preferences play a part at the first educational choice, it nonetheless tells us that, *once high school has been chosen*, adaptive preferences do not seem to be present to a large extent.

This conclusion is reinforced if we consider the distribution across classes of the other set of preferences, provided by the youth unemployment survey: they are more specific and refer to an actual sum of money for earning preferences and to particular occupations for job preferences, rather than referring to value judgements like 'high' or 'interesting'. Those subjects in the sample who had reached the end of high school around the time of the interview and could be included in the models for testing the effects of preferences (cf. n. 49) manifest the same distribution of ambitions irrespective of class: the same average scores on both five-point scales referring to the preferred and to the acceptable job as well as to the average sum of money they would request in order to accept the job they prefer. Both surveys, therefore, confirm the fact that, once high school has been chosen, the probability of developing the same preferences is similar in both social classes.

Unfortunately, the survey data offered neither the possibility of testing the effects nor the class distribution of the preferences entertained *before* a decision about high school is made. Thus, we are not in a position to say whether adaptive preferences could be present at the first post-compulsory choice, and explain the class-specific inertia discussed in chapter 3 (section 3.2.3). The difference detected in the high school pupils data, which shows a higher proportion of risk-averse subjects in the working class, is indicative of that possibility and of the fact that this difference could be wider if we took into account also those who opted out of the educational system before high school. Precisely the choice of not going to high school could pick out those working-class subjects who hold a more cautious attitude.

The youth unemployment survey, however, can provide information on *ex post* preferences at every level of education; in other words preferences which were manifested by subjects after they had reached any particular level of education. The data (table 4.17) confirm the existence of adaptive preferences in general, but they do not tell us to what extent the process of adaptation is prior rather than subsequent to the educational choices. By looking at the totals in table 4.17 we can see that, in general, working-class subjects score lower than middle-class

Table 4.17. *Mean points relative to preferred job scale and acceptable job scale, and average monthly earnings requested to accept a job offer (in 10,000 lire)*

	preferred job		acceptable job		earnings	
	working class	middle class	working class	middle class	working class	middle class
compulsory school	2.28	2.44	1.61	1.51	387	341
vocational school	2.53	2.58	1.50	1.74	373	359
istituto tecnico	3.13	3.25	2.02	2.26	369	352
liceo	3.73	3.61	2.27	2.43	395	402
university student	4.10	4.24	2.92	2.96	433	440
graduate	4.55	4.49	3.49	3.37	500	447
all	3.18	3.69	2.11	2.55	395	405

Source: youth unemployment sample

subjects on all three measures of preferences: preferred job, acceptable job, and requested earnings. We can therefore say that the probability of developing higher preferences is higher the higher the social class of origin. If, however, we examine the figures broken down by the educational level reached by subjects, the picture is considerably different: once education is controlled for, the class disparity in terms of preference disappears. As far as the requested pay is concerned, positive and negative differences are even reversed and working-class subjects, at several educational levels, express aspirations for higher pay than middle-class subjects.

The difference between the marginals and the figures broken down by educational level indicates that preferences are filtered by educational decisions and attainment.[54] Thus, although we can conclude that in general preferences are not distributed at random with respect to the social class of origin, we cannot say how exactly the process of adaptation occurs. If those reported in table 4.17 were *ex ante* preferences we could say that the class differences in ambition could explain part of the differences in education choices, especially those *inertial* differences not accounted for by constraints and probability of success.

[54] A large body of international literature suggests that education is a more powerful predictor of the level of occupation (although not of preferences) than the social level of one's family. The latter tends to influence the former through education. For an early and well-known study see Blau & Duncan (1967); for a recent assessment see Heath (1981).

However, we cannot be sure that this is really the case. For all we know, part of the process could be the result of the fact that those who, for reasons other than their initial preferences, did not or could not reach the next level would also be less likely to cultivate lofty aspirations, whereas those who did would be more likely to do so.

4.3.3 Summary

We can now summarize the results outlined in this section. The length of the temporal perspective – although only tentatively measured – appears to have a major effect upon educational decisions: the longer the perspective the higher the probability of going to university. For high school pupils, the effect of the temporal horizon is independent of class of origin, and seems itself to be formed independently from a wide range of other attributes. The findings also show that job and earnings preferences play an independent role in influencing educational decisions. However, differences were detected in the way in which subjects of different social origins respond to their own preferences, probably because they adjust to different sets of opportunities. A preference for higher earnings has the effect of sending more working-class children to university, but not more middle-class children. The latter probably expect to be able to reach their desired level of income somewhat independently of their level of education. By contrast, middle-class subjects act in direct conformity with their job preferences, whereas working-class subjects need something more, namely an unrenounceable level of job preferences, to be attracted by university studies. Finally, although for subjects who went to high school the probability of developing higher ambitions is largely unaffected by their class of origin, we cannot rule out the possibility that the same probability could well differ between classes if those subjects who chose not to go to high school were also taken into account.

Conclusions

Emerging from the last two chapters the reader may have acquired a general impression of complexity. This impression is essentially correct. Making sense of all significant differences in educational behaviour found in the evidence presented, by reference to a simple set of theoretical statements, seems problematic. The distribution of individuals across possible educational options appears to be the result of a dense combination of mechanisms.

If this is our first general conclusion, there would not seem to be much cause for satisfaction. Charles Taylor once argued that 'complexity', rather than being an excuse, may be a symptom of error, 'for any subject matter is complex in the light of a wrong theory once we try to apply it, in that we are forced to complicate our theory with *ad hoc* hypotheses' (1964: 271). Moreover – for quite separate reasons – a justifiable desire of scholars and laymen alike is that science, even if it enjoys (or suffers from) the mitigating adjective of 'social', should offer simplifying insights, leading us by the hand through the dismal intricacies of reality. Steven Lukes (1985) has even suggested that some degree of monomaniac obsessiveness is a desirable requirement for producing good results in the social sciences: those who have made significant contributions in the field 'have all been in their several ways, one-sided, one-eyed, exaggerating, unreasonable and unjudicious focusing obsessively on certain relationships or aspects of social life and blind to others. Indeed their very one-sidedness and obsessiveness is a precondition for whatever insight they attain' (p. 1163). Lukes' remarks were aimed at those whose theoretical reflections tend to acknowledge something worthwhile in many competing theoretical views and turn out to be 'too' reasonable and charitable at the expense of passion and innovative insights.

There is a further reason why a conclusion which claims 'complexity' could be suspect. The social sciences are often plagued by a form of criticism which attacks other people's work by pointing out that things are really more complex than they make out and that 'true, on the one hand, they dealt with X and Y, but on the other they have unforgivably omitted dealing with W and Z'. This is a standard objection which is bound to be always to some extent true as well as useless, for most of the time we are left in the dark as to why W and Z should be at all relevant to X and Y. The underlying view in this criticism is one of complexity as an essentially 'additive' result: on the one hand it charitably stresses the merits of some theoretical statements in whatever collection of statements, and on the other it laments that some are missing and that they should be added from some other collection to make the picture complete.

With such premises one could easily end up feeling paralysed whenever encountering the word 'complexity', let alone using it. In any case, given that that word does not always necessarily carry those unattractive connotations, one ought at least to feel somewhat uncomfortable in making the claim that educational choices are complex events – more complex than generally represented – and even more uncomfortable in believing, as I do, that they probably reflect a complexity which is a common feature of many other socially relevant decisions, not adequately allowed for by any one alone of the three approaches we met in chapter 1. This claim must be duly supported if the feeling of discomfort is to disappear.

First, it is a claim that rather than emerging from mere speculation is generated through empirical analysis. When the research reported in this book began, my personal obsessions – notably with rational choice theory – were considerably greater than they are now after having repeatedly stumbled into hard evidence. Second, it is not a weak claim whereby by simply piling up bits of different theories one would get a better picture of decision processes. Although still in a fairly preliminary way, the empirical results point towards the possibility of formulating, as well as the need to formulate, a theoretical, novel and empirically viable approach to decision mechanisms. In what follows, while summarizing the broad set of the empirical findings, I shall try to articulate such an approach.

Educational decisions are the joint result of three main processes: of

what one can do, of what one wants to do and, indirectly, of the
conditions that shape one's preferences and intentions. They are the
result partly of causality and partly of intentionality. It seems hardly the
case that decisions are generated by either of these two forces alone. The
form in which they combine to produce a given educational choice merits
some detailed attention.

The most basic model which can make some sense of schooling choices
consists in saying that *educational behaviour is predominantly the result of
constraints*. This statement expresses the basic features of the
structuralist approach. Subjects can only choose among a finite number
of options which are institutionally defined. In addition, they may
directly face constraints of an economic and cultural nature which can
further limit their opportunities. We could then proceed to suppose that
if the set of various constraints is broad enough to admit more than one
feasible option, subjects select one according to their preferences and
intentions. For the moment let us not be concerned with what these
preferences are. Suffice it to say that in this preliminary model we can
expect that, holding preferences constant, constraints make a difference
even if only for the subset of those who would have preferred some
option which the constraints did not allow.

Up to a point this model will do. We have seen that – *ceteris paribus* –
the variations of constraints modify the probability of making given
educational choices: subjects tend to act consistently with the intensity of
their constraints and a great deal of evidence shows that they take them
into account consciously, also by anticipating their future appearance.
Even in a structuralist model subjects cannot be seen as merely pushed. I
shall begin, then, by reviewing the effects of constraints.

Educational institutions shape the set of feasible options for everyone,
irrespective of their social background. They establish length of
compulsory education, types of high school, selective procedures and so
on. Subjects distribute themselves among options which are on offer, and
it would not make sense to ask why they did not choose a course of
education that does not exist. It may be an interesting question to ask
why a certain course of education does not exist – why, for instance, the
technical branch of middle school was abolished in Italy in 1963, in spite
of the fact that it had an increasing number of pupils (section 2.1.2). But it
is an entirely different question from asking why subjects choose one

particular option among those which are available, and it involves considering the decisions of social actors – such as government, parties, and unions – other than those who face the prospect of educational choices for the following year. The power to alter the feasible set does not lie with any one individual alone. It is exclusively in this broad and special sense that institutions 'explain' individual acts. To the extent to which the institutional set-up is of universal significance within a society (i.e. it applies to everyone indiscriminately), differences in individuals' educational behaviour *within* that society cannot be explained by the presence of institutions of a given form.

There is nonetheless one way in which institutions operate in a discriminating fashion, but rather than directly acting as constraints they do so by not lifting constraints which exist independently, for instance, by not providing economic aid or by indirectly increasing the costs of education through a particular selection system. Neither the Italian nor the British educational institutions provide economic support for poorer students at the crucial point at which they leave compulsory education. The Italian system, furthermore, still maintains the practice of keeping down children of poor academic performance, a fact that – as I have shown beyond any reasonable doubt (section 4.1.1) – has severe consequences in reducing the probability of a long educational career for anyone, but particularly for subjects of working-class origin.

More important than institutional constraints seem to be the economic constraints, which are indeed unequally distributed within most societies. These constraints play a crucial part in explaining educational decisions, particularly at the beginning of high school: the tighter they are the lower the probability both that education will be continued and, if continued, that it will be in the longer and more demanding types of high school. In this respect education can be seen as a consumption commodity subject to budget constraints.

The importance of the family budget is linked not simply to the current level of family income but also to the level expected in the future. We have seen clear evidence – by using father's age as a 'proxy' – that subjects are capable of responding *ex ante* to their expected level of economic constraints (section 3.3.2). One does not need to hit one's nose against constraints to perceive their presence.

There are relevant differences between the way in which working-class and middle-class families react to variations in income when deciding about their children's education: the lower the income the lower the probability that a working-class child will go to high school; if he or she does go to high school income is less relevant in determining which type of high school is chosen. By contrast, middle-class children are more likely to continue to high school even when income is low, but here the economic pressure is then felt on the choice of the type of high school: the lower the income the shorter or the less demanding the type of high school selected. This inter-class difference, which is matched by several others which we shall review shortly, cannot be adequately accounted for by the structuralist model with which we have started. It means that the effect of economic constraints of similar entity is also *filtered* by other mechanisms which are related to the class of origin and, possibly, to class-specific preferences. Before we come to the model that can make sense of this difference in the responsiveness of the social classes to income variations, we still have to take a few steps.

Cultural constraints – or the amount of 'cultural capital' children find at their disposal in the family – appear as generally less important than economic constraints, and, particularly for the working class, the latter seem to have a binding effect which overrides that of the former (section 3.2.1). Working-class children do not seem to be able to reach that point in which cultural constraints could make themselves directly felt. Only the most deprived section of the working class – constituted by Southern migrants – does seem to run into cultural difficulties. While in fact working-class migrant families send their children to high school as much as any other working-class family, they meet a less fortunate educational fate during the course of high school (section 3.3.1).

More generally, cultural constraints operate strongly mainly upon the ambitious and culturally ill-equipped section of the middle class whose children seem to share a fate which, *mutatis mutandis*, is analogous to that of the migrants' children in the working class. This part of the middle class seems to act on the basis of a lexicographic preference for having its children sent to high school, a preference that, if not accompanied by an adequate amount of 'cultural capital', leads them to a high risk of failure and of abandoning high school before completion. In this case cultural constraints really seem to act as a barrier which is encountered without foresight. They explain why children of poorly educated middle-class families are pushed out of school. They do not explain, however, the reasons why the middle class seems to be so light-heartedly prone to expose its children to failure – especially if compared with the extreme caution shown by the working class, whose children, if they go to high school at all, are comparatively more likely to make it through to the end. Once again the structuralist model can explain educational behaviour only up to a point.

Let us now take a further step and introduce a second model, which, unlike the previous one, essentially refers to intentional rather than causal processes. In deciding about their education subjects take into account *the expected probability of success of a given course of action relative to the other available options.* Here we are in the realm of the 'economic approach to human action', which, as we have already pointed out, constitutes a particular version of the rational approach to action. In this model the assumption is that – once the effects of constraints on opportunities are taken into account – what really discriminates between available alternatives is a standard preference for 'the more the better', where the more refers essentially to material benefits. It does not necessarily deny the explanatory value of constraints, whose role it can easily incorporate, but it stresses that – beyond constraints – what explains differences in individual choices are the differences in the structure of the expected rewards that can fulfil that basic preference. This model too exhibits considerable explanatory power.

I have been able to analyse the effects of the expected probability of success in two ways. The *first* was to measure the effects of past school achievement on future educational choices: independently of social class and of specific economic constraints, the higher the perceived level of personal ability – 'signalled' by school reports, failures and successful survival in the educational system – the higher the probability that education is continued for longer periods and in more demanding types of school (section 4.1).

This evidence has relevant theoretical implications. If subjects' decisions were in fact governed to any large extent by class-specific values or preferences one would expect to find no response to changes in the perceived probability of success: if, in other words, education were either rejected or pursued 'at all costs', variations in the structure of expected rewards should not be accompanied by variations in behaviour. The fact that this is not the case unequivocally shows that, irrespective of other conditions, if subjects have good reasons to feel confident about their ability in school they tend to adjust to that feeling and opt intentionally for longer educational careers.

We should add, however, that although the working and the middle class are both responsive to variations in the perceived level of ability, the former group appears to be considerably more responsive than the latter, not to school success but to school failures. If a working-class child suffered from a failure at middle school his probability of not choosing the *liceo* is no less than one and a half times greater than the corresponding chances of a middle-class child. Subsequently, if high school is chosen and a failure is suffered during its course, a working-class child has nearly three times as many chances as a middle-class child of opting out as a consequence. The greater *caution* of working-class families – which seems to apply to political choices too (cf. Przeworski 1985) – emerges once more.

The data were not particularly helpful in explaining the reasons for these inter-class differences in responsiveness. However, when these differences are compared with several other inter-class differences encountered throughout the analysis there seems to be a well-grounded suspicion that there are other mechanisms at work which curb or enhance responsiveness to probabilities of success – as well as to economic constraints – and which cannot be explained *prima facie* either by the structuralist model or by a rational choice model. Although the fact that subjects *are* responsive to the level of ability irrespective of their class of origin indicates that class-specific values or preferences cannot constitute a generalized explanation of educational decisions, the inter-class differences in the intensity of the responses nonetheless suggest that they could still be effective to a limited extent: depending on which social class we focus on, it could either be that relatively more subjects in the middle class feel a greater normative pressure to resist the temptation to abandon school after a failure or, on the other hand, that relatively more subjects in the working class do not attach as high a value to education.

The *second* way in which the effects of the probability of success were measured was by considering labour market prospects. The specific hypothesis here was that education, besides representing a consumption commodity subject to budget constraints, also has an investment value and, *ceteris paribus*, is acquired in greater quantities the higher the expected returns. If education were just a consumption commodity then variations in its likely benefits should not be relevant. A wide range of evidence was presented to show that subjects do indeed choose their education consistently with the labour market prospects they are likely to observe in the area where they live (section 4.2.1). This evidence further reinforces the idea that individuals, irrespective of many other conditions, are capable of purposeful action.

In this case too, however, there are several indications that there are limits to the explanatory value of the 'economic approach to human behaviour'. First there is a problem of *supra-intentional* causality generated by a 'game' where there is no stable solution. The benefits of education that a subject can expect also depend on the educational decisions made by everybody else: for any one level of education the chances of finding employment and the level of wages are negatively correlated with the number of people reaching that particular level. The problem, though, is that for any one subject it is very difficult to act strategically and make the right guess as to the number of people who are likely to stay on to the next educational level and compete later on in the labour market. If the predominant expectation is that a lot of people are going to stay on, it becomes relatively less worthwhile to continue one's education, with the result that fewer people than initially expected will actually stay on. Processes of supra-intentional causality of this kind mean that – in spite of the capacity to act purposefully – there are situations in which subjects genuinely are not in a position to choose on the basis of *the* right expectations. This process can also perhaps make sense of the evidence highlighted by the 'parking theory', where in markets with fewer opportunities people end up acquiring more education, for in such markets those who achieve a higher level of education obtain a relatively greater advantage and can compete for a less limited number of job openings.

The second limit which emerged from the evidence depends on how exactly the rational choice model which we adopt is formulated. In the formulation put forward by Becker (1976), what count are essentially the expected rates of return: if one is black, female, or handicapped then one is likely to be paid less and have greater difficulties in finding a job. Thus, rational individuals in these positions can be expected to invest less in education. The point here is not really that being in these positions modifies one's personal preferences. Preferences, in this approach, are largely irrelevant, for they are considered to be stable over time and above all similar among different individuals. In the course of the analysis we have met with strong evidence which runs counter to this view.

Very telling in this respect are the interactions between subject's sex and social class of origin. Whereas women of middle-class background were found to be less prone than their male counterparts to go to high school, women of working-class origin were found to behave exactly in the same way as men of their social origin. According to Becker's model one should infer that between men and women of working-class origin there is no difference in the expected returns from education, while such a difference existed at the expense of middle-class women as compared with middle-class men.

Exploring women's labour force participation rates broken down by class we were able to see that there are very significant differences (table 4.11): women of working-class origin who achieved a high school diploma are both more frequently to be found in paid employment and devote more hours to it, to an extent which is very similar to that of men of whichever social class. Thus, in a sense it is correct for them to expect higher returns. However, the stress should fall on *expectations* rather than on objective possibilities of achieving significant returns once on the labour market, for these – it would seem reasonable to believe – would be there for women of middle-class origin too if *they planned* to pursue them. In conclusion, this evidence seems to suggest that educational choices vary not only as a consequence of variations in returns, but also as a consequence of variations in the expectations and plans that a subject entertains about his or her life. A woman may decide to acquire more education not only because objective prospects for women are encouraging, but also because she can count on her resolve to take full advantage of these possibilities after she obtains her diploma.

This evidence is significant because it simultaneously suggests (1) that preferences and life-plans are important over and above changes in the reward structure and (2) that, in part at least, they are not equally distributed between the classes. Let us take these conclusions one at a time.

It is possible to hold the view that all our preferences are causally shaped. Thus, action would intentionally follow from our preferences, but in turn these would be causally shaped and constrained by the outside world we live in. It is also plausible to believe that we may sometimes be aware of the causal influences on our preferences and able to interact with them, to the point of exercising some control over the relevant processes. However, it would be an impossible task – as well as a useless one from the point of view of a social scientist – to try to map the potentially infinite set of causes to which we are randomly exposed or to which we may intentionally expose ourselves. The only preferences whose explanation is crucial for the social sciences are those which are shaped according to some social pattern. But preferences which are generated at random with respect to relevant social conditions have to be taken as given, and action must be accounted for exclusively as the intentional product of these preferences.

This leads us to introduce a third explanatory model: *educational choices result from how subjects plan their future lives*, irrespective of whether these are primarily based on economic preferences and irrespective of relevant social conditions that could shape preferences behind the subjects' backs. In the last section of chapter 4, I was able to show that preferences whose origin cannot be traced to social class of origin or to other unevenly distributed social attributes play a part in explaining educational choices. The most basic condition for planning one's life, i.e. the length of the time perspective within which a subject projects him or herself into the future, was shown as having a dramatic effect on the probability of going to university. Similarly, the degree of one's ambitions relative to one's career has very much the same consequences. In essence, what one *wants* to do does count.

However, what is striking is not so much that subjects are capable of manifesting purposeful behaviour as the fact that the spectrum of possible actions associated with any given preference is modified by differences in opportunities: thus, within the same social class of origin, more ambitious preferences result in more ambitious educational decisions, but, between classes, the same preference acts in a different direction and with a different intensity. A middle-class pupil with a preference for an interesting job is significantly more likely to go to university than those other middle-class pupils who do not have such a preference, whereas for a working-class pupil going to university is associated with that preference only when it is held to be unrenounceable (section 4.3.2). Similarly, a preference for higher earnings is associated with a higher probability of going to university only when it is entertained by working-class subjects, for middle-class subjects probably enjoy more opportunities of satisfying that preference without necessarily gaining higher educational credentials.

Here, the explanation of educational decisions comes full circle and the third model, higher-order purposeful behaviour, brings us back to the model we started with – i.e. constraints as the key variable. The question is now whether the models we have sequentially reviewed can be merged in one single explanatory apparatus. Given that each of them separately can make theoretical sense of different empirical findings and that all together can account for a large part of the empirical findings, this question is indeed central.

The three models we have considered so far are all to varying degrees based on an *intentional agent* capable of purposeful behaviour. Even when the focus is on constraints as in the structuralist model the evidence suggests that actors evaluate them rather than being mechanically pushed by their presence. Thus at the centre of an overall explanatory model we must place subjects' preferences and life-plans. Let us postpone a little longer the problem of how these preferences are generated and concentrate on their general features.

Life-plans and preferences can be seen as including a basic set of elements such as the length of the time perspective on the basis of which subjects project themselves into the future and expectations concerning the intensity and quality of their working career as well as their cultural and economic ambitions. A useful way of representing educational and other preferences within a population is to imagine that they are distributed along a bell-shaped continuous line: at one extreme we have those who entertain life-plans which strongly exclude education, verging on a lexicographic preference for other options; at the other extreme there are those whose life-plans contemplate education 'at all costs'. Most subjects will tend to be distributed somewhere between these extremes and we can expect the distribution to be skewed towards the latter extreme (figure 5.1). In other words, we can expect that more people would have a general interest in education, but they would initially tend to be somehow uncertain about whether or not to pursue that interest and up to what level of education. In other words, fewer people would tend to seek education taking little or no account of other circumstances.

The next step is to suppose that that distribution of life-plans is *filtered* by constraints which may limit the opportunities for their fulfilment. In certain circumstances constraints can be of a binding nature and, irrespective of preferences, make some options altogether unfeasible. Thus, planning a life with no education is considerably more difficult when the institutional set-up enforces some degree of education; similarly, a life-plan that contemplates higher education can require unacceptable sacrifices when subjects are in conditions of extreme poverty. When binding, constraints necessarily dominate the explanation of behaviour and annihilate the possibilities of fulfilling one's preferences intentionally.

Except for extreme circumstances, however, the effect of constraints on opportunities is not binding but is better represented as a cost. The more severe the constraints the higher the costs of certain options relative to others and the higher the sacrifices required to be able to choose them. Whether or not a certain level of costs is met partly depends on the point of the preference distribution at which subjects are located. For instance, the more unrenounceable the appeal of an interesting working career the higher the probability of going to university, irrespective of all other conditions.

The final outcome, though, also depends on a second filtering process which involves the evaluation of the expected probability of success of choosing a given educational option. The higher the probability of success – which is variously assessed by subjects through their perceived

Figure 5.1 *Hypothetical distributions of educational preferences*

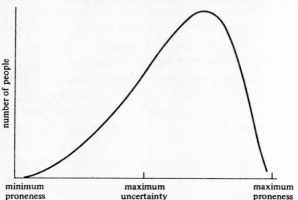

number of people

minimum proneness   maximum uncertainty   maximum proneness

level of ability and through the labour market prospects – the higher the attractiveness of the cultural and economic benefits associated with education.

The conclusion of this general model is that the closer the subjects are to the extremes of the basic preference distribution, i.e. the higher their basic determination either to leave education as soon as possible or to stay on as long as possible, the less the constraints and the probability of success affect their decisions. Correspondingly, the closer the subjects are to the middle point of the distribution, where the uncertainty of one's preferences towards education is maximum, the higher the influence of those circumstances which determine the rewards associated with education. Thus, for example, given the same level of constraints and expected benefits, subjects with more ambitious life-plans are more likely to seek a longer educational career; similarly, given the same level of ambition, the lower the constraints and the higher the expected returns the higher the amount of education that will be acquired.

Although the statistical models I have used unproblematically assume that all relevant factors in the decision process – constraints, probability of success, and preferences – are additively related by possible trade-offs, we can imagine conflictual and uncertain situations arising in which the crucial factors tend to diverge dramatically and in which decisions become problematic: thus, a child with scarce economic resources, a good school performance and a reasonably high preference for continuing his education is, when facing attractive immediate work prospects, likely to meet a painful basic decision as to whether to let his or her preference govern. Similarly, a child with sufficient economic resources, some ambitions for a future career, good immediate employment prospects and a not very brilliant performance at school would have to decide whether or not he could seriously cultivate his ambitions further in the face of discouraging circumstances.

This model differs from the standard economic model in two respects. One is essentially a matter of emphasis; the other is more substantive. The first is that the economic model is generally more reluctant to attach any great importance to budget constraints for, when the returns from investing in education are high enough, people in the economist's ideal world should be able to overcome the lack of 'internal financing' by borrowing money. As it turns out, though, this possibility is readily available only in few countries and, above all, people seem reluctant to view education exclusively as an investment commodity. The second is that, unlike 'the economic approach to human behaviour' (Becker 1976), this model takes into account the relevant effect of preferences, over and above those 'built-in' preferences which are supposed to adjust mechanically to variations in the objective feasibility of returns. With respect to the latter feature it also differs from Boudon's model (1974); this is essentially an expansion of the economic model which takes into account a socially stratified structure of costs and benefits (see below for further discussion). Empirically, furthermore, it differs from Boudon's approach because it allows for an effect of cultural capital on educational opportunities, which, however limited, seems to affect the most deprived section of the working class as well as some sections of the middle class. Yet, as I have presented it so far, this general model shares with each of these approaches, Becker's and Boudon's, both the centrality of rational-intentional choice and the lack of concern with the formation of preferences in general and, more particularly, with the presence of *behind-the-back* mechanisms which might conceivably contribute to their genesis.

After a long postponement it is time to face the crucial question of whether it is simply by postulating a fully intentional agent – subject to constraints and adjusting to the expected level of probability of success – that we reach a satisfactory explanation of educational decisions. Although we can generally expect that people's behaviour is typically the result of intentional choice taken on the basis of preferences and cost-benefit calculations, we can nonetheless ask both (1) whether there are instances of behaviour where the selected option is directly and *atypically* caused by sub-intentional mechanisms and (2) whether there are socially significant causes that shape people's intentions *behind their backs*. The answer to this twofold question must go through a preliminary review of the empirical differences found in the course of the analysis and which looked more resistant to being explained by postulating the general model we have considered above.

First of all we have to clear away an hypothesis which has been repeatedly put forward to explain educational as well as other socially relevant individual decisions. All the evidence I found goes strongly against the idea that *traditional values* play any role in accounting for educational choices, for those groups whose behaviour could be suspected of being governed by such values do not seem to behave in any way consistently with that suspicion. If one expected traditional values to keep women away from education, one would be disappointed to find that working-class girls behave in the same way as boys of their social background. If, somewhat similarly, one expected people from a less developed society to be traditionally less keen on education, then one could hardly make sense of why Southern Italians – whether boys or girls – are more rather than less prone to pursue longer educational careers than their Northern counterparts. Also when they migrate, they do not show any pattern of educational behaviour which could be plausibly interpreted as deriving from traditional values.

The major empirical differences which do not seem to fit the general model we have elaborated are related to other dimensions, particularly to the social class of origin as measured by father's occupation. We have already encountered two interesting differences along these lines, indicating that working-class children are more responsive both to variations in family income and to bad school reports. The most important difference, though, was found by looking at the net effects associated with father's occupation (section 3.2.3): independently of cultural and economic constraints, of ability and labour market prospects, there seems to be a specific effect whereby working-class children are less likely to stay on both at high school and at university. At the same time, middle- and upper-class children are generally more prone to stay on both before high school and at university, but they seem comparatively more likely to drop out during high school. Furthermore, there is a basic proneness of all classes to avoid the *liceo*, except for the upper class, which seems strongly attracted by this type of school.

The fundamental question is whether this set of differences is better explained by assuming further opportunity costs specific to the social class of origin which would not be allowed for by the variables specified in the models, or by assuming the existence of other mechanisms which have more to do with the conditions in which subjects' preferences are formed.

Boudon has chosen the former line, which does away with preferences and class values entirely; educational ambition would differ between classes, not because some non-rational mechanism is governing the processes through which it comes to be formed, but essentially because ambition itself would be a function of class-specific costs and benefits. In this model, one should not only take into account family income, academic ability, and labour market prospects, but also the *social* costs and benefits associated with the distances in status which children from different social classes have to travel in order to reach a given level of education: from the point of view of upward social mobility, according to Boudon, a working-class child aiming at university would face both higher costs and lower benefits *relative* to his or her point of social departure. By contrast a middle- or upper-class child aiming at university would face lower costs and also expect relatively higher benefits. To look at the same process from the point of view of downward mobility, a working-class child would suffer lower costs than a child from the other classes when leaving school earlier, because the prospects of demotion would be lower for the former than for the latter.

The main implication to be derived from this model is that – even assuming ambition to be constant throughout the social ladder – in order to bring about the same educational choice each class needs different incentives: for instance the higher the educational level aimed at, the relatively higher the income, the level of ability and the labour market returns required to 'convince' a working-class child to reach that level. Thus, one does not really need to postulate different levels of ambition to explain why the social classes have specific differentials in educational decisions.

Most of the findings summarized above do not generally contradict this model: bad school reports are more effective for working-class subjects than they are for middle-class ones; working-class subjects need a greater dose of job ambition to choose university, and, above all, every social class shows an *inertia* which is consistent with the predictions of the model. The overall pattern of such inertia (cf. section 3.2.3), however, strongly suggests the presence not so much of adaptive as of *over-adaptive* behaviour, i.e. subjects tend either to try *too little* or *too much* relative to what their respective constraints and probabilities of success would indicate as advisable.

Thus, even if Boudon's model were correct, the effect of the differential social costs could be better understood, therefore, as activating not so much a process of rational adaptation implying optimal and conscious adjustment as one of *behind-the-back* preference formation, which would result either in excessive caution, within the working class, or in excessive boldness, within the other classes. In section 3.2.3 we considered several hypothetical mechanisms that could plausibly govern the effects of constraints on preferences rather than on opportunities: in the working class there could be cognitive constraints which would inhibit the emergence of certain preferences or a general sense of risk aversion acquired through difficult past experiences. In the upper class there could be a strong normative pressure deriving from restricted reference groups. Furthermore, in all classes, a psychological intolerance of ambiguity could prejudice fine preference tuning.

Quite apart from the empirical signs, there are theoretical reasons that suggest that Boudon's model may be more than marginally inadequate in accounting for educational choices. Boudon does not go into much detail when explaining what exactly are the latent social costs and benefits to which the class-specific ambition could be reduced via a process of rational adjustment. He mainly mentions social and psychic costs related to reference groups and family solidarity. Costs would be higher the lower the social status because by choosing a prestigious curriculum or by going to university children could endanger their bonds with friends and relatives. However, saying that costs of this kind are higher does not also imply, as Boudon suggests, that 'the higher the social status the higher the anticipated benefits' (Boudon 1974: 30) associated with a given level of education. Precisely on the basis of initial social distances one could infer the opposite, i.e. that relative to their point of departure the benefits in terms of social mobility of a university degree are higher the lower the social status.

When there are discouraging circumstances – such as a low income or bad school performance – it may well be true that a working-class subject may find it relatively easier to leave school also because he faces lower social sanctions in doing so. The relative weakness of sanctions, however, could simply provide greater scope for *ex-post* rationalization of what nonetheless remains a non-desirable outcome. The idea that subjects may be maximizing on the basis of 'psychic' costs might be just to impose an *ad hoc* rational choice explanation on mechanisms that are not necessarily rational. Furthermore, in the absence of discouraging circumstances, there is no reason why children of a lower social background should not find education *at least* as attractive. Working-class families, in contradiction to the predictions of Boudon's model, do not need a greater income increase to compensate for their supposedly greater losses in terms of solidarity in order to modify their probabilities of staying on in high school: the *same* income increase brings about a greater positive probability change in the working than in the middle class. This greater elasticity of education with respect to income variations in the working class could suggest several possibilities (cf. section 3.2.2), but certainly not that benefits are lower. In particular, it could suggest that the distribution of basic preferences for education in the working class is less skewed towards the extreme where education is a lexicographically superior option and that subjects are generally more uncertain (figure 5.2). Moreover, we have seen that a preference for high income in the future leads to a higher proneness to go to university *exclusively* when entertained by working-class subjects, and we have concluded that middle-class subjects with a similar preference are likely to have relatively better opportunities for high earnings even *without* a university degree (section 4.3.2).

The conclusion could thus be that the different social costs and benefits to which social classes are exposed could run against each other: the working class may feel weaker sanctions but it may also have higher relative benefits from education because of the longer mobility jump that this could provide and because of the absence of alternatives. Conversely, the middle class may feel a stronger normative pressure to stay on 'at all costs', but at the same time, if these costs become too exacting, it can more easily have recourse to alternative routes for preventing social

Figure 5.2 *Hypothetical distributions of educational preferences broken down by social class.*

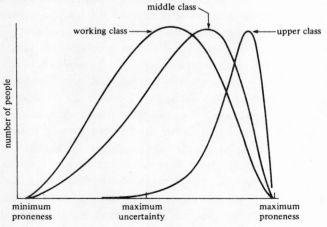

demotion. If this were the case we could not *a priori* predict the sign of class differences in the educational behaviour of fully rational agents. The opposing forces could even offset each other and we would then expect to find *no* relevant unexplained class differences beyond those accounted for by the variables specified in the statistical models, and almost certainly no differences that bring educational behaviour to the extremes.

But given that we do find such differences, the conclusion must be different, for even the expanded version of the rational choice model we have elaborated above will not do by itself. Before we draw such a conclusion, however, let us briefly recall two further signs that the filter of constraints, in this case cultural constraints, could shape preferences themselves rather than simply and directly altering the opportunities for their fulfilment. These were found in some particular effects that parents' education has on schooling decisions. One such effect is that at the two opposite extremes of parental education the capacity to respond to differences in labour market prospects appears as considerably reduced: children with either an illiterate or a highly educated father are less sensitive to employment and earning prospects when deciding about their education (figure 4.1, section 4.2.1). At the highest level of parental education families are more likely to consider children's education as a necessary consumption commodity which has to be acquired irrespective of the level of expected economic benefits. In this case, parents' education could be seen as shifting the distribution of basic preferences towards the extreme of maximum educational proneness. At the lowest level of parental education, by contrast, the effect of an almost complete lack of cultural capital might be not so much to inhibit the opportunities for fulfilling pre-existing preferences or to shift them towards the extreme of maximum dislike for education, but rather to limit the capacity to process the minimum necessary information to be able to *form* preferences themselves.

The second effect of parents' education that suggests the presence of *culturally determined preferences* is the following: within the working class, the level of parental education – while it affects neither the general choice of whether to stay on at high school nor the probability of dropping out during high school – nonetheless strongly influences the type of high school chosen and, to a lesser extent, whether university is chosen. It would therefore seem that here parents' education does not measure the effects of the basic endowment of cultural instruments which children meet in their families and which could limit their learning ability, as the effect of culturally determined preferences and life-plans.

In this case too, it does not seem plausible to believe that a working-class father with a relatively higher level of education would have his children sent to school more frequently than a less educated one *because* he feels somehow higher up on the social ladder and would feel a greater sense of demotion if he did not. It seems more plausible to believe that he will do so because generally less ignorant of the intrinsic as well as instrumental advantages of staying on at school for longer periods. It would, in other words, be more a matter of preferences than of cost-benefit calculation.

We are finally in a position to amend the overall model elaborated above and sum up our theoretical conclusions: subjects tend to evaluate rationally the various elements for making educational decisions, which include economic constraints, personal academic ability and expected labour market benefits. This process of evaluation takes place on the basis of their personal preferences and life-plans, which are partly the result of personal characteristics subject to socially random influences. Preferences and life-plans, though, are in turn 'distorted' by specific class biases which act as weights that subjects sub-intentionally apply to the elements of their rational evaluation. The formation of these class-specific preferences may be due to a variety of processes, such as a tendency to extremizing behaviour, a cautious 'view of the world' related to difficult past experiences, or normative effects of reference groups. Furthermore, *within* each class – particularly the working class – there are shifts of the distribution which depend on the amount of parents' education: poorly educated parents would push the specific class distribution further to the left, whereas more educated ones would correct it by shifting it to the right. The distribution of educational ambitions broken down by social class could look somewhat as in figure 5.2 and could explain why essentially rational agents from different social classes, even when confronted with the same circumstances, still manifest an inertia of their own.

The impression of complexity may, by this stage, appear less worrying than initially feared, and we can conclude by returning to our original question. So, *were they pushed or did they jump?* If anything, they jumped.

They jumped as much as they could and as much as they perceived it was worth jumping. The trouble, though, is that not all children can jump to the same extent and the number of pushes they receive in several directions, shaping their opportunities as well as preferences, varies tremendously in society. What does not seem to vary is that the pushes are likely to push in the wrong direction: wrong in general because of the strong degree of social inequality involved. But wrong in particular too, because several of those who are pushed upwards risk failures later on and are often in no position to make good use of the education they receive, other than for satisfying tenacious family pride; and because some of the others, those who are pushed downwards and do not simultaneously enjoy the relaxing gift of self-deception, are left wondering whether they could not have made a better job of it had they been given a better chance.

Appendix 1
The high school pupils survey

The survey was carried out during the school year 1977–8, by two research fellows, Luca Ricolfi and Loredana Sciolla, of the University of Turin under the supervision of Professor Guido Quazza.

The survey, which interviewed 1,031 high school pupils from Turin, was not only an academic initiative. In fact, besides the Facoltà di Magistero and the Facoltà di Scienze Politiche, three non-academic associations sponsored the initiative: Il Circolo della Resistenza (a cultural association of partisans), Il Centro Studi Piero Gobetti, and a progressive parents' association (COGIDAS). The aim of the survey was that of analysing the political and cultural orientations of high school pupils. The findings associated with the main purpose of the research project have been published in a book along with a full description of the various statistical and methodological details (Ricolfi & Sciolla 1980: 259). In what follows I have summarized the major points of that description.

The sample

The aim was to have a representable sample of the population of high school pupils in Turin. It was judged too costly and complicated to get a random sample of the pupils and to carry out the survey over a large number of schools. Therefore an alternative strategy was devised.

1. All schools were classified according to a 3×2 typology, combining the social composition of the school (whether it was predominantly upper, middle, or working class according to the data given by the school authorities) and the degree of 'politicization' (ranked as high or low according to factual criteria such as degree of internal election participation and number of political associations present within the

school). Six schools were then selected, one for each of the possible combinations.

2. In each school a number of classrooms were randomly selected, in such a way that the number of pupils included from each school was proportional to the number of pupils of the corresponding typology in the whole population; for example if all Turin schools which were ranked as 'middle class – low politicization' had 20% of the total number of pupils, then in the sample the classrooms selected from the school corresponding to that particular typology contained 20% of the pupils in the sample.

The interviews

A questionnaire of 78 precoded questions was then given in each classroom to the pupils who completed them individually and without the direct help of an interviewer. They could ask for clarification from the interviewers, who were present in the classroom. The questionnaires were then collected, checked and eventually returned if missing or mis-specified items were found. The rate of success was extremely high and only one pupil refused to fill in the questionnaire. The proportion of missing data was also kept within very low limits (2–3%). A further sign of the active participation of the pupils is given by the high proportion of those who filled in the blank space which is usually left for comments at the bottom of each questionnaire.

Appendix 2
The youth unemployment survey

The survey was carried out in December 1978 and led by three researchers, U. Colombino, F. Rondi, and myself. It was commissioned by the Regional Government of Piemonte. The main findings, along with a full description of the sampling methodology adopted, have been published in a book (Colombino, Gambetta & Rondi 1981); here I present a summary of that methodological description and a few further considerations concerning more specifically my own work.

The sample

The aim was that of having a sample representative of all those individuals aged 14–29 of both sexes who had registered in the special unemployment lists between 1 June 1977 and 12 June 1977 and who constituted the first large group of people to take advantage of the '285 Act'. We wanted to be able to assess what had happened to them in employment terms a year after they had started to look for a job. It was a cheap way of getting a sort of longitudinal survey where the only previous information available was that a year before the interview all subjects were unemployed and in search of a job.

Registration in the lists took place by communes, and since in Piemonte there are over a thousand communes it was not feasible to sample from all communal lists; this in fact would have meant actually visiting all the communes involved. A purposive p.s.u. of 28 communes was then selected, including Turin and its surrounding communes plus all chief towns of provinces and districts with more than 25,000 inhabitants. They included 64% – 18,774 in absolute terms – of the individuals of the original population of all communes. A final unit sample of 1,746 individuals was then randomly selected from the 28 lists.

The selection of a sub-universe was clearly biased against the small, mostly rural communes where the remaining 36% of the young unemployed were scattered. (Only 4% of the young people interviewed had an agricultural family background, whereas if the regional proportion of agricultural families had been respected the figure would have been 11%; the difference, however, might also be partly due to a lower propensity of young people in rural areas to register in the lists.) Thus the sample can be said to represent the metropolitan (Turin) and urban areas of the region.

Stratification and weighting

The sample was stratified according to four groups, reflecting the official designations the young people had acquired after a year in the lists:

(1) young people who had found a job through the special unemployment lists
(2) young people who had turned down a job offered by the employment office
(3) young people who had found a job through the ordinary unemployment lists
(4) young people not in A, B or C.

The stratification was not carried out in proportion to size, with strata A and B oversampled to make sure that we had enough cases to assess the results produced by the Youth Unemployment Act. As a consequence the strata had to be weighted in order to restore the original sample–population proportions.

All analyses have been performed weighting each observation by a factor

$$W_h = n/N * N_i/n_i$$

where
$h = 1 \ldots 4$ strata
$n =$ individuals in the sample
$N =$ individuals in the population
$n_i =$ individuals in the ith stratum of the sample
$N_i =$ individuals in the ith stratum of the population
For a demonstration of how this factor restores the correct sample–

population relationship see Colombino, Gambetta & Rondi (1981: 184–7).

The interviews

The interviews were carried out in December 1978 by a specialized firm, whose work was directly controlled by the researchers. The interviews, which took approximately one hour each, were carried out at the subjects' homes by trained interviewers. Over 10% of the interviews were checked by telephone subsequently to ensure that they had actually been carried out and that some of the most relevant items had been correctly recorded. The rate of success was very high and 1,739 interviews were performed out of 1,746 names sampled.

Representativeness of the sample

The survey was designed to analyse employment conditions and occupational preferences of those young people who a year before (1) were unemployed and (2) had registered in the special unemployment lists. It was not designed to analyse educational behaviour. The 'secondary' way in which I use the data creates some problems, which cannot be completely resolved. In what follows they will be presented and some tests made as to the extent to which they might affect my results. The testing also has some relevant substantive implications.

Prima facie it would seem quite unlikely that the population from which the sample is taken could actually represent a sound source for the analysis of educational choices. It would be somewhat surprising if the individuals who were registered in the unemployment lists represented – as far as the variables that I use are concerned – a faithful image of the whole population aged 14–29 at that time in Piemonte, which could be considered as the population of primary concern in analysing educational decisions. The population to which the sample directly refers can be imagined as separated from its original population by two decisions that individuals had to make: the first concerns whether to enter the labour market, and the second whether to register in the unemployment lists. The subjects in the sample were all people who had answered both questions positively a year before being interviewed.

In general these two steps might have introduced in Population 3 (see figure A.1) three biases: the first in some of the independent variables irrespective of educational behaviour (for example relatively more women than men moved from P1 or P2 to P3); the second in some of the levels of educational characteristics (the dependent variable) irrespective of any independent variable (for instance relatively more people educated in vocational schools moved from Population 1 to Population 3); the third in a dependent variable in correlation with one or more of the independent ones (for example relatively more women *with* a vocational school education registered). The first and second type of biases need not concern us directly, because neither of them alters the effects as measured by multivariate analysis. It should be remembered that my analysis aims mainly at estimating the effects of the independent variables upon educational behaviour rather than at observing single variable means and distributions. The bias that might be more problematic for my results is the correlated one.

In general terms there is no way of knowing whether a correlated bias is contained in my data. The possibility of such knowledge would mean having access to better data, which would of course make redundant the use of those in question.

There are, however, encouraging signs which give some confidence in the data. There was only one choice which could be analysed on both samples, that between *liceo* and *istituto tecnico*. The two logit analyses performed on exactly the same variables on both the youth unemployment sample and the high school pupils sample give similar coefficients. Since there is no reason to expect the high school pupils sample to have the same bias as the youth unemployment one, it seems fair to conclude that as far as the particular variables that can be compared are concerned

Figure A.1 *Relationships between the youth unemployment sample and its original population*

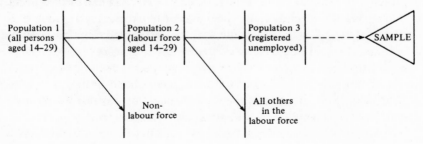

the youth unemployment sample is sound. However, it is not possible to jump to the further conclusion that, as a consequence, all educational choices not between *liceo* and *istituto tecnico* and all variables additional to those which could be used in both samples simultaneously (class of origin, parents' education and sex) would also produce unbiased estimates.

This rather surprising finding suggests that to some extent the two decisions which separate the actual population of the sample from the original population might have been taken randomly with respect to possible correlated combinations of education with class, parents' education and so on. As an explanation going beyond the statistical problems, one could consider the fact that the setting up of special lists led almost three times as many young people as normal to register in public unemployment lists; thus the novelty of the initiative might have exercised an attraction at random across the potential population and brought into the open different categories of people from the 'usual' unemployed.

The other test relative to the possible existence of a correlated bias in my data which I could attempt concerns sex and the choice of the type of school. According to a survey carried out in Piemonte in 1977, people from vocational schools are those who experience most difficulties finding a job, and among them women in particular (Federpiemonte-Doxa 1978: 54). This group of unemployed people usually look for non-manual routine jobs which are much in demand and much preferred to manual occupations. As a consequence, if we assume that people with greater unemployment difficulties are likely to have registered more frequently in the lists, we should expect to find in the lists (1) more people from vocational schools and among them (2) a relatively greater number of women than men. In this case the effect of being a female on the probability of going to vocational schools – which is one of the effects that sex has on educational behaviour according to my logit models (see section 4.2) – would be considerably overestimated: coming from a vocational school would increase the chances of being on the unemployment lists (second bias), and being a woman educated at a vocational school would increase them even further (correlated bias).

With the help of another source I managed to test this hypothesis, which clearly has substantive implications. The other source is a survey based on a random sample of 1,000 families carried out in Turin in 1979

Table A.1. *Level of education by sex in the 1,000 families sample*

	women	men	total	differences
middle school	.475	.531	.505	+ .056
vocational school	.150	.053	.097	− .097
istituto tecnico	.189	.204	.197	+ .015
liceo	.174	.185	.178	+ .011
university	.034	.028	.031	− .060
all	.456	.544	1.000	—

Table A.2. *Level of education by sex in the youth unemployment sample*

	women	men	total	differences
middle school	.282	.392	.328	+ .110
vocational school	.283	.093	.204	− .190
istituto tecnico	.238	.301	.264	+ .063
liceo	.145	.133	.140	− .012
university	.051	.081	.063	+ .030
all	.586	.414	1.000	—

(Martinotti 1982); I was given permission to extract some information from the data.

I selected the families with at least one child above 14 years of age (338 families) and considered the information concerning all children in the relevant age group (596 individuals between 14 and 30 years of age). With these cases I produced a cross-tabulation of sex by level of education and adjusted the distributions by age, applying to the original distributions of educational levels the age distribution of the young unemployed as a weighting factor (table A.1). There is some hope that this set of individuals might sufficiently approximate a random cross-section of the population to be compared with the data of my sample, though the fact that among the 596 individuals there were brothers – whose educational behaviour is correlated (Blau & Duncan 1967) – makes the whole test more uncertain. From the youth unemployment sample I produced an equivalent table (table A.2), selecting only those young people who lived in Turin (979 cases), as in the other sample.

Table A.3. *Father's education*

	1,000 families	youth unemployment
elementary	52.5	54.9
middle	18.9	21.8
vocational	4.1	5.2
high	17.1	13.0
degree	7.4	5.1
all	100.0	100.0

Table A.4. *Mother's education*

	1,000 families	youth unemployment
elementary	64.2	65.5
middle	19.2	24.6
vocational	3.8	2.4
high	11.0	6.2
degree	1.8	1.3
all	100.0	100.0

If we examine tables A.1 and A.2 it appears that the major overall difference is that among the young unemployed there are many more people from vocational schools and many fewer from middle schools, a result which is consistent with expectations. Furthermore, from the frequency distributions broken down by sex and from their differences, it can be seen that my data generally overestimate the effect of sex on educational behaviour and particularly on the choice of vocational schools: in the reference sample being a woman makes it 9.7% more likely to have been to a vocational school, whereas in the youth unemployment sample the same effect is as high as 19%. On the other hand, the 1,000 families sample seems to confirm the ordinal results of my analysis, i.e. that being a female positively affects going to vocational school more than any other educational decision.

The availability of some of the data from the 1,000 families sample also gave me the opportunity to answer a general question concerning the nature of my data and whose value is merely suggestive. The question is: how different is the socio-economic status of the youth unemployment families with respect to all families with children over 14 years of age?

It appears that on average the young unemployed belong to a lower

Table A.5. *Class of origin according to father's occupation*

	1,000 families	youth unemployment
upper class	11.0	6.0
middle class	27.3	23.6
self-employed	15.5	9.7
working class	46.2	60.7
all	100.0	100.0

Table A.6. *Father's area of origin*

	1,000 families	youth unemployment
North-West	43.3	37.9
North-East	8.0	9.7
Centre	5.3	3.7
South	39.6	44.2
abroad	3.8	4.5
all	100.0	100.0

socio-economic background, although the striking fact is that the difference is not particularly marked. Their origins are more frequently working class (table A.5); their family income is 10% lower; both parents are on average slightly less educated and the fathers are more frequently immigrants from the South of the country (tables A.3, A.4, A.6). This suggests that the movement from Population 1 – here represented by the family sample – to Population 3 – represented by the youth unemployment sample – might be correlated with social origins, in the sense either that fewer individuals from a higher socio-economic background entered the labour market, or that fewer of them, once there, registered on the unemployment lists.

Finally, we should say something about other possible biases which could result from age and cohort effects. In the sample there are young people from 14 to 29 years of age. If we take into account the fact that the longer the time since they left school the higher the probability of their finding a job and the lower the probability of their being on the unemployment lists, it follows that – among those who are in the sample – the majority of those who left school with a lower level of education are on average younger and reached that level of education in more recent years than those who stayed on and reached higher levels of education. Thus, for example, the university graduates in the sample are on average older than the high school graduates who stopped after high school, and they met the choice of whether to stop or stay on at university earlier. Because the overall tendency to stay on has increased over time (cf. table 2.1), when I analyse any given choice I group subjects who stayed on but had an overall lower probability of doing so because their choice was made closer to 1963 together with subjects who left, but had an overall lower probability of leaving because their choice was more frequently made in recent years. The consequence is that the models implicitly end up considering a measure close to an average probability of staying on over the whole period and that the constant terms in the models tend to be somewhere in between the constant terms that would be found if we compared the same cohorts facing the same choice: lower than that which would be obtained for the older cohorts and higher than that which would be obtained for the younger cohorts.

If one suspected further that there could be interactions between the specific period of the choice and the other independent variables, such as social background, these should be implicitly taken into account by the fact that I ran different models for each class.

A related bias could result from the fact that also among those who made the same decision there are subjects who met the decision point in different years; thus the model cannot take into account whether some of them made one particular decision rather than another also because they made it in a particular year, where labour market or other conditions might have been different.

If I had introduced age into the model, obviously I would have obtained a positive effect on the probability of staying on at school, but I would not have been able to distinguish what in that effect was genuinely due to year-specific factors from what was due to the selectivity of the unemployment lists. In principle I could have used secondary sources and weighed each case by applying the attendance rate in Piemonte specific to the year the choice was made. In principle this could have 'freed' age from the selectivity bias. But given that there are separate models by class, one would have needed year-specific attendance rates for each social class. Unfortunately, annual attendance rates are barely available in Italy for the whole country in some non-consecutive years, and they are not available broken down by class or region, let alone by both.

Appendix 3
Independent variables

In this appendix I consider only those independent variables which either required some particular work to be done or which need a more detailed description of their definition. I shall consider the following variables:

(1) per capita income (youth unemployment sample only)
(2) labour market indicators (youth unemployment sample only)
(3) preferences (both samples)
(4) social classes (both samples).

Per capita income of the family

In the questionnaire presented to the unemployed young people, subjects were asked to give the monthly income of their family; this was precoded as a level variable of nine possible categories (in thousands of lire these were: 0–150, 151–300, 301–450, 451–600, 601–750, 751–1,000, 1,001–1,500, 1,501–2,000, and 2,001 and above).

In the analysis I gave each case the value of the mid-point of the category (for the highest income class I took the arbitrary value of 3,000) and, in order to obtain the *per capita* (or per child) income of the family, I divided the mid-point value by the number of family members living in the same household at the time of the survey.

Unfortunately the question concerning the income of the family remained unanswered in many cases: while over the whole questionnaire the rate of missing answers remained remarkably low (2–3%), on this variable the rate of missing values was over 20% (377 cases). This was due partly to the ignorance of some of the subjects, who were normally not the heads of their families, and partly to reticence. In order to avoid such a heavy loss of cases in my multivariate analysis I decided to try to use linear regression to estimate the income of the missing families by

Table A.7. *Regression coefficients of the equation estimating family income*

predictors	coefficients
father's occupation:	
manager, entrepreneur, professional	1.61 (5.19)*
white-collar worker	1.11 (4.13)
blue-collar worker	0.55 (2.19)
menial occupation	−0.79 (1.72)
self-employed worker	0.48 (1.74)
mother works	0.71 (8.44)
father works	0.53 (5.70)
father's age (years)	0.01 (0.98)
father's education (years)	0.06 (5.40)
constant (*a*)	2.40

$R2 = 0.228$; $F = 42.46$; sample size = 1,362
* The t values are shown in parentheses

predicting it on the basis of other information I had about them. The variables I used were: five different levels of father's last occupation, father's and mother's labour market status (work/non-work), and father's age and education. All predictors, apart from father's age and education, which were measured in years, were dummy variables. The dependent variable I used was the number of the category of income to which the family belonged. In principle it would probably have been safer to use the mid point of each category, because this would have eliminated the non-linearity with respect to money resulting from the fact that not all categories referred to the same amount of money. *De facto*, however, a regression on the mid-point showed that the differences were very small and therefore for computational reasons I preferred to use the number of the category.

The results of the estimation (which are shown in table A.7) turned out to be satisfactory: all coefficients but father's age were significant and R squared was 0.228; I therefore computed the estimated values for those cases where the family income was missing. In the estimation I included father's age despite the fact that it was non-significant. The reason is that there are solid grounds both theoretical and empirical for considering age as a key explanatory variable, positively related to the level of income (see for instance Becker 1975 and Blaug 1970). In my data the effect of age came out positive, as expected, and the fact that it was non-significant has a plausible explanation. The average age of fathers in the sample is 55, and the great majority fall between 45 and 65; at these ages individuals in many countries no longer enjoy a rapid increase in earnings and as they become older will often face a decrease in their incomes (see Blaug 1970). The imbalance in the age distribution of respondents' fathers could therefore be the cause of the low significance of the coefficient.

I also introduced a further correction in the original data. The income which was recorded in the interview referred to the time of the survey, which did not necessarily correspond to the time of educational choice. As a consequence changes – notably retirements – had probably occurred in the interval between the educational choice and the interview such as to affect the income of the family. Since the data allowed me to reconstruct the parents' employment position at the time of the choice I corrected for this lag, by applying the same coefficients estimated for the missing values. Thus for all those cases where one or both parents worked at the time of the educational choice but not at that of the interview (45 cases) I applied the coefficients corresponding to the net effect on family income of having parents employed.

A similar problem concerned the number of family members used to calculate per child and *per capita* income; this number might have been different at the time of the choice with respect to the time of the interview. Unfortunately I could not correct for this possible difference and to obtain *per capita* income I had to use the number in the family at the time of the survey. This might have upwardly biased *per capita* income; the families are likely to have been larger in the past owing to the presence in the household of elder siblings and grandparents, both of whom – if via different routes – may have left in the mean time.

In the text, as a measure for family income, I have used per child income weighting older and younger children differently by attributing a factor of 2 to children below 14 years of age. In addition, I have also carried out tests using three other measures. In Table A.8 the whole set of results is shown. The measures of income are as follows:

(1) *per capita*
(2) per child
(3) per child, including only children below the age of 14
(4) per child, weighting children below 14 twice (used in the text).

Table A.8. *Tests on the effects of four measures of family income*

	CHOICE 1: Staying on to high school vs leaving					
	working class			middle class		
	coefficients	t-stat	LLR	coefficients	t-stat	LLR
income						
per capita	1.13	5.20	142.1	0.10	0.33	91.8
per child	0.96	6.29	156.1	0.36	1.52	94.0
per child < 14	0.90	5.47	144.6	0.25	0.90	92.5
per child-weighted	0.91	6.85	164.2	0.44	2.24	96.7

	CHOICE 2: Staying on during high school vs leaving					
	working class			middle class		
	coefficients	t-stat	LLR	coefficients	t-stat	LLR
per capita	0.89	2.50	133.2	0.50	0.97	58.6
per child	0.68	2.82	135.0	0.66	1.72	60.7
per child < 14	0.69	2.51	133.3	0.48	1.98	58.9
per child-weighted	0.49	2.45	133.0	0.26	0.87	58.5

	CHOICE 3: Staying on to university vs leaving					
	working class			middle class		
	coefficients	t-stat	LLR	coefficients	t-stat	LLR
per capita	− 0.06	0.31	104.2	0.62	2.40	155.7
per child	0.27	1.05	106.0	0.10	0.54	150.0
per child < 14	− 0.14	0.44	104.9	0.54	2.24	154.9
per child-weighted	0.18	0.83	105.4	− 0.04	0.30	149.9

The coefficients associated with each of these measures are reported in the tables, along with the log likelihood ratio of the corresponding model. In terms of fitting, the most outstanding improvement is obtained for either class by introducing per child income weighted in the first choice. Some improvement in the fitting is obtained also by *per capita* income, in the model concerning the third choice for the middle class where these measures increase the log likelihood ratio and bring the coefficient to a statistically significant level. On the whole, the pattern of results is such that it is only in the first choice that weighted per child income is outstandingly a better measure.

Geographical differences in employment chances and in returns to education

My original intention was to construct two dummy variables singling out respectively (1) all those areas of Piemonte where the probability of high-school-leavers finding a job was higher than average and (2) all those areas where the wage differentials between individuals with a high school certificate and individuals with a university degree were lower than average, or, in other words, where the pecuniary advantage of going to university was relatively lower. In both cases the condition singled out could be expected to decrease the probability of going to university and increase that of leaving the educational system. As the reader knows, the purpose of constructing the two dummy variables was to create indicators of the relative importance of material factors on educational choice. The two dummy variables singled out virtually the same set of areas – the correlation coefficient between the two variables is as high as 0.73 – although I used two different ways of creating them. Since the fact that they are the same set of areas has some theoretical relevance which I have discussed in the text it is probably worth explaining in some detail the procedure used.

The best way to determine those areas would have been through some secondary source unrelated to my data, but no such alternative was available for the entire region. As a consequence I had to use the data from the survey on unemployed young people in such a way as to obtain an indirect measure of the state of the labour market in the 16 different geographical areas – communes or groups of communes – from which the sample had been drawn all over Piemonte. This use of data was made possible because, as I have explained in Appendix 2, over half the subjects when interviewed had already found a job. In order to find out in which of the 16 areas high-school-leavers were at an advantage in terms of speed in finding a job I calculated a linear regression for subjects with a high school certificate but not enrolled in university. The dependent variable is constituted by a dummy variable taking value 1 if the subject was employed at the time of the survey and value 0 otherwise; the predictors were a set of personal characteristics and 15 of the 16 different areas coded as dummy variables (the left-out member was Turin, whose effect is incorporated in the constant term of the equation). All

Table A.9. *Regression coefficients of the equation estimating probability of employment of individuals with a high school certificate*

predictors	coefficients
age (years)	0.01(0.96)*
female	−0.05(0.84)
married	−0.16(1.47)
with children	0.28(2.17)
born in Piemonte (not Turin)	−0.05(0.18)
born in Northern Italy (not Piemonte)	−0.45(3.62)
born in Southern Italy	−0.14(1.88)
working-class family	−0.04(0.40)
self-employed family	−0.11(1.26)
upper-class family	−0.10(0.56)
parents' years of education	0.08(1.79)
accepts manual work	0.05(0.83)
areas:	
Turin belt	0.23(2.72)
Ivrea	0.42(1.82)
Pinerolo	0.41(1.86)
Vercelli	0.37(2.12)
Biella	0.27(1.52)
Borgosesia	0.46(1.04)
Novara	0.28(1.83)
Verbania-Domodossola	0.20(0.78)
Alessandria-Novi-Tortona	0.00(0.0)
Casale Monferrato	0.00(0.0)
Asti	−0.23(1.58)
Cuneo	−0.02(0.0)
Alba-Bra	−0.02(0.0)
Mondovi'	−0.10(0.30)
Fossano-Savigliano-Saluzzo	−0.06(0.0)
constant	0.374

$R^2 = 0.173$; $F = 2.819$ (significant 0.01); sample size = 378
* The t values are shown in parentheses

predictors, apart from subject's age and father's education, which are expressed in years, are dummy variables.

Since the coefficients relative to the areas are computed controlling for several personal characteristics there is reason to believe that the effects corresponding to each area are actually measuring the net effect of the demand for labour in that particular area. The regression results (see table A.9) show that the first seven areas listed appear to be associated with strongly and, most of the time, significantly increased chances of

Table A.10. *Areas of overlap between the two labour market indicators*

+ employment chances	no. of cases		earnings differentials
Turin belt	50		Turin belt
Ivrea	7		Ivrea
Biella	12		Biella
Novara	26		Novara
—	—		—
Vercelli	15	15	Novi Ligure
Pinerolo	5	9	Tortona
Borgosesia	2		

finding a job: all else being equal, a subject living in any of these areas could be expected to have a probability of being employed 31% higher than if he lived elsewhere, a substantial difference. The selection of areas appears to be plausible, for they are among the more industrialized of the region.

I could in principle have applied the same procedure to wage differentials by running two regressions on the wages of high-school-leavers and university graduates respectively, estimating the net effect of different areas on wages and then selecting those areas where the ratio between the two corresponding estimated values was higher than average. But the small number of employed subjects – especially graduates, of whom there were only 69 – made a multivariate estimation of any significance impossible. As a consequence I used a simpler and less satisfactory direct procedure, tabulating the average wages by level of education and by area, and selecting those areas where the ratio of graduates' to high-school-leavers' earnings was below average. There turned out to be six such areas out of 16, and four of these were also in the group of areas selected for having higher than average employment chances.

In these areas the pecuniary rewards attached to going to university were considerably lower than elsewhere in the region: here in fact an average graduate earned only 959,000 lire more per year than an average high-school-leaver, whereas in the rest of the region graduates earned 1,535,000 lire more than their less educated counterparts. In other words, in these six areas individuals holding only a high school certificate had earnings which were relatively closer to those of graduates than would have been the case elsewhere in the region. This situation was the product of both possible reasons simultaneously, i.e. in the six areas graduates earned less and high-school-leavers more. Unfortunately there is no certainty as to whether the difference in wage differentials is really due only to labour market conditions or also to differences in the characteristics of the subjects.

As an *ex post facto* control – i.e. not to make the selection but to check whether the selection made also held under more restrictive conditions – I ran two regressions on the wages of individuals of both levels of education including three variables as predictors: the age and the sex of the subject plus a dummy variable taking value 1 when the subject lived in one of the 6 selected areas and value 0 otherwise. The results were consistent with my rudimentary grouping, suggesting that even when sex and age were controlled for, in these areas graduates earned less and high-school-leavers more. However the F test on the whole fitting of the two regressions was in both cases below the acceptable level of significance.

Preferences

Data on respondents' preferences on school and work were available in both samples. In the sample of *high school pupils* I used two questions. The first question was 'Which, among the following, is for you the most important attribute of your future job?'

(1) high earnings
(2) success
(3) good career prospects
(4) interesting
(5) security of the job.

With this question I created three dummy variables, singling out answers 1, 2 and 3, and 4. The left-out member is made up of those subjects who gave the fifth answer. The second question was 'What is the role you will attribute to your future work with respect to your life?'

(1) the most important thing in life
(2) important among other things
(3) it's important only because it allows me to survive
(4) I haven't yet thought about work because it is too far ahead to say.

Selecting the fourth answer I created one dummy variable, in an attempt to measure subject's time perspective.

The variables I used to construct job and money preferences among the *unemployed young people* are contained in a special section of the questionnaire where the subjects were asked a set of related questions concerning:

(1) preferred hours of work
(2) preferred type of job (among 11 pre-defined types)
(3) type of job least preferred but still acceptable
(4) monthly earnings required to accept preferred type of job
(5) monthly earnings required to accept the lowest acceptable type of job.

The list of 11 types of job from which the subject had to choose both the preferred and the unacceptable job was presented not as a scale but as an unordered set of types of job. However, I ordered them in two equal scales – one for the preferred and the other for the acceptable job – and reduced the number of categories from 11 to five, compressing in particular the bottom categories concerning the manual jobs. The reason for this was that few of the subjects used in the analysis – who were the most educated half of the sample – selected their preferred job from the lower categories. The categories on the scale are as follows:

(1) manual unskilled (including menial occupations, manual unskilled work in industry, agriculture and services)
(2) manual skilled
(3) non-manual ordinary work
(4) non-manual skilled work
(5) managerial, professional, university teaching.

As far as the *earnings preferences* are concerned, in the analysis I considered the monthly pay the subject had indicated he would require in order to accept the preferred job.

Social class of origin

In both samples social class of origin is based on father's occupation at the time of the surveys (or the last occupation he had before retirement).

The variable in general is organized in the following way:

(1) upper class (higher grade professional, managers, entrepreneurs)
(2) middle class (salaried non-manual workers in skilled and routine occupations)
(3) self-employed workers (artisans, shopkeepers, farmers)
(4) working class (salaried manual skilled and unskilled workers, including foremen, salesmen, porters, messengers *et sim.*)

(People in the Army have been distributed according to their rank.)

The criteria adopted to define social class of origin separate first of all manual from non-manual workers; then, in both groups, dependent from independent; finally, in the non-manual-dependent group, I applied the criterion of prestige vs non-prestige occupation.

Appendix 4
Logit models: summary tables

Models A: youth unemployment sample

MODELS FOR THE WORKING CLASS
CHOICE: *staying on vs leaving*

	after compulsory education			during high school			after high school		
	coeff.	st.err.	T-stat.	coeff.	st.err.	T-stat.	coeff.	st.err.	T-stat.
parents' years of education	0.03	0.02	1.56	0.01	0.03	0.44	0.09	0.03	3.54
per child income (weighted)	0.91	0.13	6.85	0.49	0.20	2.45	0.18	0.21	0.83
father retired	-0.98	0.50	-1.96	-1.61	0.60	-2.65	0.06	0.98	0.06
subject migrated to Piemonte	-0.32	0.24	-1.34	-1.21	0.41	-2.94	0.55	0.40	1.37
father migrated to Piemonte	-0.30	0.22	-1.38	-1.47	0.37	-3.94	0.20	0.27	0.75
subject kept down	-1.11	0.17	-6.53	-1.94	0.31	-6.20	-0.05	0.27	-0.18
subject attended *liceo*	—			—			1.97	0.30	6.55
female	0.16	0.17	0.93	0.97	0.25	3.76	-0.38	0.24	-1.51
constant	-3.52	0.79	-4.44	0.76	1.23	0.62	-2.78	1.34	-2.07
log likelihood ratio	164.2			133.0			105.4		
degrees of freedom	7			7			8		
sample size	920			681			379		

CHOICE: *type of school*

	liceo vs istituto tecnico			liceo vs vocational school			istituto tecnico vs vocational school		
	coeff.	st.err.	T-stat.	coeff.	st.err.	T-stat.	coeff.	st.err.	T-stat.
parents' years of education	0.14	0.04	3.89	0.17	0.03	6.06	0.03	0.02	1.21
per child income (weighted)	-0.09	0.26	-0.34	0.38	0.21	1.79	0.47	0.16	2.94
father retired	-4.07	5.33	-0.76	-5.55	5.26	-1.05	-1.48	0.88	-1.68
subject migrated to Piemonte	0.16	0.47	0.34	-0.22	0.37	-0.58	-0.38	0.29	-1.33
father migrated to Piemonte	0.40	0.39	-1.02	-0.87	0.32	-2.80	-0.47	0.23	-2.05
subject kept down	-1.45	0.40	-3.63	-1.59	0.34	-4.71	-0.14	0.21	-0.65
female	0.34	0.41	0.84	-1.13	0.32	-3.48	-1.47	0.25	-5.95
constant	-1.87	1.62	-1.16	-3.08	1.30	-2.37	-1.21	0.96	-1.27

log likelihood ratio   166.4
degrees of freedom   15
sample size   583

MODELS FOR THE MIDDLE CLASS
CHOICE: *staying on vs leaving*

	after compulsory education			during high school			after high school		
	coeff.	st.err.	T-stat.	coeff.	st.err.	T-stat.	coeff.	st.err.	T-stat.
father self-employed worker	-1.22	0.32	-3.84	0.84	0.54	1.55	-0.04	0.30	-0.15
father upper class	0.31	0.66	0.47	-1.73	0.63	-2.71	0.32	0.39	0.81
parents' years of education	0.02	0.03	0.79	0.24	0.05	5.33	0.05	0.02	2.27
per child income (weighted)	0.44	0.20	2.24	0.26	0.30	0.87	-0.04	0.17	-0.30
father retired	-1.30	0.57	-2.28	-1.19	1.14	-1.05	-0.71	0.49	-1.46
subject migrated to Piemonte	-1.45	0.37	-3.96	-0.28	0.58	-0.49	-0.68	0.40	-1.70
father migrated to Piemonte	-0.95	0.32	-2.96	-0.18	0.48	-0.37	0.43	0.28	1.54
subject kept down	-1.03	0.28	-3.72	-0.74	0.42	-1.76	-0.17	0.24	-0.70
subject attended *liceo*	—			—			2.15	0.26	8.41
female	-0.81	0.31	-2.64	1.08	0.43	2.52	-0.37	0.23	-1.61
constant	1.48	1.22	1.21	-1.73	1.99	-0.87	-0.64	1.08	-0.60
log likelihood ratio	96.7			58.5			149.9		
degrees of freedom	9			9			10		
sample size	686			636			476		

CHOICE: *type of school*

	liceo vs istituto tecnico			liceo vs vocational school			istituto tecnico vs vocational school		
	coeff.	st.err.	T-stat.	coeff.	st.err.	T-stat.	coeff.	st.err.	T-stat.
father self-employed worker	0.19	0.45	0.42	0.49	0.34	1.45	0.30	0.29	1.02
father upper class	1.09	1.02	1.06	2.23	0.72	3.10	1.14	0.73	1.56
parents' years of education	0.09	0.03	3.18	0.13	0.02	5.23	0.04	0.02	1.81
per child income (weighted)	0.27	0.28	0.95	0.86	0.21	4.05	0.59	0.19	3.06
father retired	1.68	1.61	1.05	1.90	1.19	1.60	0.22	1.22	0.18
subject emigrated to Piemonte	0.78	0.64	1.22	1.21	0.47	2.59	0.46	0.43	1.06
father emigrated to Piemonte	0.34	0.49	0.69	0.86	0.36	2.37	0.52	0.33	1.57
subject kept down	-0.87	0.38	-2.27	-1.22	-0.29	-4.16	-0.35	0.25	-1.39
female	-0.25	0.21	-1.22	-1.78	0.33	-5.45	-1.53	0.31	-5.06
constant	-3.38	1.87	-1.80	-5.52	1.39	-3.95	-2.14	1.26	-1.70

log likelihood ratio 187.54
degrees of freedom 19
sample size 596

Models B: youth unemployment sample (models with three alternatives)

(Here the sample is in the restricted version used for testing the effects of labour market conditions and preferences.
See chapter 4, nn./28 and 49.)

GENERAL MODEL

CHOICE: *staying on to university vs leaving* (3 alternatives)

	university vs university & work			university vs leaving			university & work vs leaving		
	coeff.	st.err.	T-stat.	coeff.	st.err.	T-stat.	coeff.	st.err.	T-stat.
father working class	-0.28	0.37	-0.75	-0.23	0.26	-0.87	0.05	0.27	0.20
father self-employed worker	0.18	0.52	0.34	-0.57	0.35	-1.61	-0.75	0.39	-1.94
father upper class	-0.60	0.69	0.82	-0.02	0.49	-0.06	0.52	0.48	1.08
parents' years of education	0.00	0.03	0.00	0.06	0.02	3.16	0.06	0.02	2.82
per child income (weighted)	-0.03	0.22	0.13	0.09	0.16	0.59	0.12	0.16	0.71
subject attended *liceo*	-0.04	0.30	0.13	1.71	0.21	7.99	1.76	0.21	8.21
female	-0.61	0.30	2.01	-0.55	0.21	-2.53	0.06	0.22	0.27
areas with better labour market opportunities	0.03	0.35	0.08	-0.44	0.25	-1.78	-0.47	0.25	-1.87
scale for preferred job	-0.07	0.14	0.49	0.45	0.14	3.24	0.52	0.14	3.75
scale for acceptable job	-0.12	0.11	1.06	0.18	0.08	2.13	0.04	0.08	0.08
wage wanted for the preferred job	-0.01	0.01	0.70	0.01	0.01	1.05	0.02	0.01	1.78
constant	0.74	1.60	0.46	-4.77	1.12	-4.26	-5.51	1.14	-4.82

log likelihood ratio 285
degrees of freedom 23
sample size 733

MODEL FOR THE WORKING CLASS

CHOICE: *staying on to university vs leaving* (3 alternatives)

	university vs university & work			university vs leaving			university & work vs leaving		
	coeff.	st.err.	T-stat.	coeff.	st.err.	T-stat.	coeff.	st.err.	T-stat.
parents' years of education	0.01	0.04	0.24	0.11	0.03	3.15	0.10	0.03	3.17
per child income (weighted)	0.49	0.37	1.31	0.40	0.28	1.45	-0.09	0.25	0.35
subject attended *liceo*	-0.10	0.48	-0.20	1.67	0.34	4.80	1.77	0.34	5.09
female	0.00	0.47	0.00	-0.12	0.34	-0.34	-0.12	0.32	-0.39
areas with better labour market opportunities	0.68	0.50	1.35	0.05	0.35	0.15	-0.63	0.36	-1.73
scale for preferred job	-0.30	0.33	-0.90	0.21	0.24	0.88	0.51	0.23	2.21
scale for acceptable job	0.51	0.20	2.69	0.43	0.15	2.83	-0.08	0.13	-0.59
wage wanted for the preferred job	-0.03	0.02	-1.75	0.01	0.02	0.86	0.04	0.01	2.96
constant	-2.24	2.58	-0.87	-7.63	1.91	-3.98	-5.39	1.73	-3.12

log likelihood ratio 129
degrees of freedom 17
sample size 343

MODEL FOR THE MIDDLE CLASS

CHOICE: *staying on to university vs leaving* (3 alternatives)

	university vs university & work			university vs leaving			university & work vs leaving		
	coeff.	st.err.	T-stat.	coeff.	st.err.	T-stat.	coeff.	st.err.	T-stat.
father self-employed worker	0.05	0.54	0.09	-0.69	0.38	-1.82	-0.63	0.39	-1.58
father upper class	-0.75	0.64	-1.16	-0.36	0.47	-0.77	0.39	0.44	0.88
parents' years of education	0.00	0.04	0.00	0.02	0.03	0.97	0.02	0.03	0.92
per child income (weighted)	-0.24	0.29	-0.81	-0.36	0.21	-1.76	-0.12	0.21	-0.57
subject attended *liceo*	0.03	0.38	0.08	1.63	0.27	5.93	1.60	0.27	5.81
female	-0.97	0.42	-2.32	-1.00	0.29	-3.37	0.03	0.30	0.08
areas with better labour market opportunities	-1.16	0.49	-2.34	-1.25	0.37	-3.34	-0.14	0.33	-0.44
scale for preferred job	0.23	0.27	0.86	0.68	0.19	3.58	0.45	0.19	2.36
scale for acceptable job	-0.10	0.16	-0.64	0.04	0.11	0.42	0.14	0.11	1.21
wage wanted for the preferred job	0.01	0.01	0.71	0.01	0.01	0.84	0.00	0.01	0.42
constant	1.57	2.17	0.72	-1.73	1.50	-1.15	-3.30	1.57	-2.10

log likelihood ratio 159.9
degrees of freedom 21
sample size 394

Models C: high school pupils sample

CHOICE: *staying on to university vs leaving*

	general model			middle-class model			working-class model		
	coeff.	st.err.	T-stat.	coeff.	st.err.	T-stat.	coeff.	st.err.	T-stat.
father working class	-0.51	0.29	-1.78	—	—	—	—	—	—
father self-employed worker	-0.57	0.36	-1.59	-0.63	0.37	-1.70	—	—	—
father upper class	0.56	0.55	1.02	0.54	0.56	0.97	—	—	—
parents' years of education	0.03	0.02	1.19	0.03	0.03	0.86	0.02	0.04	0.55
subject kept down	-0.34	0.20	-1.70	-0.04	0.32	-0.13	-0.49	0.26	-1.87
subject with good school records	1.02	0.26	3.89	1.09	0.43	2.54	0.96	0.34	2.82
subject's age	0.17	0.07	2.28	0.17	0.12	1.33	0.16	0.09	1.71
subject attending *liceo*	3.81	0.54	7.11	3.48	0.59	5.90	3.45	6.28	1.34
female	0.20	0.21	0.97	-0.23	0.34	-0.67	0.45	0.28	1.62
subjects' preferred job attribute:									
interesting	1.02	0.25	4.01	1.38	0.41	3.37	0.78	0.33	2.37
good career prospects	0.37	0.38	0.95	0.79	0.59	1.34	0.11	0.52	0.22
high earnings	0.82	0.49	1.70	0.46	0.70	0.66	1.28	0.72	1.79
subject with short time horizon	-1.86	0.69	-2.75	-1.71	0.84	-2.03	-1.77	1.05	-1.68
constant	-3.85	1.23	-3.12	-3.87	2.04	-1.90	-4.07	1.50	-2.71
log likelihood ratio	323.2			159.2			112.0		
degrees of freedom	13			12			10		
sample size	669			325			344		

References

Acland H. 1980. Research as stage management: the case of the Plowden Committee. In M. Bulmer, *Social research and royal commissions.* London: Allen & Unwin.

Ainslie G. 1975. Specious reward. *Psychological Bulletin* **82**, 463–97.

Alberoni F. 1970. Aspects of internal migration related to other types of Italian migration. In C. J. Jansen, *Readings in the sociology of migration.* Oxford: Pergamon Press.

Alexander P. 1974. Rational behaviour and psychoanalytic explanation. In R. Wollheim (ed.), *Freud.* New York: Anchor Books.

Althusser L. & Balibar E. 1970. *Reading capital.* London: New Left Books.

Andorka R. 1978. *Determinants of fertility in advanced societies.* London: Methuen.

Antonelli G. 1980. Income distribution and labour factor quality. Model and applications at a regional level. Paper presented at the International Conference on School and Labour Market, *Fondazione Giorgio Cini*, November 1980. Venezia.

Archer M. S. 1979. *Social origins of educational systems.* Beverly Hills: Sage.

Arlacchi P. 1980. *Mafia, contadini e latifondo nella Calabria tradizionale.* Bologna: Il Mulino.

Armor J. D. 1972. Characteristics of black and white schools compared. In F. Moerteller & P. D. Moynihan (eds.), *On equality of educational opportunity.* New York: Random House.

Arrow K. 1973. Higher education as a filter. *Journal of Public Economics*, July.

Atkinson J. W. 1964. *An introduction to motivation.* Princeton: D. van Nostrand.

Atkinson J. W. & Feather N. T. (eds.). 1966. *A theory of achievement motivation*. New York: Wiley.

Balbo L. & Chiaretti G. 1972. Le classi subordinate nella scuola di massa. *Inchiesta* 2, 6, 23–38.

Banks O. 1976. *The sociology of education*. London: Batsford.

Banks O. & Finlayson D. 1973. *Success and failure in secondary school*. London: Methuen.

Barbagli M. 1973. Scuola e mercato del lavoro in Italia. In Atti del Convegno, *Scuola e mercato del lavoro*. Bologna: Il Mulino.

Barbagli M. 1974. *Disoccupazione intellettuale e sistema scolastico in Italia*. Bologna: Il Mulino.

Barr R. & Dreeben R. 1983. *How schools work*. Chicago: Chicago University Press.

Barry B. M. 1970. *Sociologists, economists and democracy*. London: Macmillan.

Beaton A. E. 1975. The influence of education and ability on salary and attitudes. In T. Juster (ed.), *Education, income, and human behaviour*. n.p.: NBER.

Becker G. S. 1975. *Human capital*. 2nd edn. Chicago: Chicago University Press.

Becker G. S. 1976. *The economic approach to human behavior*. Chicago: The University of Chicago Press.

Becker G. S. 1981a. Altruism in the family and selfishness in the market place. *Economica* 48, 1–15.

Becker G. S. 1981b. *A treatise on the family*. Harvard: Harvard University Press.

Benadusi L. & Gandiglio A. 1978. *La scuola in Italia: valutazioni e statistiche*. Firenze: La Nuova Italia.

Ben David J. 1966. The growth of the professions and the class system. In R. Bendix & S. M. Lipset (eds.), *Class, status and power*. London: Routledge & Kegan Paul.

Bernstein B. 1977. Social class, language and socialization. In J. Karabel & A. H. Halsey (eds.), *Power and ideology in education*. New York: Oxford University Press.

Binmore K. G. 1977. Mathematics, games and society. *Bulletin of the Institute of Mathematics and its application* 13, 257–300.

Blackburn R. M. & Mann M. 1979. *The working class in the labour market*. London: Macmillan.

Blau P. M. and Duncan O. D. 1967. *The American occupational structure*. New York: Wiley.

Blaug M. 1970. *An introduction to the economics of education*. Harmondsworth: Penguin Books.

Bogetti M. 1982. Famiglie e istruzione: diseguaglianze e rendimenti. In G. Martinotti (ed.), *La città difficile*. Milano: Franco Angeli.

Boskin M. J. 1974. A conditional logit of occupational choice. *Journal of Political economy* **82**, 389–98.

Boudon R. 1974. *Education, opportunity and social inequality*. New York: Wiley.

Boudon R. 1977. *Effets perverses et ordre social*. Paris: Presses Universitaires Françaises.

Boudon R. 1979. *La Logique du social*. Paris: Librairie Hachette. (English translation 1981: *The logic of social action*. London: Routledge & Kegan Paul.)

Bourdieu C. 1966. L'Ecole conservatrice. *Revue Française de Sociologie* **7**, 3, 325–47.

Bourdieu C. 1977. Cultural reproduction and social reproduction. In J. Karabel & A. H. Halsey (eds.), *Power and ideology in education*. New York: Oxford University Press.

Bourdieu C. & Passeron J. C. 1964. *Les Héritiers*. Paris: Les Editions de Minuit.

Bourdieu C. & Passeron J. C. 1977. *Reproduction*. London: Sage.

Bourricaud F. 1975. Contre le sociologisme. *Revue Française de Sociologie* **16**, 583–603.

Bowles S. 1970. Migration as investment: empirical tests of the human investment approach to geographical mobility. *Review of Economics and Statistics* **52**, 356–62.

Bowles S. & Gintis H. 1976. *Schooling in capitalist America*. New York: Basic Books.

Braverman H. 1974. *Labor and monopoly capital*. New York: Monthly Review Press.

Brown G. W. & Harris T. 1978. *Social origins of depression*. London: Tavistock.

Brusco S. 1982. The Emilian model: productive decentralization and social integration. *Cambridge Journal of Economics* **6**, 2, 164–84.

Busfield J. & Paddon M. 1977. *Thinking about children*. Cambridge: Cambridge University Press.

Camera di Commercio di Torino 1978. *L'occupazione irregolare in*

Piemonte. Torino.

Campbell D. T. 1979. Reforms as experiments. In J. Brymmer & K. M. Stribley (eds.), *Social research: principles and procedures.* New York: Longman.

Capriolo L., Luccitelli E. & Pratesi C. 1980. *Il lavoro sbagliato.* Torino: Rosenberg & Sellier.

Cartwright A. 1976. *How many children.* London: Routledge & Kegan Paul.

CENSIS 1976 to 1981. La situazione educativa del paese. *Quindicinale di Note e Commenti,* 1 January of the corresponding year.

Colasanti G., Mebane B. & Bonolis M. 1976. *La divisione del lavoro intellettuale.* Bologna: Il Mulino.

Coleman J. 1973. *The mathematics of collective action.* London: Heinemann.

Colombino U., Gambetta D. & Rondi F. 1981. *L'offerta di lavoro giovanile in Piemonte.* Milano: Franco Angeli.

Consiglio di Zona CGIL–CISL–UIL 1977. *Disoccupazione giovanile e piena sottoccupazione.* Roma: Seusi.

Contini B. 1982. The second economy in Italy. In V. Tanji (ed.), *The underground economy in the United States and abroad.* Washington: Lexington Books.

Corbetta P. 1975. Classi sociali e scuola media superiore. *Inchiesta* 5, 19, 43–7.

Cottle T. J. & Klineberg S. L. 1974. *The present of things future.* New York: The Free Press.

Craft M. 1970. Family, class and education: changing perspective. In M. Craft (ed.), *Family, class and education.* London: Longman.

Craig J. E. 1981. The expansion of education. *Review of research in education* **9**, 151–213.

Craig J. E. 1984. Schooling and migration. Paper presented at the Annual Meeting of the Social Science History Association, Toronto, Canada.

Craig J. E. & Spear N. 1982. Explaining educational expansion: an agenda for historical and comparative research. In M. S. Archer (ed.), *The sociology of educational expansion.* London: Sage.

Cumings B. 1981. Interest and ideology in the study of agrarian politics. *Politics & Society* **10**, 467–95.

Deaton A. & Muellbauer J. 1980. *Economics and consumer behaviour.* Cambridge University Press.

De Francesco C. & Trivellato P. 1977. I dropouts nell'università italiana. In A. Cefarelli *et al. I giovani ad elevato livello di istruzione e i mercati del lavoro in Italia*. Milano: Franco Angeli.

Dei M. & Rossi M. 1978. *La sociologia della scuola italiana*. Bologna: Il Mulino.

De Masi D. & Signorelli A. (eds.). 1978. *La questione giovanile*. Milano: Franco Angeli.

De Meo P. 1970. *Evoluzione della forza lavoro in Italia*. Roma: ISTAT.

Diggory J. C. 1966. *Self-evaluation*. New York: Wiley.

Domencich T. & McFadden D. 1975. *Urban travel demand: a behavioral analysis*. Amsterdam: North Holland.

Dore R. 1976. *The diploma disease*. London: Allen & Unwin.

Downes D. M. 1966. *The delinquent solution*. London: Routledge and Kegan Paul.

Durkheim E. 1956. *Education and sociology*. New York: The Free Press.

Easterlin R. A. 1978. The economics and sociology of fertility: a synthesis. In C. Tilly, *Historical studies of changing fertility*. Princeton: Princeton University Press.

Edwards R. C., Reich M. & Gordon D. (eds.). 1975. *Labour market segmentation*. Lexington, Mass.: D. C. Heath.

Elster J. 1976. Boudon, education and the theory of games. *Social Science Information* 15, 733–40.

Elster J. 1978. *Logic and Society*. New York: Wiley.

Elster J. 1979. *Ulysses and the sirens*. Cambridge: Cambridge University Press.

Elster J. 1980. Irrational politics. *London Review of Books*. 21 August–3 September 1980.

Elster J. 1983. *Sour grapes*. Cambridge: Cambridge University Press.

Emma R. & Rostan M. 1971. *Scuola e mercato del lavoro*. Bari: De Donato.

EUROSTAT 1978. *Educational statistics*. Bruxelles.

EUROSTAT 1–1979. *Hourly earnings*. Bruxelles.

EUROSTAT 1980. *Education and training*. Bruxelles.

EUROSTAT 1981. *Economic and social position of women in the community*. Bruxelles.

Evans F. B. & Anderson J. G. 1973. The psychocultural origins of achievement and achievement motivations: the Mexican American family. *Sociology of Education* 46, 396–416.

Fadiga Zanatta A. L. 1978. *Il sistema scolastico italiano*. 3rd edn. Bologna: Il Mulino.

Feather N. T. 1966a. Subjective probability and decisions under uncertainty. In J. W. Atkinson & N. T. Feather (eds.), *A theory of achievement motivation*. New York: Wiley.

Feather N. T. 1966b. Effects of prior success and failure on expectation of successes and subsequent performance. *Journal of Personality and Social Psychology* 3, 287–98.

Federpiemonte-Doxa 1978. Occupazione giovanile e lavoro qualificato. *Quaderni della Federazione delle Associazioni industriali del Piemonte* 5, 1–85.

Ferrarotti F. 1967. La scuola media come fattore di cultura e di democrazia. *La Critica Sociologica* 1, 3.

Festinger L. 1957. *A theory of cognitive dissonance*. Stanford, California: Stanford University Press.

Floud J. 1970. Social class factors in educational achievement. In M. Craft (ed.), *Family, class and education*. London: Longman.

Foa V. *et al.* 1969. *I lavoratori studenti*. Torino: Einaudi.

Foerster J. F. 1979. Mode choice decision process models: a comparison of compensatory and non compensatory structures. *Transportation Research* 13A, 17–28.

Fofi G. 1970. Immigrants to Turin. In C. J. Jansen (ed.), *Readings in the sociology of migration*. Oxford: Pergamon Press.

Fofi G. 1976. *L'immigrazione meridionale a Torino*. Milano: Feltrinelli.

Gambetta D. 1981. The Fiat strike, Turin, Sept.–Oct. 1980. Cambridge: mimeo.

Gambetta D. & Moretti E. 1981. Il lavoro fra gli studenti delle scuole medie superiori. *Quaderni di Sociologia* 29, 1, 115–44.

Gambetta D. & Ricolfi L. 1978. *Il compromesso difficile*. Torino: Rosenberg & Sellier.

Gans H. J. 1962. *The urban villages*. New York: The Free Press.

Gattullo M. 1976. L'andamento della selezione in Italia. *Inchiesta* 6, 23, 53–61.

Giddens A. 1979. *Central problems in social theory*. London: Macmillan.

Gilbert J. P. & Mosteller F. 1972. The urgent need for experimentation. In F. Mosteller & P. Moynihan (eds.), *On equality of educational opportunity*. New York: Random House.

Goldthorpe J. *et al.* 1980. *Social mobility and class structure in modern*

Britain. Oxford: Clarendon Press.

Gordon A. 1980. Leaving school: a question of money? *Educational Studies* **6**, 43–4.

Gordon D. 1972. *Theories of poverty and underemployment*. Lexington, Mass.: Lexington Books.

Gronau R. 1973. The effect of children on the housewife's value of time. *Journal of Political Economy* **82**, 1119–43.

Halsey A. H. & Floud J. 1961. English secondary school and the supply of labour. In A. H. Halsey *et al.* (eds.), *Education, economy and society*. New York: The Free Press.

Halsey A. H., Heath A. & Ridge J. M. 1980. *Origins and destinations*. Oxford: Clarendon Press.

Hanushek E. A. & Jackson J. E. 1977. *Statistical methods for social scientists*. New York: Academic Press.

Hausman J. A. R. & Wise D. 1978. A conditional probit model for qualitative choice. *Econometrica* **46**, 403–26.

Hawthorn G. 1970. *The sociology of fertility*. London: Macmillan.

Haystead J. 1974. Social structure, awareness contexts and processes of choice. In M. W. Williams (ed.), *Occupational choice*. London: Allen & Unwin.

Heath A. 1976. *Rational choice and social exchange*. Cambridge: Cambridge University Press.

Heath A. 1981. *Social mobility*. Glasgow: Fontana.

Heath A. & Clifford P. 1980. The seventy thousand hours that Rutter left out. *Oxford Review of Education* **6**, 3–19.

Heidegger M. 1967. *Being and time*. Oxford: Blackwell.

Hicks J. 1979. *Causality in economics*. Oxford: Blackwell.

Hirsch F. 1977. *Social limits to growth*. London: Routledge & Kegan Paul.

Hirschman A. O. 1967. *Development projects observed*. Washington: Brookings Institution.

Hirschman A. O. 1970. *Exit, voice and loyalty*. Cambridge, Mass.: Harvard University Press.

Hirschman A. O. 1973. The changing tolerance for income inequality in the course of economic development. *Quarterly Journal of Economics* **87**, 544–56.

Hirschman A. O. 1977. *The passions and the interests*. Princeton: Princeton University Press.

Hobbes T. 1980. *Leviathan.* Harmondsworth: Penguin Books.

Hollis M. 1976. *Models of man.* Cambridge: Cambridge University Press.

Homans G. C. 1961. *Social behaviour: its elementary forms.* London: Routledge & Kegan Paul.

Homans G. C. 1967. *The nature of social science.* New York: Harcourt, Brace & Jovanovich.

Hughes G. A. 1980. On the estimation of migration equations. Cambridge Faculty of Economics: mimeo.

Husserl E. 1970. *The crisis of European sciences and the transcendental phenomenology.* Evanston: Northwestern University Press.

Hyman H. H. 1966. The value system of different classes. In S. M. Lipset & R. Bendix (eds.), *Class, status and power.* London: Routledge & Kegan Paul.

Hyman H. H., Wright C. R. & Reed J. S. 1975. *The enduring effects of education.* Chicago: Chicago University Press.

Ishikawa T. 1975. Family structures and family values in the theory of income distribution. *Journal of Political Economy* **83**, 987–1008.

ISTAT 1947–78. *Annuario statistico italiano dell'istruzione.* Roma.

ISTAT 1959. Indagine sulle scelte scolastiche e professionali degli alunni delle scuole medie inferiori. *Note e Relazioni* **6**.

ISTAT 1966–80. Supplemento al Bollettino mensile di Statistica dell'istruzione. Roma.

ISTAT 1968. Distribuzione per età degli alunni delle scuole elementari e medie nell'anno scolastico 1966–67. *Note e Relazioni* **38**.

ISTAT 1969a. Indagine speciale sui diplomati di scuole medie superiori. *Supplemento al Bollettino Mensile di Statistica* **8**.

ISTAT 1969b. Indagine speciale su alcuni aspetti della vita scolastica italiana. *Note e Relazioni* **39**.

ISTAT 1975. Indagine speciale sui diplomandi di scuole secondarie superiori. *Supplemento al Bollettino mensile di Statistica* **8**.

ISTAT 1976a. Distribuzione per età della popolazione scolastica. *Note e Relazioni* **54**.

ISTAT 1976b. Indagine speciale sulle caratteristiche degli studenti universitari iscritti al primo anno di corso. *Supplemento al Bollettino Mensile di Statistica* **16**.

Istituto di Sociologia, Università di Torino 1979. *Lavorare due volte.* Torino: Book Store.

Jackson B. & Marsden D. 1962. *Education and the working class.* London: Routledge & Kegan Paul.

Jahoda M., Lazarsfeld P. F. & Zeisel H. 1933. *Marienthal: the sociography of an unemployed community.* (First published in Britain in 1972, London: Tavistock.)

James S. 1985. Louis Althusser. In Q. Skinner (ed.), *The return of grand theory in the human sciences.* Cambridge: Cambridge University Press.

Jencks C. 1972a. The Coleman report and the conventional wisdom. In F. Moerteller & P. D. Moynihan (eds.), *On equality of educational opportunity.* New York: Random House.

Jencks C. 1972b. *Inequality, a reassessment of the effect of family and schooling in America.* New York: Basic Books.

Juster T. F. (ed.). 1975. *Education, income and human behaviour.* National Bureau of Economic Research.

Kahl J. A. 1961. 'Common man' boy. In A. H. Halsey *et al.* (eds.), *Education, economy and society.* New York: The Free Press.

Keller S. & Zavalloni M. 1964. Ambition and social class: a respecification. Social Forces **43**, 58–70.

Kelsall R. K. & Kelsall H. M. 1971. *Social disadvantage and educational opportunity.* New York: Holt, Rinehart & Winston.

Klineberg S. L. 1971. Modernisation and the adolescent experience: a study in Tunisia. *The Key Reporter* **37**.

Kohn M. L. 1969. *Class and conformity.* Homewood, Illinois: The Dorsey Press.

Lane M. 1972. Explaining educational choice. *Sociology* **6**, 255–66.

Layard R. & Psacharopoulos G. 1974. The screening hypothesis and the returns to education. *Journal of Political Economy* **82**, 985–98.

Lazear E. 1976. Education: consumption or production. *Journal of Political Economy* **92**, 569–97.

Leibowitz A. 1977. Family background and economic success: a review of the evidence. In P. Taubman (ed.), *Kinometrics: determinants of socioeconomic success between and within families.* Amsterdam: North Holland.

Lerner D. 1958. *The passing of traditional society.* New York: The Free Press.

Levy Garboua L. 1976. Les Demandes de l'étudiant ou les contradictions de l'université de masse. *Revue Française de Sociologie* **17**, 53–80.

Lewin K. *et al.* 1944. Level of aspiration. In J. Hunt (ed.), *Personality and the behaviour disorders.* New York: The Ronald Press.

Lindblom C. E. 1965. *The intelligence of democracy.* New York: The Free Press.

Livi Bacci M. 1977. *A history of Italian fertility.* Princeton: Princeton University Press.

Luhmann N. 1976. The future cannot begin: temporal structures in modern society. *Social Research* **43**, 130–52.

Luhmann N. 1979. *Trust and power.* New York: Wiley.

Luhmann N. & Habermas J. 1973. *Teoria della società o tecnologia sociale.* Milano: Etas Compass.

Lukes S. 1985. Subject to survey. *The Times Literary Supplement* 18 October.

McFadden D. 1976. A comment on discriminant analysis 'versus' logit analysis. *Annals of economic and social measurement* **5**, 363–90.

McFadden D. 1980. Qualitative response models: handout. Paper given at the Econometric Society World Congress. Aix-en-Provence.

McLelland D. C. 1973. Testing for competence rather than for intelligence. *American Psychologist* **28**.

Mahon E. 1985. When is a difference not a difference? A reply to J. Murphy. *The British Journal of Sociology* **36**, 1, 73–6.

Mann M. 1973. *Workers on the move: the sociology of relocation.* Cambridge: Cambridge University Press.

March J. C. 1974. For a technology of foolishness. In H. Leavit *et al.* (eds.), *Organizations for the future.* New York: Praeger.

Marsh C. 1983. *The survey method.* London: Allen & Unwin.

Martinotti G. (ed.) 1982. *La città difficile.* Milano: Franco Angeli.

Marx K. 1974. *Capital.* London: Dent (Everyman's Library).

Marx K. & Engels F. 1930. *The communist manifesto.* London: Martin Lawrence.

Merton R. K. 1932. The unanticipated consequences of purposive social action. *American Sociological Review* **1**, 894–904.

Michael R. T. 1975. Education and consumption. In T. Juster. *Education, income and human behaviour.* n.p.: NBER.

Miegge M. 1971. Sviluppo capitalistico e scuola lunga. *Inchiesta* **1**, 1, 23–35.

Mill J. S. 1979. *Utilitarianism.* Glasgow: Collins.

Miller L. & Radner R. 1970. Demand and supply in U.S. Higher

Education. *American Economic Review* **60**, 326–34.

Ministero del Lavoro. 1979. *Rassegna di statistiche del lavoro*. Roma.

Moss L. & Goldstein H. 1979. *The recall method in social surveys*. University of London Institute of Education.

Murphy J. 1981. Class inequality in education. *The British Journal of Sociology* **32**, 182–201.

Musgrave P. W. 1972. *The sociology of education*. London: Methuen.

Nisbett R. E. & Wilson T. D. 1977. Telling more than we know: verbal reports on mental process. *Psychological Review* **84**, 231–59.

Nisbett R. E. & Ross L. 1980. *Human inference: strategies and shortcomings in social judgement*. Englewood Cliffs: Prentice Hall.

OECD 1969. *Development of secondary education*. Paris.

Olson M. 1965. *The logic of collective action*. Cambridge, Mass.: Harvard University Press.

Paci M. 1973. *Mercato del lavoro e classi sociali*. Bologna: Il Mulino.

Padoa Schioppa F. 1974. *Scuola e classi sociali in Italia*. Bologna: Il Mulino.

Padoa Schioppa F. 1977. *La forza lavoro femminile*. Bologna: Il Mulino.

Park W. 1980. Modernity and views of education. *Comparative Education Review* **24**, 35–47.

Parkin F. 1974. Strategies of social closure and class formation. In F. Parkin (ed.), *The social analysis of class structure*. London: Tavistock.

Pindyck R. & Rubinfeld D. 1981. *Econometric models and economic forecasts*. New York: McGraw-Hill.

Piore M. J. 1979. *Birds of Passage*. Cambridge: Cambridge University Press.

Piselli F. 1981. *Parentela ed emigrazione*. Torino: Einaudi.

Pissarides C. A. 1981a. Staying-on at school in England and Wales. *Economica* **48**, 345–63.

Pissarides C. A. 1981b. From school to university: the demand for post-compulsory education in Britain. London School of Economics: mimeo.

Plowden Report 1967. *Children and their primary schools*. London: HMSO, vol. 1.

Popper K. R. 1963. *Conjectures and refutations*. London: Routledge & Kegan Paul.

Popper K. R. 1965. *Of clouds and clocks*. St Louis, Missouri: Washington University.

Post D. 1985. Student expectations of educational returns in Peru. *Comparative Education Review* **2**, 189–203.

Przeworski A. 1985. *Capitalism and social democracy.* Cambridge: Cambridge University Press.

Psacharopoulos G. & Sanyal B. 1981. Student expectations and labour market performance: the case of the Philippines. *Higher Education* **10**, 449–72.

Psacharopoulos G. & Tinbergen J. 1978. On the explanation of schooling, occupation and earnings: some alternative path analyses. *The Economist* **126**, 505–20.

Rawls J. 1972. *A theory of justice.* Oxford: Oxford University Press.

Record R. G., McKeown T. & Edwards J. G. 1970. An investigation of the difference in measured intelligence between twins and single births. *Annals of Human Genetics* **30**, 11–20.

Ricolfi L. & Sciolla L. 1980. *Senza padri ne' maestri.* Bari: De Donato.

Roberts K. 1968. The organization of education and the ambitions of school leavers: a comparative review. *Comparative education* **4**, 87–96.

Rosen S. 1977. Human capital: a survey of empirical research. In R. G. Ehrenberg (ed.), *Research in labor economics.* Greenwich, Connecticut: Jai Press, vol. 1.

Rubery J. 1978. Structured labour markets, market organization and low pay. *Cambridge Journal of Economics* **2**, 17–36.

Rubery J. & Wilkinson F. 1981. Outlook and segmented labour markets. In F. Wilkinson (ed.), *The dynamics of labour segmentation.* New York: Academic Press.

Runciman W. G. 1972. *Relative deprivation and social justice.* Harmondsworth: Penguin Books.

Rutter M. *et al.* 1979. *Fifteen thousand hours.* London: Open Books.

Sabel C. 1982. *Work and Politics.* Cambridge: Cambridge University Press.

Sartre J. P. 1943. *L'Etre et le néant.* Paris: Librairie Gallimard.

Schmitt N. *et al.* 1978. Prediction of post high school labour force decisions. *Human Relations* **31**, 727–43.

Schramm W. 1964. *Mass media and national development.* Stanford: Stanford University Press.

Schwarzweller H. K. 1967. Educational aspirations and life chances of German young people. *Comparative Education* **4**, 35–49.

Sen A. 1973. Behaviour and the concept of preference. *Economica*, May, 241–59.

Sewell W. H. & Hauser R. M. 1975. *Education, occupation and earnings*. New York: Academic Press.

Shultz T. W. 1980. Nobel lecture: The economics of being poor. *Journal of Political Economy* **88**, 639–51.

Simon H. A. 1957. *Models of man*. New York: Wiley.

Simon H. A. 1976. *Administrative behavior*. 3rd edn. New York: The Free Press.

Simon H. A. 1979. From substantive to procedural rationality. In F. Hahn & M. Hillis, *Philosophy and economic theory*. Oxford: Oxford University Press.

Simon J. L. 1977. *The economics of population growth*. Princeton: Princeton University Press.

Smith M. S. 1972. The basic findings reconsidered. In F. Moerteller & P. D. Moynihan (eds.), *On equality of educational opportunity*. New York: Random House.

Spilerman S. 1971. Raising academic motivation in lower class adolescents: a convergence of two research traditions. *Sociology of Education* **44**, 103–18.

Stewart A. & Blackburn R. M. 1975. The stability of structural inequality. *Sociological Review* **23**.

Stewart A., Prandy K. & Blackburn R. M. 1980. *Social stratification and occupations*. London: Macmillan.

Stigler G. J. & Becker G. S. 1977. De gustibus non est disputandum. *The American Economic Review* **67**, 76–90.

Strodbeck F. L. 1961. Family integration, values and achievement. In H. A. Halsey *et al.*, *Education, economy and society*. New York: The Free Press.

Tagliaferri T. 1980. Il lavoro minorile in provincia di Milano. *Economia e Lavoro* **1–2**.

Taylor C. 1964. *The explanation of behaviour*. London: Routledge & Kegan Paul.

Taylor C. 1969. Responsibility for self. In A. O. Rorty (ed.), *The identities of persons*. Berkeley: University of California Press.

Thurow L. 1975. *Generating inequality*. New York: Basic Books.

Trivellato U. 1978. L'evoluzione della scolarizzazione e delle disuguaglianze sociali nella partecipazione all' istruzione in Italia (1953–1973), *Economia, Istruzione e Formazione Professionale* **2**.

Turner R. H. 1960. Sponsored and contest mobility and the school system. *American Sociological Review* **25**, 855–67.

Turner R. 1964. *The social context of ambition*. San Francisco: Chandler.

Tversky A. 1972. Elimination by aspects: a theory of choice. *Psychological Review* **79**, 281–99.

Tversky A. & Sattath S. 1979. Preference trees. *Psychological Review* **86**, 542–73.

Tyler W. 1977. *The sociology of educational inequality*. London: Methuen.

Veyne P. 1976. *Le Pain et le cirque*. Paris: Editions du Seuil.

Von Wright G. H. 1973. On the logic and epistemology of the causal relation. In P. Suppes *et al.*, *Logic, methodology and philosophy of science*. Amsterdam: North Holland.

Westergaard J. & Little A. 1970. Educational opportunity and social selection in England and Wales. In M. Craft (ed.), *Family, class and education*. London: Longman.

Wiezsäcker C. C. von. 1971. Notes on endogenous change of tastes. *Journal of Economic Theory* **3**, 345–72.

Williams B. A. O. 1962. The idea of equality. In Laslett and Runciman (eds.), *Politics, philosophy and society*. Oxford: Blackwell.

Williams B. A. O. 1976. Persons, character and morality. In A. Rorty, *The identities of persons*. Berkeley: University of California Press.

Willis P. 1977. *Learning to labour*. Westmead: Saxon House.

Willis R. J. & Rosen S. 1979. Education and self-selection. *Journal of Political Economy* **87**, 5, part 2.

Index of names

About the Book and Author

Like few other decisions in life, educational choices must be made by virtually everyone growing up in industrial societies. The consequences of these choices for individual lives are momentous, yet decisions about schooling can be treacherous. They are made during the teen years, at a time when personal preferences are unstable and there is little past experience to draw upon; once made, they are not easy to change. Diego Gambetta offers a refined exploration of the mechanisms that influence educational decisions between compulsory school and college.

Gambetta tests two fundamental and opposed explanations, which he applies to the study of educational and other personal choices. One approach holds that individuals are essentially passive, either constrained by a lack of alternatives or pushed by factors they are unaware of. The other approach regards individuals as capable of purposive action, able to weigh the available alternatives against the prospects of future rewards.

Applying sophisticated statistical models to two surveys conducted in northwest Italy, Gambetta provides an integrated assessment of the specific effects of a variety of factors on educational decisionmaking: family economic and cultural capital, previous academic achievements, labor market prospects, and personal aspirations. From this analysis emerges a subtler, more realistic approach to individual decisionmaking that brushes aside either extreme. The author concludes that rational adaptation is the predominant operating mechanism in making choices, but that it generates different effects depending on class-related values and personal preferences.

Diego Gambetta is reader in sociology and fellow of All Souls College, Oxford.